LIBRARY OF PHILOSOPHY AND RELIGION

General Editor: John Hick, Danforth Professor
Claremont Graduate School, Claremont, California 91711

This series of books explores contemporary religious understandings of humanity and the universe. The books contribute to various aspects of the continuing dialogues between religion and philosophy, between scepticism and faith, and between the different religions and ideologies. The authors represent a correspondingly wide range of viewpoints. Some of the books in the series are written for the general educated public and others for a more specialised philosophical or theological readership. - UNOTT

ZEN AND WESTERN THOUGHT *Masao Abe*
THE RELEVANCE OF NATURAL SCIENCE TO THEOLOGY
William H. Austin
CHRISTIAN BELIEFS ABOUT LIFE AND DEATH *Paul Badham*
IMMORTALITY OR EXTINCTION? *Paul and Linda Badham*
INCARNATION IN HINDUISM AND CHRISTIANITY
Daniel E. Bassuk
THE FRAGILE UNIVERSE *Patrick Burke*
GANDHI'S RELIGIOUS THOUGHT *Margaret Chatterjee*
THE *KALÁM* COSMOLOGICAL ARGUMENT
THE COSMOLOGICAL ARGUMENT FROM PLATO TO
LEIBNIZ
William Lane Craig
LOGIC AND THE NATURE OF GOD *Stephen T. Davis*
THE PROBLEM OF THE SELF IN BUDDHISM AND
CHRISTIANITY *Lynn A. de Silva*
AN INTRODUCTION TO BUDDHIST PSYCHOLOGY
Padmasiri de Silva
THE AVAILABILITY OF RELIGIOUS IDEAS
Pamchandra Gandhi
HUME'S PHILOSOPHY OF RELIGION *J. C. A. Gaskin*
THE CONCEPT OF THE KNOWLEDGE OF GOD *Brian Haymes*
THREE FAITHS – ONE GOD *John Hick & Edmund S. Meltzer*
(*editors*)
GOD BEYOND KNOWLEDGE *H. A. Hodges*
THE COGNITIVITY OF RELIGION *J. Kellenberger*

THE POSSIBILITY OF AN ALL-KNOWING GOD
Jonathan L. Kvanvig
PERSONS AND LIFE AFTER DEATH   *Hywell D. Lewis*
THE FACE OF TRUTH   *Julius J. Lipner*
VEDANTIC APPROACHES TO GOD   *Eric Lott*
REINCARNATION AS A CHRISTIAN HOPE   *Geddes MacGregor*
AN INTRODUCTION TO THE PHILOSOPHY OF
BERNARD LONERCAN   *Hugo A. Meynell*
THE PSYCHOLOGICAL BASIS OF MORALITY   *F. C. T. Moore*
THE USE AND ABUSE OF THE BIBLE   *Dennis Nineham*
RELIGION AND ULTIMATE WELL-BEING   *Martin Prozesky*
BELIEF, CHANGE AND FORMS OF LIFE   *D. Z. Phillips*
HEGEL'S PHILOSOPHY OF RELIGION
KANT AS PHILOSOPHICAL THEOLOGIAN
Bernard M. G. Reardon
REASON, RELATIVISM AND GOD   *Joseph Runzo*
EXPERIENCE, INFERENCE AND GOD   *John J. Shepherd*
RELIGION, TRUTH AND LANGUAGE GAMES
SPIRIT, SAINTS AND IMMORTALITY   *Patrick Sherry*
CONCEPT AND EMPATHY
RELIGION AND THE WESTERN MIND   *Ninian Smart*
TOWARDS A WORLD THEOLOGY   *Wilfred Cantwell Smith*
RELIGION AND RATIONAL CHOICE   *Shivesh Chandra Thakur*
FREEDOM, RESPONSIBILITY AND GOD   *Robert Young*

Further titles in preparation

Series Standing Order

If you would like to receive future titles in this series as they
are published, you can make use of our standing order
facility. To place a standing order please contact your
bookseller or, in case of difficulty, write to us at the address
below with your name and address and the name of the
series. Please state with which title you wish to begin your
standing order. (If you live outside the UK we may not have
the rights for your area, in which case we will forward your
order to the publisher concerned.)

Standing Order Service, Macmillan Distribution Ltd,
Houndmills, Basingstoke, Hampshire, RG21 2XS, England.

Hume's Philosophy of Religion

J. C. A. Gaskin

Fellow of Trinity College
Dublin

Second Edition

M

MACMILLAN
PRESS

First published 1978 by
THE MACMILLAN PRESS LTD
Houndmills, Basingstoke, Hampshire RG21 2XS
and London
Companies and representatives
throughout the world

1000458199

ISBN 0–333–42329–1
ISBN 0–333–39346–5 Pbk

A catalogue record for this book is available
from the British Library.

Printed in Hong Kong

Second edition 1988
Reprinted 1993

To

To a' the men, and women too,
   That dine wi' me and have no view
Of how the world should be put right,
   Or pulled to bits with virtuous spite;

To a' the friends that walked wi' me
   O'er heather hills where men are free,
And turning hame, when comes the night,
   Would talk by fires we kindled bright;

To a' who formed this book for print
   And gave me thoughtful help or hint;
To a' on whom I've long relied –
   These arguments are new inscribed.

J.C.A.G.

Contents

Preface   ix

List of Abbreviations   xii

1   Introduction: Hume on Religion   1
    Publications and Controversy   1
    The Object of the Revised Exercise   5

PART ONE   NATURAL RELIGION AND
NATURAL BELIEF

2   ×Order and Design   11
    The Structure of the Argument   12
    Restrictions on the Conclusion   17
    The Unique Cause Objection   24
    Weakness in the Analogy   27
    Possible Sources of Order   41
    'Principles of Order' and 'Irregular Arguments'   47

3   Evil, Freedom and the Religious Hypothesis   52
    The Inference Problem of Evil   53
    The Consistency Problem of Evil   58
    The Free Will Problem   69

4   Being and Necessity   74
    Necessary Beings   76
    ×The Infinite Chain of Insufficient Reasons   84
    Existence and the Conception of a Thing   90

5   Meaning, School Metaphysics and Divinity   94
    Words and Ideas   94
    A Meaning Which Confounds Everything   101
    The Immense Abyss   104

6   Scepticism and Natural Belief   108
    Varieties of Scepticism   110
    Reasonable Belief   113
    Natural Belief   116

viii   *Contents*

7 God and Natural Order   120
     Belief in God as a Natural Belief   120
   X The Feeling of Design   126

PART TWO   REVEALED, HISTORICAL AND PERSONAL
RELIGION

 8 Miracles and Revelation   135
     The Significance of Miracles and Contrary Miracles   136
     The Eighteenth-Century Controversy   143
     The Reliability of Witnesses   152
     Laws of Nature   159

 9 The Revelation of Immortality   166
     Species of Immortality   166
     Hume's Arguments   169

10 The Causes and Corruptions of Religion   183
     An Origin in Human Nature   184
     True and Corrupt Religion   187

11 The Corruptions Caused by Religion   192
     Sick Men's Dreams   193
     Frivolous Species of Merit   194
     If Suicide be Criminal   203

12 The Dispassionate Sceptic   209
     Hume's Beliefs and Philo's Arguments   209
     The Attenuated Deist   219
     The Citizen of the World   229

Notes   232

Index   247

Preface

Whether this edition of *Hume's Philosophy of Religion* is closer to a new book or to a rewrite of the 1978 text others will judge. It follows the same overall purpose but restructured, extended, much revised in detail and, at one point, significantly modified.

The purpose is to gather Hume's thought about religion from its diversity of sources, published and unpublished by him, and to display it as the coherent and systematic critique of all religious belief and activity which it undoubtedly is. In this way the book is intended to be read as a whole. But it is not primarily or exclusively intended as a contribution to the history of ideas, and I trust it retains the characteristic noted by critics of the first edition: namely that of being useful on particular topics as an introduction to critical issues in Hume's philosophy.

The detailed amendments are in points of style and to achieve additional accuracy. Wherever practicable they also take note of relevant publications which have appeared since the original manuscript was completed in 1976. The text has been made longer by additional material concerning the design argument. This is in Chapter 2 and in the largely new Chapter 7. New sections have been added to Chapters 8 and 11, and the notes to Chapter 12 develop further my thesis that Hume was an 'attenuated deist'. A section on personal identity originally in Chapter 9 has been omitted, and there are a number of other minor abbreviations.

The modification in the argument has been brought about by my reading (or re-reading) of publications by Nelson Pike, P. S. Wadia, Stanley Tweyman, D. F. Norton and others, but particularly of those by Terence Penelhum. This has resulted in refinement and restatement of my original position that belief in god is not a natural belief. Partly to facilitate this restatement, partly because I now think a better presentation of the material results, the work is now divided into two (originally three) parts: I trust their titles explain the division.

CONVENTIONS

On first mention I give Hume's major works their full titles. I subsequently refer to them by the abbreviated titles and in the editions specified on page xii. In order to minimise the irritation of end notes, references are given in brackets after quotations. In all quotations the punctuation and spelling of the originals have been retained.

Quotations from the Bible are from the Authorised Version of King James. Apart from a personal aversion to the dated modernity of some recent translations, for Hume, as for almost all who have written in the English language since the beginning of the seventeenth century, the Authorised Version *is* the Bible.

One other convention needs to be noted. When I refer to God in the normal theistic sense I shall use a capital 'G' or speak of 'the theistic God'. When this God is given any of the specific characteristics which associate the deity with a particular theistic religion, I shall use a qualifying phrase such as 'the Christian God'. When a god (or gods) are referred to in any other sense, or indeterminately (as will usually be the case) I shall write 'god' without the capital letter.

ACKNOWLEDGEMENTS

Earlier versions of parts of certain chapters in this book have appeared in article form. I am indebted to the editors of the following journals and publications for their permission to adapt the material for use in the present publication (the date of original appearance is given in brackets): *Hermathena* (1964 and 1978); *Philosophy* (1974); *Journal of the History of Philosophy* (1976); *Religious Studies* (1976); *McGill Hume Studies* (1979); *Archiv für Geschichte der Philosophie* (1983); *Hume Studies* (1985).

I remain indebted to Antony Flew for his critical reading of the original manuscript of this work: a salutary experience which delivered me from many errors. My thanks are also due to Pheroze Wadia for his detailed comments on the first edition.

BIBLIOGRAPHIC NOTE

Hume is so exceptionally well served by the bibliography in
Rowland Hall's *Fifty Years of Hume Scholarship* (Edinburgh, 1978),
together with its continuations in various issues of *Hume Studies*,
that the attachment to the present book of a large and
undifferentiated list of 'works consulted' seems entirely unnecessary. I would however wish to record my general debt to the
following publications (given in chronological order) which must
remain of importance to anyone working on Hume's philosophy of
religion: Kemp Smith's edition of Hume's *Dialogues* (Oxford, 1935;
Edinburgh, 1947 etc.); Antony Flew, *Hume's Philosophy of Belief*
(London, 1961); Nelson Pike's commentary contained in his edition
of the *Dialogues* (New York, 1970); R. M. Burns, *The Great Debate on
Miracles* (Lewisburg, 1981); Terence Penelhum, *God and Skepticism*
(Netherlands, 1983). All the articles by Penelhum, together with
some by P. S. Wadia and M. A. Stewart, are also interesting and
important to certain aspects of the present subject.

List of Abbreviations

Reference to Hume's major works and to certain other standard texts will be given by means of an abbreviation followed by a page number (and volume where necessary). The following abbreviations are used:

Dialogues *Dialogues concerning Natural Religion*, edited by N. Kemp Smith, 2nd edn (Edinburgh, 1947), reprinted with the same pagination, New York 1947 (Library of Liberal Arts).

N.H.R. *The Natural History of Religion*, edited by H. E. Root (London, 1956).

Enquiry *An Enquiry concerning Human Understanding.* The first number given is the page in the edition by Selby-Bigge (Oxford, 1902; 3rd edn Oxford, 1975, with same pagination). The second number is the page in the edition by C. W. Hendel (New York, 1955). Quotations follow the text of the former which is itself a reprint of the 1777 edition.

Moral *An Enquiry concerning the Principles of Morals.* The first
Enquiry number given is the page in the Selby-Bigge edn as above. The second number is the page in Hendel's edn (New York, 1957).

Letters *The Letters of David Hume*, edited by J. Y. T. Greig, 2 vols (Oxford, 1932).

New Letters *New Letters of David Hume*, edited by R. Klibansky and E. C. Mossner (Oxford, 1954).

History *History of England*, 8 vols (London, 1778). This edition contains Hume's final corrections.

A Letter *A Letter from a Gentleman*, edited by E. C. Mossner and J. V. Price (Edinburgh, 1967).

Treatise *A Treatise of Human Nature*, edited by L. A. Selby-Bigge (Oxford, 1888).

Other minor abbreviations will, I hope, be intelligible. Unusual editions of Hume's works, where used, will be specified in full. Essays by Hume will be referred to by their titles, and wherever possible will be quoted from *Essays and Treatises on Several Subjects*, two volumes (London, 1777).

1

Introduction: Hume on Religion

[Hume] seems to me one of those philosophers that think to spin out Systems, out of their own brain, without regard to religion, antiquity or Tradition sacred or profane. (The Chevalier Ramsey)

PUBLICATIONS AND CONTROVERSY

In the totality of his work Hume wrote more about religion than about any other single philosophical subject. Almost all of what he wrote was critical; some of it has since been recognised as terminally destructive.

His earliest remarks on the subject, which might have settled many biographical puzzles, were destroyed by their author. Writing to Elliot of Minto in 1751 he remarks:

And tis not long ago that I burn'd an old Manuscript Book, wrote before I was twenty; which contain'd, Page after Page, the gradual Progress of my Thoughts on that head. It begun with an anxious Search after Arguments, to confirm the common Opinion: Doubts stole in, dissipated, return'd, were again dissipated, return'd again; and it was a perpetual Struggle of a restless Imagination against Inclination, perhaps against Reason. *Letters*, I, 154[1]

But his 'Early Memoranda' – notes and paraphrases taken while reading Cicero, Xenophon, Bayle and others – do survive,[2] and indicate Hume's interest in religion even in the years which preceded the *Treatise of Human Nature*, his first published work.

The *Treatise* (Books I and II appeared anonymously in 1739; Book III in 1740) is not overtly concerned with religion, although we do know that Hume removed from it before publication a chapter on miracles and possibly other sections (see below, p. 182) which he had reason to believe would provoke hostility from Scottish ecclesiastics or involve him in religious controversy. A few brief and apparently inoffensive references to the existence of god and to religion remain, but with the exception of the section called 'Of the Immateriality of the Soul' they occur only incidentally in sections dealing with other subjects. Nevertheless these passages, together with the construction which was put upon some of his arguments, were sufficient to fuel a 'Charge' against him during his (unsuccessful) candidature for the Professorship of Moral Philosophy at Edinburgh University.

A modern reader might find it a little puzzling to know what aspects of the *Treatise* could possibly cause offence, but fortunately an answer of a kind is to be found in *A Letter from a Gentleman*. This is a thirty-four page pamphlet drafted by Hume's kinsman Henry Home (later Lord Kames) from an actual letter of Hume's written to John Couts (the Lord Provost of Edinburgh who had proposed Hume for the Chair). The *Letter* was 'so hastily composed that I scarce had time to revise it' (*New Letters*, 15) and Hume regretted its publication. A copy of this pamphlet came to light in 1966 and has been reprinted in facsimile.[3] In it Hume defends himself on six 'charges' arising from his arguments in the *Treatise*. These are: (1) That he maintains 'the Folly of pretending to believe any Thing with Certainty'; (2) that his principles lead to 'downright Atheism, by denying the Doctrine of Causes and Effects'; (3) that his account of the idea of existence involves 'Errors concerning the very Being and Existence of God'; (4) that he commits errors 'concerning God's being the first Cause, and prime Mover of the Universe'; (5) 'He is chargable with denying the Immateriality of the Soul, and the Consequences flowing from this Denial'; (6) that he is chargeable with 'sapping the Foundations of Morality, by denying the natural and essential Difference betwixt Right and Wrong, Good and Evil, Justice and Injustice; making the Difference only artificial, and to arise from human Conventions and Compacts' (pp. 17f). It is not necessary to decide whether these accusations can be justified on the basis of what is said in the *Treatise*, but several of them were certainly given more substance by Hume's later publications beginning with the two *Enquiries*.

In *An Enquiry concerning Human Understanding* (1748) Hume rewrote and clarified some of the material contained in Book I of the *Treatise* as well as adding new sections and giving the whole a much more obvious and deliberate anti-metaphysical and anti-theological content. Problems relating to free will and responsibility, miracles, the argument from design, the comprehensibility of theological statements, the character of scepticism and the possibility of excluding metaphysics out of the scheme of things are examined, sometimes at length.

In *An Enquiry concerning the Principles of Morals* (1751) Hume developed an account of social morality which is in effect a well-qualified form of utilitarianism. The work is of interest to a study of his philosophy of religion not only because of its sharp asides at the expense of the clergy and the church, but because the moral philosophy which it contains makes no reference whatever to divine sanctions or authority: the connection between moral conduct and religious belief is portrayed as purely contingent and generally bad. The outcome of this contingent connection, according to Hume, shows itself in historical events, some of which he chronicled in his lengthy and successful *History of England* (published between 1754 and 1762).

The *History* is good 'philosophical history' in the manner followed by Robertson and Gibbon. That is to say it contains both an account of events and the author's enlightened comments upon them. This convention allows Hume opportunities to observe that the social and political manifestations of organised religion and of impassioned religious belief, as they have shown themselves in history, have almost always been bad. In another work, *The Natural History of Religion*, published in 1757 in the middle of writing the *History*, Hume generalises the lesson:

> What a noble privilege is it of human reason to attain the knowledge of the supreme Being; and, from the visible works of nature, be enabled to infer so sublime a principle as its supreme Creator? But turn the reverse of the medal. Survey most nations and most ages. Examine the religious principles, which have, in fact, prevailed in the world. You will scarcely be persuaded, that they are any thing but sick men's dreams: . . . Hear the verbal protestations of all men: Nothing so certain as their religious tenets. Examine their lives: You will scarcely think that they repose the smallest confidence in them. *N.H.R.*, 75

The *N.H.R.* is the first of the two major works which Hume devoted exclusively to religion. In it he discusses the psychological and environmental causes which might have brought about belief in divine power independently of any good reasons for such belief. He concludes that fear of the unknown causes which control man's environment could, in primitive societies, lead to belief in malevolent or capricious powers. Only at a later stage in man's understanding of his environment do the regularities of nature suggest the activity of a single omnipotent god. Even then the ignorant man 'will tell you of the sudden and unexpected death of such a one: . . . The excessive drought of this season: . . . These he ascribes to the immediate operation of providence: And such events, as, with good reasoners, are the chief difficulties in admitting a supreme intelligence, are with him the sole arguments for it' (*N.H.R.*, 41).

When Andrew Millar, Hume's London publisher, first printed the *N.H.R.* he did so as one of *Five Dissertations*; the other four included the celebrated (or perhaps one should say infamous) essays 'Of the Immortality of the Soul' and 'Of Suicide'. In the first of these Hume sets out in aphoristic form most of the traditional arguments to show that man does not have an immortal soul; in the second he argues that circumstances may arise which make suicide a moral duty notwithstanding the dictates of religion. Why these essays were never published is not precisely known,[4] but it would seem that a copy got into the hands of the polemical and vindictive Warburton, and that Millar was warned by Warburton or his agents that the volume as it stood would provoke prosecution. All Hume tells us is that 'from my abundant Prudence I suppress'd [them] . . .' and that 'Mr Millar and I agreed to suppress them at common Charges . . .' (*Letters*, II, 253). His efforts to suppress them were, however, less than effective and pirated copies appeared. But he himself never again offered these essays to the public although he did leave a copy of the suppressed pages to William Strahan with authority to print them if he thought fit. This copy is now in the National Library of Scotland.[5] The essays are of interest since they contain opinions on matters relating to religion which are not mentioned elsewhere in Hume's published work. I shall return to them in Chapters 9 and 11.

During the 1750s Hume's literary reputation waxed great but did so against a background of very dangerous opposition from those who thought his writings a threat to both religion and morality. It is possible that Hume's experience in 1745 when he was rejected for the Chair of Moral Philosophy at Edinburgh determined him to act in the character he had been given. It is possible that maturity and the beginnings of success gave him the confidence to disregard the unanimous advice of his friends. It is certain that having been very cautious about what was included in the *Treatise* he suddenly became relatively incautious about what went into the *Enquiries*, the *History*, the *N.H.R.*, and the miscellaneous essays (see, for example, his astonishingly tactless footnote on the character of the clergy in 'Of National Characters'). But the boldness of his writings in the 1750s did not pass without adverse effect. In 1752 the united opposition of the Glasgow clergy and the influential Duke of Argyll prevented Hume from being given the Chair of Logic at Glasgow University. But it is at least to the credit of Scotland that the Great Infidel was *considered* for Glasgow as he had earlier been for Edinburgh: a consideration he would scarcely have been granted at either English university or in Dublin where Trail, the Bishop of Down and Connor, begged him in 1765 not even to set foot since 'His Character as a Philosopher is an object of Universal Disgust not to say Detestation in this Country.' Even at home he was not entirely secure. Between 1755 and 1757 an attempt was made to excommunicate Hume from the Church of Scotland. In 1757 semi-official pressure resulted in the suppression of the essays on immortality and suicide, and in 1759 there was an outcry against the volumes of the *History* dealing with the Tudors. Whether Hume became alarmed at the intensity of this hostility or whether he respected the emphatic advice of his friends is not known; but having written the first draft of his greatest and most extensive work on religion in 1751, and having revised it twice, he kept the manuscript unpublished until his death.

The *Dialogues concerning Natural Religion* finally appeared in print in 1779, three years after Hume's death. They form a complement to the discussion contained in the *N.H.R.* That work had dealt with the social and psychological causes of religious belief: the *Dialogues* examine some of the arguments used to maintain that religious belief is reasonable and true. In the *Dialogues* Hume discusses at length the argument from design, the problem of evil, the character of religious scepticism, one version of an *a priori* argument for the existence of god, the meaning of language used to make statements about god's nature and the moral value of religious belief.

THE OBJECT OF THE REVISED EXERCISE

From the foregoing it will be seen that Hume's discussion of religion is both diverse and comprehensive. In the *Enquiry* and *Dialogues* he

discusses the reasons for religious belief. In the *N.H.R.* he examines
the causes. In the *Moral Enquiry* and in the *History* he traces the
ethical and social effects of religion. His critique of religion is in
fact much more comprehensive than the best-known of his
philosophical works might suggest or apparently do suggest
to some philosophers. (See, for example, Warnock's un-
characteristically misleading remark that some philosophical
visions bear 'as with Hume, on morality perhaps but on religion not
at all'.[6]) But the diversity has the disadvantage that most critics and
commentators have been content with self-contained articles and
piecemeal development of some particular item in Hume's account
of religion without making any serious attempt to relate the item to
the rest of his account. Even books devoted to Hume on religion
have had a tendency to treat one aspect of his thought. R. H.
Hurlbutt's *Hume, Newton and the Design Argument*[7] gives a scholarly
account of the Newtonian origins of the particular type of design
arguments which Hume attacks. A. Jeffner's *Butler and Hume on
Religion*[8] contains an exposition and comparative analysis of both
Hume's and Butler's thought. Stanley Tweyman's recent *Scepticism
and Belief in Hume's Dialogues concerning Natural Religion* (The Hague,
1986) is also, as its name suggests, a critical (and important)
examination of *one* section of Hume's work.[9]

My purpose is somewhat different. It is to bring Hume's various
critiques and accounts of religion into a single coherent picture. The
main features in that picture include Hume's attempts to establish
that the arguments of natural religion provide by themselves no
sufficient reasons for belief in a god (Chapters 2 to 5); that the
credentials of revelation will convince no reasonable man (Chapters
8 and 9); that belief in god(s) has causes in human nature and
adverse effects on morality (Chapters 10 and 11) and that, over and
above these causes, we have a strong – but not irresistable –
propensity to believe in god(s) from the fact of natural order: a
propensity we misread as the soundness of the design argument
(Chapters 6, 7 and 12).

I shall try to show that Hume's critique as a whole moves steadily
towards a consistent position which is short of atheism but has
chilling consequences for personal religion. This position is that a
vestigial design argument establishes a weak probability that
natural order originates in the activity of something with
intelligence remotely analogous to our own. This feeble *rational*
datum is united with an insistent *feeling* in most of us that natural

order springs from a designer. When our philosophical assent to the existence of this designer has been given (that is to say our assent qualified by the exercise of mitigated scepticism) we recognise that it has no moral claim upon us, nor we upon it. I call this position 'attenuated deism'.

The attempt to give such a comprehensive account of Hume's philosophy of religion must result in a book which comprehends very diverse material. The greater part of it is philosophical discussion and argument; but historical, social, moral and personal material provided by Hume or relevant to what he says cannot be ignored for the sake of a convenient homogeneity of treatment.

I begin with an examination of what Hume has to say about the reasons for belief in god. In eighteenth-century thinking (but not only in eighteenth-century thinking) these reasons were regarded as twofold: the arguments of natural religion and the evidence which authenticated the Christian revelation. Of the former, by far the most prominent was the design argument.

Part One
Natural Religion and
Natural Belief

2
Order and Design

The spacious firmament on high,
With all the blue etherial sky,
And spangled heav'ns, a shining frame,
Their great Original proclaim.
The unwearied sun from day to day
Does his Creator's power display,
And publishes to every land
The works of an almighty hand.

Addison

The occurrence of purpose or order in the natural world provides, in both pagan and Christian traditions, by far the most widely used and generally accepted ground for arguing from the world to the existence of an intelligent and powerful designer-god. The argument, in various forms, is to be found in Plato, Xenophon and Cicero; in Aquinas, Newton and Berkeley; and in almost all eighteenth-century attempts to establish the reasonableness of religion.[1] Paley's version of it was recommended reading for most undergraduates throughout the nineteenth century. In the twentieth century the argument still has philosophical advocates and thrives in the reflections of scientists who feel that their ability to describe the intricate working of the world argues that it is in some way the product of an intelligence vastly greater than but in some respects similar to the human. Thus Einstein is able to write that the scientist's 'religious feeling takes the form of a rapturous amazement at the harmony of natural law, which reveals an intelligence of such superiority that, compared with it, all the systematic thinking and acting of human beings is an utterly insignificant reflection'.[2] It is the various forms of the design argument, some of which still give rise to thinking of this sort, which Hume subjects to searching and devastating criticism in Section XI of the *Enquiry*,[3] and throughout the *Dialogues*.

11

THE STRUCTURE OF THE ARGUMENT

In eighteenth-century writers it is common to find such confidence in the design argument that its conclusion is stated without discussion. The titles 'The Master Craftsman', 'The Divine Artificer', 'The Designer' or 'The Great Architect of the Universe' are found as synonyms for 'god'. Even a careful writer like Butler speaks of the argument as if its validity were too obvious to need discussion '. . . the manifold appearance of design and final causes, in the construction of the world, prove it to be the work of an intelligent mind . . .'.[4] But when a search is made for a definitive version of the argument it is hard to find or devise one. In 1751, when he was working on the *Dialogues*, Hume wrote complainingly to a friend: 'I cou'd wish that Cleanthes' Argument [the design argument] could be so analys'd as to be render'd quite formal and regular' (*Letters*, 1, 155). The version which he gave to Cleanthes in Part II of the *Dialogues* is as follows.

Causal Effect :

> The curious adapting of means to ends, throughout all nature, resembles exactly, though it much exceeds, the production of human contrivance; of human design, thought, wisdom and intelligence. Since therefore the effects resemble each other, we are led to infer, by all the rules of analogy, that the causes also resemble; and that the Author of nature is somewhat similar to the mind of man; though possessed of much larger faculties, proportioned to the grandeur of the work, which he has executed.
>
> *Dialogues*, 143

Note that this is an argument from experience and analogy. It starts by observing that there is an analogy between a typical feature of nature and a typical feature of what is produced by human contrivance. From this analogy it concludes that the causes of the features are probably similar. All three speakers in the *Dialogues* agree that the argument has this character. Cleanthes thinks that the analogy is close and the probability of similar causes is therefore a virtual certainty; Philo that the analogy is remote and the probability of the weakest sort. Demea, on the other hand, objects to the whole enterprise of resting our knowledge of god on a less than demonstrable certainty.

Note also that Hume is not only concerned with argument from the feature of nature which is 'the curious adapting of means to

Ambivalence of design arg (handwritten margin note)

ends' (or 'purposive contrivance'), but also with argument from the feature of nature which is simply 'order'. The ambivalence comes from the convention of using the phrase 'design argument' to refer to at least two distinct (but not always clearly distinguished) sub-arguments. In one – apparent in parts of Cicero's *De Natura Deorum* – the feature of nature appealed to is *order*. In the other – originally Xenophon's version – it is *purpose*. I shall call the former the *regularity* or *nomological argument* (from *nomos*, 'law'). I shall follow common usage in calling the latter the *teleological argument* (from *telos*, 'end').

The *regularity* or *nomological argument* takes its start from the discovery that regular temporal patterns or processes (Richard Swinburne calls them 'regularities of succession') operate on a vast scale throughout the known universe and are expressable as relatively simple physical laws. Swinburne puts it thus:

Pervasive natural regularities (handwritten margin note)

> The orderliness of the universe to which I draw attention here is its conformity to formula, to simple, formulable, scientific laws. The orderliness of the universe in this respect is a very striking fact about it. The universe might so naturally have been chaotic, but it is not – it is very orderly.[5]

From this striking fact that the universe is subject to regularities of succession on a vast scale, the regularity argument proceeds with one or other of two emphases. One follows out the analogy with regularities of succession established by human agents. In this version the regularity argument has the same form as Cleanthes' argument quoted above, but with 'order' substituted for 'the curious adapting of means to ends'. The other maintains that it is not possible to explain how regularities of succession arose from the presumed original chaos of matter unless an intelligent designer had established the regularities.

to Order in world - reflects that of human contrivance. (handwritten margin note)

The regularities of succession which are expressed in physical laws might, nevertheless, have given rise to no entities persisting over any period of time, to no settled structures ('regularities of copresence' is Swinburne's term). But this is not what has happened. Many entities have been established with a relatively stable existence so that their parts display to each other a fixed spatial order. If these entities are almost entirely static (a crystalline structure for instance) a design argument from analogy with the semi-static entities established by human activity may be set up. But in many of the most striking instances of natural order, regularities of succession operate to produce machine-like entities which also display regularities of copresence (for example: at one extreme, the solar system; at the other, a molecule of DNA). But when the parts of the entity combine to serve a purpose in the whole entity (as the lungs in a mammal), or when the entity furthers the end of life or man's existence in particular (as the helium layer in the atmosphere), then the particular design argument given to Cleanthes – the *teleological argument* – results.

But the teleological argument is vulnerable to any scientific advance which might show that the appearances of purpose in nature are explainable by reference to the operation of physical laws which have no foresight of the ends to be achieved.[6] The regularity argument is not vulnerable in this way. It could be argued (as Philo argues with a slightly devious purpose in *Dialogues*, 165) that every advance in the natural sciences which displays another or more general law-governed aspect of the universe is further evidence in its support. The more successful the natural sciences become, the less plausible it looks to say 'all this regularity came by chance alone', and the less intellectually satisfactory it is to say 'the regularities of succession which science discovers are ultimate brute facts about the way things are'. As Swinburne and others have pointed out, the regularity argument offers an ultimate agent explanation of why things are as science finds them to be.

In much eighteenth-century writing the teleological argument is more prominent than the regularity argument. Thus Paley's classic statement of the design argument in 1802 is given almost exclusively in terms of examples which fit the teleological argument, and almost all writers in the preceding century pay considerable attention to the means-end adaptation of the parts of plants and animals. But from this prominence of the teleological argument it does not follow either that eighteenth-century writers were unaware of the regularity argument or that Hume's criticisms have little modern interest because they are largely directed at the now largely abandoned teleological argument. Indeed they are not so directed. The subject of discussion in most of the *Dialogues* is the origin and significance of order, not merely the inference from purposive structures.

In Newton, perhaps the most considerable influence upon this area of eighteenth-century thought, both arguments are to be found. In the *Opticks*, Query 31, he writes '. . . the first contrivance

Newton ~~Supreme~~
Supreme being.

of those very artificial parts of animals, the eyes, ears [etc] . . . can be the effects of nothing else than the wisdom and skill of a powerful and ever living Agent'. This is the attention to the purpose served by the parts of animals which was to become so typical of the teleological argument. But in the 'General Scholium' to the second edition of the *Principia* he lays emphasis on the system and order discernible in the universe: 'This most beautiful system of the sun, planets and comets could only proceed from the counsel and dominion of an intelligent and powerful being.' (It is this near awe at the cosmic observance of physical laws, not the purposes observable in living structures, which moved Addison in the hymn quoted as the motto to this chapter.) When Maclaurin was expounding Newton's system in 1748 he attributes to him what we tend to think of as a very twentieth-century version of the regularity argument: the version which sees god as the explanation of the laws of nature being what they are: 'It appeared to him [Newton] much more just and reasonable, to suppose that the whole chain of causes or the several *series* of them, should centre on him [god] as their source and foundation; and that the whole system appear depending on him the only independent cause.'[7] What is remarkable and in need of an agent explanation is the lawfulness and regularity of succession of the universal system, not merely the occurrence of those parts of it which appear to fulfil some purpose.

In Hume, as in Newton, the design argument is sometimes formulated as the teleological argument, sometimes as the regularity argument, sometimes as a mixture of both. In Cleanthes' statement already quoted from the beginning of the *Dialogues*, he speaks of 'the curious adapting of means to ends, throughout all nature' – a formula which appears to confine the discussion to the teleological argument. But in other places in the *Dialogues* Hume speaks of 'the order and arrangement of nature' or simply of 'order' and in the *Enquiry* he writes:

> [The religious philosophers] paint, in the most magnificent colours, the order, beauty, and wise arrangement of the universe; and then ask, if such a glorious display of intelligence could proceed from the fortuitous concourse of atoms, or if chance could produce what the greatest genius can never sufficiently admire.
>
> *Enquiry*, 135: 145

Elsewhere he again emphasises the *order* rather than the *purpose* to be found in nature:

Were men led into the apprehension of invisible, intelligent power by a contemplation of the works of nature, they could never possibly entertain any conception but of one single being, who bestowed existence and order on this vast machine, and adjusted all its parts, according to one regular plan or connected system.   N.H.R., 26

But although it is possible to show Hume attending to one or other of the sub-arguments in the design argument, or to both at the same time (e.g. *Dialogues*, 146: 'Order, arrangement or the adjustment of final causes . . .') It is apparent from his discussion that he does not generally distinguish or need to distinguish between the two. What he does is to provide criticisms of immense subtlety and penetration which either apply mainly to the regularity or to both the sub-arguments. These criticisms I shall now consider.

In what follows I shall take it that Hume in the *Dialogues* is any speaker who appears to be making a good philosophical point and I shall treat the *Enquiry* and the *Dialogues* as a continuous body of philosophical argument. I shall speak of the 'design argument' whenever it is unnecessary to distinguish between the two sub-arguments and, in order to keep clear of gratuitous and, at this stage, unimportant complications in the discussion, I shall take it that no feature of nature (purpose, order, fitness of means to ends etc.) used to state the argument will analytically imply the activity of an agent. For example, if it is observed that nature is *orderly* this will not analytically imply the existence of an *orderer*.

I also take it that when something is said to be orderly, or to display order, this will mean that *both* regularities of succession *and* regularities of copresence are discernible. When it is important to indicate one type of order rather than the other, I shall speak of regular *processes* (regularities of succession) or of regular *structures* (regularities of copresence).

Precisely how many criticisms of the design argument can be individuated in the *Dialogues* and the *Enquiry* depends upon how Hume's continuous flow of argument is sub-divided. For the purposes of discussion in this chapter, I have distinguished ten interrelated criticisms. They are set out in groups according to their influence upon the argument. The first imposes restrictions upon what could be concluded from the design argument if it were valid, the second is a special objection arising from Hume's account of causation, the third group is concerned with the quality of the analogy in the argument, and the last with alternative explanations of the order to be found in the natural world. The ten criticisms, (A) to (J), are as follows.

RESTRICTIONS ON THE CONCLUSION

(A) *If the gods are the cause of order in the universe, then they possess that degree of power, intelligence and benevolence which appears in their known effect (the world) and nothing more (Enquiry, 135: 145 et seq.).*

Hume expresses the bones of this criticism in two sentences in the *Enquiry* which I shall denote P_1 and P_2.

P_1 When we infer any particular cause from an effect, we must proportion the one to the other, and can never be allowed to ascribe to the cause any qualities, but what are exactly sufficient to produce the effect.   *Enquiry*, 136: 145

P_2 If the cause be known *only* by the effect, we never ought to ascribe to it any qualities, beyond what are precisely requisite to produce the effect: Nor can we, by any rules of just reasoning, return back from the cause, and infer other effects from it, beyond those by which alone it is known to us (my italics).   *Enquiry*, 136: 146

Thus, for example, if we find in a junk shop a painting of an arcadian landscape, we can confidently conclude from what we have seen or heard about the origin of paintings that its origin lies in the activity of an artist, and from what we know about human beings we can infer that the artist had a body temperature of approximately 98.4°F. But from the arcadian landscape alone we cannot conclude that the artist was also an architect who kept bees. In general, we can know more about a cause than that it is just sufficient to produce a given effect when we know from experience what kind of thing the cause is. But in the case of arguing from the world to a god, we are not, it is to be assumed, already familiar with what gods are like and, if our inspection of the world suggests a designer of limited power who is indifferent to human welfare, we cannot then conclude that he is a god of infinite power concerned with human good. It will be noticed that this consideration does not attempt to invalidate the design argument. It only restricts its conclusion to what can actually be inferred from the phenomena.

In an influential article[8] on Hume and the design argument, Swinburne comments here.

> the universal adoption, of this celebrated principle [P_1] would lead to the abandonment of science. Any scientist who told us only that the cause of E had E-producing characteristics would not add an iota to our knowledge. Explanation of matters of fact consists in postulating on reasonable grounds that the cause of an effect has certain characteristics other then those sufficient to produce the effect.

But Hume would be in complete agreement with this as is shown, for example, by his comments (*Dialogues*, 162–3) on the unsatisfactory character of explanations which have recourse to faculties or occult qualities in accounting for effects.

The important question to settle is when am I in the *common* situation (which Swinburne characterises) of knowing more about or being able to postulate on reasonable grounds more about a cause than that it is just sufficient to produce a given effect, and when am I in the *special* situation (which Hume states in P_2) of knowing the cause *only* through its effects? Hume's answer is that I am in the special situation when the cause is the only one of its kind as far as I can know. Thus when I infer the cause of something to be a human agent I am in the common situation and I can at once infer other human type activities in the cause because I know from experience what humans are like and what they can do: 'man is a being, whom we know by experience' (*Enquiry*, 143: 152). On the other hand with the cause of the regularities in the world I am in the special situation. This cause is unique, as far as I can know, and is known to us only from the given effect: 'The Deity is known to us only by his productions, and is a single being in the universe, not comprehended under any species or genus, from whose experienced attributes or qualities, we can, by analogy, infer any attribute or quality in him' (*Enquiry*, 143: 153).

It will be noticed that Hume does not propose the universal adoption of the principle P_1 since it describes an inference pattern which is immediately qualified in his remarks by P_2. Swinburne's comment does not allow for this qualification. Hume is himself very much alive to the dangers of mixing up the common and the special situations. If you saw a half-finished house (*Enquiry*, 143: 151–2), would you not infer that it was a work of intelligent contrivance and that it would be completed? Likewise if you saw one human footprint in the sands would you not infer that there had been another? Why then when you see a world displaying very great signs of contrivance but falling short of perfection do you hesitate to infer that its cause is limitlessly good and powerful, or that the world is moving towards perfection? Because in the former case you know what finished houses are like, and that they are designed, and you know that human beings generally have two legs. This is the common situation. But in the latter case the degree of completeness of the world is not known by comparison with anything else like it and neither is the power and perfection of its cause. Gods are not beings known to us by experience. This is the special situation (which Hume underlines in a footnote which reiterates P_2; see *Enquiry*, 145: 154).

What the religious philosophers are tacitly assuming, as Hume points out, is that they *do* know more about their God than the design argument could establish if it were valid. In particular they claim that God has moral attributes. Hume's general response to this claim is a rhetorical challenge: 'I ask; who carried them into the celestial regions, who admitted them into the councils of the gods, who opened to them the book of fate, that they thus rashly affirm, that their deities have executed, or will execute, any purpose beyond what has actually appeared?' (*Enquiry*, 138: 147). The possible answer to this challenge, that the Christian revelation admitted the religious philosophers to the councils of God, will be considered in Chapter 8. At the moment what is being argued by Hume is that the design argument, if valid, does not itself establish that the designer has attributes beyond those which appear in the world. In particular it does not show that the designer has perfect moral attributes. Indeed the situation is worse.

(B)   *If the design argument is valid then the existence of natural evil in the world is evidence against god having the moral characteristics attributed to him in theistic religions* (*Dialogues*, 193–213).

What I here distinguish as a separate criticism of the design argument is clearly a particular and very important application of the first. Swinburne dismisses it: 'this does not affect the argument from design which, as Cleanthes admits, does not purport to show that the designer of the universe does have these characteristics'. I do not know where Cleanthes is supposed to admit this. The entire discussion in the *Dialogues* takes place within the agreed assumption that 'the question is not concerning the *being* but the *nature* of God' (*Dialogues*, 141; see also 128) and in Sections X and XI, where the problem of natural evil is being discussed, Cleanthes makes it very clear that he *does* wish to establish the moral attributes of the Deity from the observed character of the world: 'If you can make out the present point, and prove mankind to be unhappy or corrupted, there is an end at once of all religion. For to what purpose establish the natural attributes of the Deity, while the moral are still doubtful and uncertain?' (*Dialogues*, 199).

Cleanthes' question is not merely rhetorical. It poses a vitally important restriction on the sort of conclusion which might be established by the design argument. There is a world of difference between an argument which might establish the moral character of the designer and an argument which leads to Philo's bleakly alien god: 'The true conclusion is, that the original source of all things is entirely indifferent to all these principles, and has no more regard to good above ill than to heat above cold' (*Dialogues*, 212). Philo concedes about the problem of evil might be solvable: that the facts of the world might be shown to be *consistent* with the presumption of divine benevolence and omnipotence (especially if talk about infinite attributes is dropped) What he does not concede, and I do not see how such a concession could be defended, is that the facts of the world could themselves be used as *evidence* from which to infer divine benevolence and omnipotence. It is Hume's contention that the savage, predatory and wasteful economy of nature is alone sufficient to prevent us *inferring* the benevolence of the designing intelligence unless we give 'benevolence' a new meaning quite at variance with the normal. As Mill wrote more passionately: 'Not even on the most distorted and contracted theory of good which ever was framed by religious or philosophical fanaticism, can the government of Nature be made to resemble the work of a being at once good and omnipotent.'[9] Thus if the design argument indicates the existence of some gigantically intelligent and powerful agent, it also indicates the amoral character of that agent. If we argue from world to god, we arrive at 'nothing but the idea of a blind nature' (*Dialogues*, 211) or at a power which has 'no more regard to good above ill than to heat above cold'. As Philo and Demea both agree, the order of nature is not such as to provide *evidence* of the power *and* benevolence of its cause.

(C) *If valid, the design argument could establish a number of conclusions incompatible with monotheism, namely, that the universe is (1) the product of a committee of designers (2) a discarded experiment in universe making or the product of a second rate god, (3) a creation which has ever since been allowed to run on at its own devices.*

(1) 'A great number of men join in building a house or ship, in rearing a city, in framing a commonwealth. Why not several Deities combine in contriving and framing a world?' (*Dialogues*, 167). The standard reply to this sort of polytheistic argument is an appeal to Occam's Razor: don't multiply entities without need. The lack of any need in the case of the design argument is argued by Berkeley: 'Further, is there not in natural productions and effects a visible unity of counsel and design? Are not the rules fixed and immovable? Do not the same laws of nature obtain throughout? The same in China and here the same two thousand years ago and today?'[10] Swinburne (p. 210) provides the identical objection in modern dress:

> If there were more than one deity responsible for the order of the Universe, we should expect to see characteristic marks of the handiwork of different deities in different parts of the Universe, just as we see different kinds of workmanship in the different houses of a city. We should expect to find an inverse square law of gravitation obeyed in one part of the Universe, and in another part a law which was just short of being an inverse square law . . .

Hume is aware that a primary methodological principle of natural science reiterated by Newton in 1686 ('We are to admit no more causes of natural things than such as are both true and sufficient to explain their appearance'[11]) is against him here. Shortly after the passage already quoted he remarks: 'To multiply causes, without necessity, is indeed contrary to true philosophy: But this principle applies not to the present case.' Why? Because it is an open question whether all the attributes of deity are united in one subject. But this is not an entirely satisfactory answer. An open question between two alternatives is exactly the sort of situation where it *is* appropriate to close on the simpler alternative (in this case monotheism) by an appeal to Newton's Rule. The real dispute between Hume and Olding[12] on the one hand and Berkeley and Swinburne on the other is whether it is in fact an open question between monotheism and polytheism. Berkeley contends that monotheism is more reasonable because of the unity of natural law; Hume that polytheism is more reasonable because the analogy in the design argument works better (if it works at all) for polytheism than for monotheism. Most human artifacts results from corporate endeavours. Therefore most natural objects should result from the corporate endeavour of gods: 'This is only so much greater similarity to human affairs.'

The dispute, it appears to me, centres upon two distinct ways in which natural laws could be said to differ. It is true that different natural laws apply, for example, to planetary motions and the circulation of the blood and that these two areas cannot be subsumed under one more general law. It is false that natural laws differ in that they conflict with themselves – sometimes the inverse square law, sometimes an inverse cube law. Now critics of Hume's point about polytheism look for conflict of the latter type and fail to find any. Defenders point to differences of the former type and argue that such differences are typical of human artifacts in which many workers co-operate to an agreed end. Thus the electric system and the plumbing system in a house differ but do not (usually!) conflict, and the difference signifies the demarcation between different tradesmen. In like manner Hume could argue that electromagnetic theory and genetic theory signify the demarcation between different gods co-operating (possibly, as with humans, under a master-builder) to an agreed end. The universe *could* be a Robinson Crusoe effort by a solitary god. More probably, on the evidence of the design analogy, it is either a co-operative effort by a commune of gods or a sub-contracted job master-minded by a chief architect. It is these possibilities which give Hume what justification he has for rejecting the obvious application of Newton's Rule.

It is apparent from elsewhere in his writings that Hume in his own person does not advocate polytheism. He never speaks in its favour as a personal belief in any private statement and in the *N.H.R.*, although he speaks of it as the original religion of mankind (*N.H.R.*, 23) and as perfectly natural and reasonable (p. 54) providing we confine our attention to 'the footsteps of invisible power in the various and contrary events of human life' (p. 27), he also says, more than once and with sincerity as far as I can judge:

For though, to persons of a certain turn of mind, it may not appear altogether absurd, that several independent beings, endowed with superior wisdom, might conspire in the contrivance and execution of one regular plan; yet this is merely arbitrary supposition, which, even if allowed possible, must be confessed neither to be supported by probability nor necessity. All things in the universe are evidently of a piece. Every thing is adjusted to every thing. One design prevails throughout the whole. And this uniformity leads the mind to acknowledge one author. *N.H.R.*, 26

Hume's argument about polytheism given to Philo in the *Dialogues* should thus be understood as a way of damaging the design argument – it gives polytheism a probability at least equal to monotheism. What he says is not an affirmation of his own beliefs.

(2) 'Many worlds might have been botched and bungled, throughout an eternity, ere this system was struck out: Much labour lost: Many fruitless trials made . . .' (*Dialogues*, 167). 'This world, for ought he knows, is very faulty and imperfect, compared to a superior standard; and was only the first rude essay of some infant deity, who afterwards abandoned it, ashamed of his lame performance; it is the work only of some dependent, inferior Deity; and is the object of derision to his superiors' (*Dialogues*, 169).

These are two of the several unacceptable possibilities which Hume points out *could* be true on the basis of the ambiguous evidence provided by the design argument. Both are appeals to his more general thesis that since we have no experience of the creation of worlds (*Dialogues*, 148 etc.), or of any world other than the one given, we are not entitled to express any judgement about its merits: we literally have no standard to judge that this is the best of all possible worlds, therefore it *could* be a botched effort etc. But this thesis is somewhat less clear-cut as an objection to the design argument than it appears at first sight. The word 'World' can, among other things, mean either 'the earth or a region of it' or 'the universe or a part of it'. If the former is intended by Hume then it is now false that we have no standard of comparison whereby we can judge the excellence of the earth. As Hume himself asks 'Is not the moon another earth? . . . Is not Venus another earth?' (*Dialogues*, 150) and by the standard of these, now relatively well-known 'earths', we can confidently pronouce our earth a veritable Eden in the solar desert. But if, as seems likely, Hume intends 'world' to mean 'the universe' then it is unavoidably true that we cannot find a standard whereby to judge its merits. Indeed it is logically impossible to judge the merits of all there is by the standard of something else. This means, as Hume points out, that we cannot say this *must* be the best of all possible universes. It is logically possible that by the standard of something we cannot experience the universe we have could appear 'botched and bungled'. Hume's point is not that these logical possibilities (a botched and bungled universe, the best of all possible universes etc.) have an equiprobability based on equal positive evidence, but that the design argument leaves us with no good reason to choose one possibility rather than another. They are equiprobable through our complete ignorance, an ignorance which the design argument does nothing to alleviate.

(3) The world 'is the production of old age and dotage in some superannuated Deity; and ever since his death, has run on at adventures, from the first impulse and active force which it received from him . . .' (*Dialogues*, 169).

This is not just another in the list of logically possible universes which our ignorance leaves as equiprobable. What Hume is now pointing out (rightly I think) is that, given the universe we actually have, it could be the production of a Christian-type, immanent God who created and continues to sustain it all, or it could be the production of a deist god who made it and thereafter left it alone. In terms of the design argument the universe could be like a watch created *and* lovingly sustained by the master watchmaker; or it could be like a watch, constructed, wound up and then left to go on forever or until it breaks up with age. The importance of this ambiguity is that if the Christian theist appeals to the design argument then, even if it is valid, its conclusion is perfectly non-committal about whether the creator is immanent or not. The evidence for his immanence and his sustaining activity (highly suspect to Hume – see Chapter 8) has to be imported from elsewhere.

THE UNIQUE CAUSE OBJECTION

(D)   *It is only when two species of objects are found to be constantly conjoined, that we can infer the one from the other; and were an effect presented, which was entirely singular, and could not be comprehended under any known species, I do not see, that we could form any conjecture or inference at all concerning its cause* (*Enquiry*, 148: 156; see also *Dialogues*, 149).

This one of the few occasions in his critique of religion when Hume appeals to a thesis drawn from his own philosophy, in this case to his analysis of the causal relationship between objects. According to Hume (and this part of his analysis is not obviously objectionable) if we call *x* the cause of *y* then we have observed that *x* and *y* are contiguous, successive with respect to time and have 'constant conjunction in all past instances' (*Treatise*, 87). His contentious psychological analysis of the necessary connection we attribute to established causal relations need not concern us in this context. The vital point is his contention that for a cause-effect relation to hold between objects we must have experience of the cause and effect being frequently conjoined, that is, being 'two *species* of objects' (*Dialogues*, 149): 'Contiguity and succession are not sufficient to make us pronounce any two objects to be cause and effect, unless we perceive, that these two relations are preserv'd in several instances' (*Treatise*, 87). If this is so, then Hume's objection to the design argument follows. The argument treats the universe as a unique object and it is not possible to infer anything about the cause of a *unique* object. 'To ascertain this reasoning, it were requisite, that we had experience of the origin of worlds' (*Dialogues*, 150), that is, in more than one instance. We have of course no experience of the origin of worlds, let alone in more than one instance.

In the conclusion to his assessment of the design argument, McPherson rejects Hume's claim that argument to a supreme designer is rendered impossible by the uniqueness of the universe.[13] Swinburne too rejects the claim: 'cosmologists are reaching very well-tested scientific conclusions about the Universe as a whole, as are physical anthropologists about the origins of our human race, even though it is the only human race of which we have knowledge and perhaps the only human race there is' (p. 208). Flew, on the other hand, remarks:

Hume's second insight is to recognise that, although it is experience which provides our only possible standard for deciding any question of fact, it must from the very nature of the case be impossible for this authority to give us any decision, or even any guidance, about the Origin of the Universe itself. For if the question of its 'external' Origin – as opposed to any questions about its 'internal' development – is indeed a genuine question of fact, it is certainly one about which we can have no evidence at all.[14]

The principal question at issue is this: given that in *most* cases causal relations are established from the constant conjunctions of two species of objects, what should be concluded about those few cases in which a causal connection appears to be scientifically established by investigation of an effect which is unique as far as we know? Swinburne offers two such instances: the origin of the human race, and cosmologists' conclusions about the universe as a whole. But neither of these are instances of the same kind of thing as conclusions about the divine cause of the universe. They are both instances of what Flew calls 'internal' development whereas the divine cause of all there is would be an 'external' cause. This distinction between external origin and internal development – which Flew does not characterise in general terms – is as follows.

A statement about the internal development of the universe, even if it contains or appears to contain statements about the origin of unique collections of objects such as men or all there is, is arrived at by extrapolation from known regularities which are themselves derived from repeated or repeatable observations. A statement about its external origin is not arrived at in this way. Thus although the human race may be the only human race there is, its genetic and/or evolutionary origin is a special case of genetic and evolutionary regularities which apply to many species. Again, the cosmologists' conclusions about the origins of the universe as a whole must at some point depend upon extrapolation from known scientific regularities, for example, upon the speed of light or the calculated rate of expansion of the observable universe. I say 'must' because if they do not, then any one hypothesis, big bang, continuous creation of matter or whatever, will not, for scientists, be different from any other hypothesis. In this way, although the universe is a unique object, the scientists' accounts of its origins are generated from within it by extrapolation of regularities which are far from unique. This is what distinguishes a seriously presented scientific cosmology from a (seriously presented) mythological or religious account of the origin of the universe. The latter is given in terms of an 'external' cause – god, the great spider etc. – which *does* make the universe a unique effect in just that sense which entitled Hume to distinguish it as 'Not comprehended under any known species' and to conclude that we cannot 'form any conjecture or inference at all concerning its cause'. What Hume is saying, surely correctly in this context, is that the design argument, because it leads to a divine *external object* as the cause of the universe, employs

So a account of origins from regularities, far from unique
(testable)

the experience-based internal causal relation in a meaningless way. Of course *if* the analogy in the argument to an agent cause is sufficiently good *then* the divine creation of a unique object would in a sense be comprehended under a causal species, namely, human acts resulting in artifacts.

In his perceptive commentary on the *Dialogues*[15] Nelson Pike points out that it is in just this way that Cleanthes anticipates Philo's argument that it makes no sense to speak of objects which are 'single, individual, without parallel' such as 'an orderly universe' being causes or effects of anything. Cleanthes' contention is that there is indeed a causal species of which the universe as a whole is a member: 'Look round the world. Contemplate the whole and every part of it: You will find it to be nothing but one great machine, sub-divided into an infinite number of lesser machines . . .' (*Dialogues*, 143). If this is so, then it becomes possible, even on Hume's account of causation, to form an analogy between the species which is natural machines (including the universe as a whole) and machines which are intelligently contrived. Hume's reply – and it is a lengthy one – is that the dissimilarities between natural and intelligently contrived machines are vast, and that we are illicitly using what is true of a tiny proportion of machines, namely that they are intelligently contrived, as a rule for all the rest.

WEAKNESS IN THE ANALOGY

(E) *The analogy between those objects known to proceed from design and any natural object is too weak and remote to suggest similar causes.* (This argument appears both in the *Enquiry* and in many locations in the *Dialogues*.)

In the article to which I have already referred, Swinburne concedes that 'if there is a weakness in the argument it is here that it is to be found' but he refuses to assess the weakness since it is perhaps more a task 'for the preacher and the poet than for the philosopher' (Swinburne, 211).[16] But this will not do in the context of Swinburne's generalisation that Hume's criticisms are 'bad criticisms of the argument in any form'. The central and most strongly urged criticism which Hume presents is that the analogy is hopelessly weak.

Swinburne gives the following account of the sort of analogical argument which the design argument is:

> Our argument thus proves . . . to exemplify a pattern common in scientific inference. As are caused by Bs. A*s are similar to As. Therefore – given that there is no more satisfactory explanation of the existence of A*s – they are produced by B*s similar to Bs. B*s are postulated to be similar in all respects to Bs except in so far as the dissimilarities between As and A*s force us to postulate a difference.
>   (p. 245)

In outline:

> A*s *are similar to* As
> As *are caused by* Bs
> *Therefore* A*s *are caused by* B*s

Where B*s are similar to Bs 'except in so far as the dissimilarities between As and A*s force us to postulate a difference' between B*s and Bs. Thus: natural objects are similar to artifacts: artifacts are caused by human agents; therefore natural objects are caused by non-human agent(s) similar to human agents except in so far as the dissimilarities between artifacts and natural objects force us to postulate a difference.

My difficulty with this otherwise very useful formulation is that the statement 'A*s are similar to As' omits reference to the main element characteristic of argument by analogy. 'How good an analogy is there?' we ask, meaning: 'how close a similarity is there between the objects compared?' Swinburne does of course allow for this question in his concluding qualification: B*s *are similar to* Bs 'except in so far as the dissimilarities between As and A*s force us to postulate a difference', a qualification which he emphasises in his reply article p. 198 (see note 16). But analogical arguments are not usually set up by conceding similarity and then noting differences after the conclusion has been reached. They are set up by establishing explicit points of similarity in the analogy and countered by disputing whether the similarities hold, are of sufficient importance, or are negated by dissimilarities. Thus it would seem desirable that the scheme for analogical argument should at least allow the points of similarity between the objects to be stated: objects are similar *with respect to certain features* which have to be specified if the similarity is challenged. A way in which this could be done in Swinburne's scheme is as follows:

A*s *are similar to* As *in features* $x_1, x_2 \ldots, \ldots x_n$
As *are caused by* Bs
Therefore A*s *are caused by* B*s

where B*s are as similar to Bs as the number and/or relative scale of x_1 to x_n allow us to suppose. Thus the analogy would be weak if either n were a very small number or if the scale of any particular x found in association with A*s were very different from the scale of the same x found in association with As. Thus both a beetle and a man can move from one place to another. But this single feature of similarity, given also the vastly different scale and complexity of its occurrence, is unlikely to be used in an analogy to show that beetles, like men, also enjoy music. It might be objected here that a beetle and a man are also *different* with respect to certain features y_1 to y_n and this constitutes an anti-analogy which further weakens the analogical force of such few similar features as can be found. Thus in formulating a full schema for analogical argument allowance should be made for stating differences between A*s and As. This is true. But I am reluctant to introduce this additional complexity for present purposes since most of Hume's objections to the analogy in the design argument do not depend upon it. This is because his points turn upon weakness in the similarities not upon the presence of dissimilarities. This same concern with strength and weakness in the positive analogy rather than with the anti-analogy shows itself in Hume's general comments on the character of analogical argument:

> Where the causes are entirely similar, the analogy is perfect, and the inference, drawn from it, is regarded as certain and conclusive [that is, it becomes an inductive conclusion] . . . But where the objects have not so exact a similarity, the analogy is less perfect, and the inference is less conclusive; though still it has some force, in proportion to the degree of similarity and resemblance.
>
> *Enquiry*, 104: 112; see also *Treatise*, 147 and *Dialogues*, 144

Now it is Hume's frequent and emphatically repeated contention that the degree of similarity between artifacts and natural objects is exceedingly slight *both* with respect to the number of features they have in common *and* with respect to the scale of these features. 'The

doesn't rely on a poor analogy.

dissimilitude is so striking, that the utmost you can here pretend to is a guess, a conjecture, a presumption concerning a similar cause (*Dialogues*, 144). And again: 'All the new discoveries in astronomy, which prove the immense grandeur and magnificence of the works of nature . . . become so many objections, by removing the effect still farther from all resemblance to the effects of human art and contrivance' (*Dialogues*, 165)

Put in this way the criticism needs neither defence nor elaboration. Anything whatever man-made is exceedingly unlike the universe at large; so unlike that Hume is moved to suggest that the cause of the universe must be beyond understanding by any possible analogy: 'But this method of reasoning [from analogy] can never have place with regard to a Being, so remote and incomprehensible, who bears much less analogy to any other being in the universe than the sun to a waxen taper' (*Enquiry*, 146: 155). But it could be argued that the analogy is not between artifacts and the universe at large. In the teleological argument the analogy is between the purpose to be found in both natural objects and artifacts (i.e. in both sorts of 'machines'). In the regularity argument it is between the order to be found in both. Thus the design argument should read 'Artifacts are caused by human agents. Natural objects are similar to artifacts in displaying the features of order and/or purpose. Therefore natural objects are caused by non-human agents *etc.*' But this, as Hume points out, is to make the analogy incredibly weak. The features of similarity named are only two (or one if we assume that the theory of natural selection has devalued the teleological argument) and the scale on which the feature(s) occur in artifacts and natural objects is almost ludicrously different: 'Admirable conclusion! Stone, wood, brick, iron, brass have not, at this time, in this minute globe of earth, an order or arrangement without human art and contrivance: Therefore the universe could not originally attain its order and arrangement, without something similar to human art' (*Dialogues*, 149).

It is, however, sometimes argued that the particular feature chosen in the regularity argument is one which experience gives us special reason to believe is closely related to the activity of an agent cause. The point was originally made, with reference to the teleological argument and with great clarity, by J. S. Mill:

The circumstances in which it is alleged that the world resembles the works of man are not circumstances taken at random, but are particular instances of a circumstance which experience shows to have a real connection with an intelligent origin, the fact of conspiring to an end [or, presumably, in the regularity argument, the fact of order – J. G.]. The argument therefore is not one of mere analogy. As mere analogy it has its weight, but it is more than analogy. It surpasses analogy exactly as induction surpasses it. It is an inductive argument.[17]

The appeal, according to Mill, is not to a bad inductive argument: the number of cases in which we know order to derive from an agent cause *versus* the much greater number of cases in which we observe order and have to infer an agent cause. The appeal is to one highly significant feature of similarity where on one side of the analogy we know that the feature *always* arises from an agent cause. Hume is aware of this move and I make his answer into a separate criticism of the analogy in the design argument.

(F)   *'Order, arrangement, or the adjustment of final causes is not, of itself, any proof of design; but only so far as it has been experienced to proceed from that principle'* (*Dialogues*, 146).

Hume speaks of *order* and *final causes* or purposes. In the present instance his objection is thus directed at both the regularity and the teleological arguments. In my discussion I largely ignore the teleological argument. This is because (a) in the *Dialogues* the context of the remarks is concerned with discussion of the origin of order and no further reference is made to purpose; and (b) Hume has no need to try to show that purpose in nature is not specially related to an agent cause (a difficult thing to do if purpose in nature is admitted) since he has an argument (see below p. 44) to explain the appearances of purpose as the consequence of non-purposive regularities of succession.

So Hume holds that there is nothing which specially relates order to an agent. Is this true? Yes, for the reasons (1) to (3) which follow. These are suggested by what Hume says but I develop them in each case.

(1) We can observe that the cause of order is the activity of an agent only in a minute percentage of the examples of order which are known to us: 'Here we may remark, that the operation of one very small part of nature, to wit man, upon another very small part,

to wit that inanimate matter lying within his reach, is the rule by which Cleanthes judges of the origin of the whole' (*Dialogues*, 176).

But as it stands this ridicule of Cleanthes' case is not decisive. It *is* sometimes possible to argue from a small sample. What is found to be a property of one sample of hydrogen in a laboratory, in the absence of any evidence to the contrary, will be presumed to be a property of all samples of hydrogen wherever found. On the other hand, if I know of one grove of trees that it has been deliberately planted this does not give me grounds for asserting that all groves of trees have been deliberately planted. When does a sample give grounds for an assertion about a whole population?

The hydrogen in the laboratory was a sample taken at random of a stuff which we have no reason to think of as other than homogeneous. What is true of it (in the absence of evidence to the contrary) would be true of *any* sample. The grove of trees on the other hand was a particular grove known to be planted and we know that groves of trees are sometimes planted and sometimes grow up by themselves; therefore the known origin of a particular grove gives us no guidance about the origin of any other grove. But this is precisely the case with the origin or order. We know, and our knowledge has the same grounds as with the grove of trees, that order is found on a vast scale in the universe at large, and sometimes imposed by man; and the known agent origin of order in the few particular cases does not give grounds for a pronouncement concerning the origin of order in general.

But, it may be said, this still fails to grasp Mill's point. In *all* cases in which we *can* explain the origin of order (or, in the teleological argument, the adaption of means to ends) its origin is found in the actions of an intelligent agent. This is a plain inductive argument of the same sort as finding – suppose that we were to find this – that *all* groves of trees *whose origin we know* are deliberately planted, and therefore concluding that the origin of all groves of trees is deliberate planting. But it is not the same sort of argument. It is not the same because in talking about explaining 'the origin of order' an undiscussed assumption is being made. The assumption is that when we have traced the origin of order to the activity of an intelligent agent we have explained it in a way in which we have not satisfactorily explained it if it is traced to the operation of some high-level natural law. Thus it is tacitly accepted that while the origin of order in a railway system is satisfactorily explained by the activity of its intelligent designers, the order in the solar system is not satisfactorily explained by the Newtonian laws of motion (or some refinement of them). This tacit assumption is not acceptable. While it may be argued at length that one of the two explanations of order (agent or natural law) should be regarded as ultimate, this cannot be assumed at the start just to give preference to agent explanation. The plain appearance of things (which may of course be modified on investigation) is that there are two sorts of order in the world: that which is brought about by intelligent agents and that which is described by natural laws. It is this well-substantiated appearance of things which makes it reasonable for Hume to conclude that 'order, arrangement, or the adjustment of final causes is not, of itself, any proof of design; but only so far as it has been experienced to proceed from that principle'.

(2) In a space-age film which otherwise stretches the credulity (and the patience) of its audience to the maximum, everyone is instantly supposed to recognise (and does recognise) that a large regularly shaped metal oblong emitting powerful radio signals and found beneath the surface of the moon is an artifact, not part of the order of nature. If order is supposed to be intrinsically, and always as a matter of fact, related to an agent cause, how is it that this distinction between artifacts and natural objects is so readily appreciated? What is it about agent-imposed order which distinguishes it from the given or naturally occurring order?

First, agent imposed order is recognised in objects which in structure and/or function are the same as or closely similar to objects we know from experience to be agent-ordered. The structural considerations which are important will include size (the order in sub-microscopic structures is never agent-given, nor is the order in cosmic systems) and regularity of shape (flat polished surfaces, regular geometrical shapes etc. are seldom – crystalline structures excepted – found in natural objects). The functional consideration of greatest importance will be the appearance of being endowed with a purpose. But as Jacques Monod points out in his very interesting discussion of these points in Chapter 1 of *Chance and Necessity*[18] the appearance of purpose is not in itself sufficient to distinguish between living beings and the artifacts produced by their activity. An additional observation has to be made: 'that the macroscopic structure of an artifact results from the application to its constituent materials of forces *exterior* to the object itself' whereas 'the source of the information expressed in the structure of a living being is *always* another, structurally identical, object'. Secondly, agent imposed order is recognised in objects which have both a macroscopic structural organisation and are either unique like a particular garden design or only repetitive (like a given make of motor car) in locally limited ways where the repetition cannot be explained by the operation of natural laws. Thus, for example, systems of concentric ring marks on flat boulders are usually attributed to intelligent agents since they are found only in localities where there have been human settlements and there is no known law of nature which could explain their occurrence. In contrast, cup holes are found in rock formations throughout the world, and in almost all geological strata, and they have a natural explanation in the action of water over long ages rocking a small stone or pebble.

Examples may of course be constructed in which the distinctions between artifact and natural object may be difficult to apply: an astronaut scatters on the moon a handful of identical sugar crystals, a handful of ball-bearings and a handful of dead but perfectly preserved ants. Later an intelligence knowing nothing of man and his ways discovers these three groups of objects. He rapidly decides the sugar crystals are natural objects because their internal structure is expressed in their shape in a way with which he is familiar as an expert on the laws of nature. But having neither anything like ball-bearings nor insects in his world he mistakenly concludes that both the ball-bearings and the ants are artifacts: he needs to see the bearings and the ants functioning before he can distinguish between the order *imposed* on the material of the artifact and the order given from within the material of the living natural objects. Furthermore he would have to be familiar with reproductive living systems. In a more mundane context: is an oddly shaped stone man-made or water eroded? But these occasional theoretical or practical difficulties neither render the distinction between the order in artifacts and the order in natural objects generally unworkable nor show that we should not try to make the distinction.

That we do use and are entitled to use criteria of this kind for distinguishing between the sort of order characteristic of artifacts and the different sort of order characteristic of natural objects sheds light on the confusion in the Shakespeare plays argument. The order in nature, it is sometimes said, could no more have occurred without an agent as cause than the intelligible order in the plays of Shakespeare could have occurred without an intelligent author. But this neglects the difference between the *kinds* of order found in a play and in nature. The plays of Shakespeare are uniquely sophisticated examples drawn from a group of objects (intelligible writings) which in our experience *always* derive from agent intelligence and which display individuality and purpose. (This is what made the writings on Belshazzar's wall so significant – *Daniel*, Chapter 5). On the other hand, the order, or multiplicity of orders, in the natural world is the repetitive, infinitely extended, non-purposeful, sub-microscopic or cosmic order which is never found in artifacts and which is never mistaken for them. So different is the order in nature from the order associated with agent intelligence that on the exceedingly rare occasions when nature does seem to display agent intelligence the occasion is dignified as a miracle.

(3) Finally, according to Hume, we have no reason to suppose that order is intrinsically and always given by an agent since we can observe in the universe other things than rational agents which bestow order: 'A tree bestows order and organization on that tree which springs from it, without knowing the order: an animal, in the same manner, on its offspring. . . . And instances of this kind are even more frequent in the world, than those of order, which arise from reason and contrivance' (*Dialogues*, 179).

Because of this it is, according to Hume, as reasonable (or as implausible) to account for the origin of natural order by reference to vegetation or generation as to account for it by reference to an intelligent agent. Recent commentators have for the most part been rather critical of this argument. Thus McPherson observes that Philo is wide of the mark when he chides: 'The world, say, I resembles an animal, therefore it is an animal, therefore it arose from generation' (*Dialogues*, 180). Swinburne too objects that 'as analogous processes to explain regularities of succession, generation or vegetation will not do, because they only produce regularities of copresence – and those through the operation of regularities of succession outside their control' (p. 210). More generally Pearl argues that there is a significant difference between the origin of artifacts from design and the origin of vegetables and animals from 'vegetation' and 'generation':

In the case of design, materials which are in a nonorderly state are transformed into an orderly system; but in the case of vegetation or generation, this is not the case. What we find instead is a process by which organized bodies generate other organized bodies. There is no genesis of order here, but rather its transmission from one body to another. Generation and vegetation are themselves orderly processes which the argument from design tries to account for. . . . The point, I am trying to make, is that vegetation and generation, unlike design, do not provide explanations for the existence of orderly systems and processes but are, in fact, themselves illustrations of that very order which requires explanation.[19]

But it appears to me that these objections do not take full account of Hume's intentions in Part VII of the *Dialogues*. He is saying that experience does not show order to be *specially* associated with the productions of an intelligent agent. It does not show this because order is also associated in our experience with vegetation and generation and 'Judging by our limited and imperfect experience, generation has some privileges above reason: For we see every day the latter arise from the former, never the former from the latter' (*Dialogues*, 180).

The crux of the matter is contained in Pearl's phrase 'the genesis of order'. What is to count as a satisfactory genesis of order? Hume's point is that, as far as our experience instructs us, reason, generation and vegetation all provide a genesis of *some* examples of order and we have no occasion to elevate reason above the rest 'otherwise than by proving *a priori*, both that order is, from its nature, inseparably attached to thought, and that it can never, of itself, or from original unknown principles, belong to matter' (*Dialogues*, 179).

The critics' point is that vegetation and generation only provide a genesis of orderly structures, not of the orderly processes which give rise to these structures. Rational agents on the other hand are sometimes responsible for orderly processes. The question is not as Hume tries to make it – whether order could belong to matter *per se* – but whether orderly processes are explained by agent causes in a way in which they are not explained by vegetable causes, and the answer has to be that they sometimes are. An intelligent agent can and does *contrive* quite complex regularities of copresence and succession; an oak tree does not. It merely follows natural regularities of succession in order to reproduce a new regularity of copresence. So agent explanations do, as a matter of experience, account for certain examples of orderly processes. But what this does not establish, and what the user of the design argument has to establish, is that these examples give a reliable guide in explaining all examples of natural order there are. What we have here is a coherent possibility, not reasonable grounds for a probability.

In summary: The general analogy between the works of nature and human artifacts is very weak. The similarities are few and where they exist the differences of scale on the two sides of the analogy further devalue the argument. When reference is made to the particular feature of order it is found: that experience does not show that order always or even frequently has an agent origin; that the order in artifacts is recognisably of a different sort from the order in nature; and that the attempt to account for the order in nature by reference to an intelligent agent shows up a possibility, not any sort of probability. But there is another difficulty in the analogy.

(G) *The balance of the analogy in the design argument between anthropomorphism and incomprehensible remoteness is difficult to maintain* (*Dialogues*, 156–60, 165–8 et al.).

There are two intersecting arguments here. Both set out to show that if valid the design argument leads to a deity unacceptably different from that worshipped in normal monothestic religions. But what sort of deity is 'normally worshipped'? Swinburne remarks that 'For the activity of a god to account for the regularities [in nature] he must be free, rational, and very powerful' (p. 209). As far as it goes this description seems to be at least compatible with normal theism. A few years ago it would have been superfluous to mention its most obvious corollary: that the deity is an *agent*. The design argument is null and void from the start unless the god is taken to be an agent, as he is always taken to be in theistic religions, some of the more rarified eccentricities of modern theologians only excepted. If then the theist takes his god to be an agent who is at least free, rational and very powerful, he cannot, according to Hume, rationally ground his belief in such a god upon an argument which wavers between the extremes of ludicrous anthropomorphism on the one hand and incomprehensible remoteness on the other. Let us consider anthropomorphism first.

The first move for Hume is to admit that the analogy in the design argument between the order in artifacts and the order in natural objects does lead us to an agent in some respects similar to man as the cause of order in natural objects. It is then asked *how similar* and the answer is *similar at least in reason*. The only sort of rational agents we know are men (and, in my experience, certain domestic cats). Therefore the deity must have a mind like the human (*Dialogues*, 166) since we cannot understand what else could count as a mind.

But since the only rational agents we know also have either two or four legs, then the deity must have two or four legs and so on: 'And why not become a perfect anthropomorphite? Why not assert the Deity or Deities to be corporeal, and to have eyes, a nose, mouth, ears, etc? Epicurus maintained, that no man had ever seen reason but in a human figure; therefore the gods must have a human figure' (*Dialogues*, 168).

Swinburne comments that this sort of argument makes Hume guilty of what he calls the supersimilarity fallacy:

> You argue by analogy from similarity of effects of human actions to other events to similarity of causes, men and a god. But the more seriously we are to take this argument, the more we must say that the god is like man, and so we are forced to become a 'perfect anthropomorphite'. The more human properties we attribute to the god, the more ridiculous does the conclusion become, and we eventually reach a stage when the whole argument can be laughed off. The error is to postulate similarities in causes in respects in which difference between effects suggests that causes are also different. I will call this error the supersimilarity fallacy (which produces death by the lack of a thousand qualifications).[20]

Thus in foisting anthropomorphism upon the design argument, Hume postulates more similarity between man and the cause of order in nature than is justified when the differences between artifacts and natural objects are fully noted. Now while this is a just comment upon what Hume does, surely the strength of his ridicule is that when and in as far as it suits his purposes this development of the similarity between god and man beyond what the design argument might establish if it were valid is precisely what the *theist* does. He is, for example, particularly inclined to argue to moral attributes which are recognisably similar to moral attributes in man and which do not appear to be manifest in the effect – the creation – which we have.[21] But 'explanation of matters of fact consists in postulating on reasonable grounds that the cause of an effect has certain characteristics other than those sufficient to produce the effect' (Swinburne, 207). Agreed, with the qualifications already given. But if this is so, it will be a little difficult to know at exactly what point it becomes reasonable to postulate a similarity between god and man which is anything more than just that degree of reason and power which is displayed in the effect we have, a similarity which, in its apparent lack of reference to moral attributes, is an insufficient account of the theist's God. However, let us accept that it is unnecessary for the theist to indulge the supersimilarity fallacy and therefore unfair for Hume to foist physical anthropomorphism upon those who hold the design argument. The other side of the coin is an excessive remoteness between man and the origin of natural order.

The first move, as with the anthropomorphism argument, is to argue that 'like effects prove like causes' and that 'the liker the effects are, which are seen, and the liker the causes, which are inferred, the stronger the argument' (*Dialogues*, 165). The second move is to accept the regularity argument, give it all the strength with which a Newton or an Einstein would invest it, and then point out that the deity thus discovered is a being so remote and incomprehensible that he 'bears much less analogy to any other being in the universe than the sun to a waxen taper' (*Enquiry*, 146: 155).

> The discoveries by microscopes, as they open a new universe in miniature, are still objections, according to you; arguments according to me. The farther we push our researches of this kind, we are still led to infer the universal cause of All to be vastly different from mankind, or from any object of human experience and observation. (*Dialogues*, 166. The same point is made on the previous page with reference to astronomical discoveries.)

Unlike Hume's teasing attempt to foist excessive physical anthropomorphism upon users of the design argument, the suggestion that the regularity argument, the most powerful and enduring version of the design argument, would lead to a deity incomprehensibly different and remote from mankind, is probably made with entire sincerity. The contention that argument has come into a fairy land 'when it leads to conclusions so extraordinary, and so remote from common life and experience' (*Enquiry*, 72: 83) is a frequently repeated refrain in Hume's philosophical writings. But the particular fairy land reached in the regularity argument presents a very real difficulty to the theist. That which is arrived at, the 'universal cause of All', may be a sufficiently free, powerful and rational agent to cause All, but is this agent in any way comprehensibly similar to the rational agents of which we actually have experience? Can the conclusion of the regularity argument and the God whom the theist speaks of as having moral and personal concern, and to whom he prays, be *identified* with each other? The answer which Hume appears[22] to give to the former question (he does not explicitly discuss the latter) is that talk of power, reason and freedom in such an agent as the cause of All is incomprehensibly far removed from the experienced situations in which such words as 'power', 'reason' and 'freedom' get their meaning.

> At least, if it appear more pious and respectful (as it really is) still to retain these terms [thought or reason], when we mention the supreme Being, we ought to acknowledge, that their meaning, in that case, is totally incomprehensible; and that the infirmities of our nature do not permit us to reach any ideas, which in the least correspond to the ineffable sublimity of the divine attributes (Philo speaking).   *Dialogues*, 157

The difficulty with total incomprehensibility of the deity is that the theist cannot accept it:

> The Deity, I can readily allow, possesses many powers and attributes, of which we can have no comprehension: But if our ideas, so far as they go, be not just and adequate, and correspondent to his real nature, I know not what there is in this subject worth insisting on. Is the name, without any meaning, of such mighty importance? Or how do you Mystics, who maintain the absolute incomprehensibility of the Deity, differ from sceptics or atheists who assert that the first cause of All is unknown and unintelligible (Cleanthes speaking).[23]   *Dialogues*, 158

But Cleanthes' refusal to accept the incomprehensibility of the deity allows Philo to develop the forked objections to the design argument we have just been considering. On the one hand, if the theist insists upon the closeness of the analogy between deity and man in order to preserve the comprehensibility of (some) of the divine attributes then he is easily led into anthropomorphism. This is both unacceptable in itself *and* incompatible with the strongest version of the design argument: that which seeks the cause of all natural order. On the other hand, if the theist relies upon the regularity argument he arrives at a cause of all order whose remoteness and incomprehensibility are unacceptable to him, both because of what else he wishes to say about his God, and because they make mysticism and scepticism indistinguishable.

The tension between personal God and ineffable Majesty pervades Christianity. Hume was perhaps the first significant philosopher to point out that it also pervades the design argument as it could be used by a Christian: according to that argument the cause of order in the universe bears less resemblance to man that the sun to a waxen taper.

POSSIBLE SOURCES OF ORDER

(H) *If an intelligent agent is required to explain the order in nature then the intelligent agent will in turn need to be explained (Dialogues, 160–4). But if we stop at the agent explanation, and go no farther; why go so far? Why not stop at the material world? How can we satisfy ourselves without going on in infinitum? And after all, what satisfaction is there in that infinite progress? (Dialogues, 161: Philo speaking).*

An answer is given by Cleanthes: 'Even in common life, if I assign a cause for any event: is it any objection, Philo, that I cannot assign the cause of that cause, and answer every new question, which may incessantly be started?' (*Dialogues*, 163). Philo agrees, with qualification, that it is not an objection if a cause cannot itself be explained (an example of such a cause might be gravitation):

Naturalists indeed very justly explain particular effects by more general causes: though these general causes themselves should remain in the end totally inexplicable: But they never surely thought it satisfactory to explain a particular effect by a particular cause, which was no more to be accounted for than the effect itself. *Dialogues*, 164

The qualification in the word 'particular' needs emphasis. An explanation is good and need not itself be explained *provided* the explanation is more general than, or known apart from, or less mysterious than, the thing which it purports to explain. Swinburne misses the significance of this qualification in his counter example:

The existence of molecules with their characteristic behaviour was 'no more to be accounted for' than observable phenomena, but

the postulation of their existence gave a neat and simple explanation of a whole host of chemical and physical phenomena, and that was the justification for postulating their existence
(Swinburne, 208).

Precisely! The postulated existence of molecules explained *more* than a particular observable effect. *More* is known about molecules than that they explain, say, why water is produced by burning hydrogen. But it is Hume's contention that the postulation of an agent cause to explain why the order in nature is what it is (or is there at all) is a postulation which does *not* explain. Such an explanation is no more general than the order in nature itself: 'No new fact can ever be inferred from the religious hypothesis; no event foreseen or foretold; no reward or punishment expected or dreaded, beyond what is already known by practice and observation' (*Enquiry*, 146: 155). Nor is the operation of an agent intelligence intrinsically any better understood or less in need of explanation than the order in nature: the explanation is arguably more mysterious than the thing explained.

> To say, that the different ideas, which compose the reason of the supreme Being, fall into order, of themselves, and by their own nature, is really to talk without any precise meaning. If it has a meaning, I would fain know, why it is not as good sense to say, that the parts of the material world fall into order, of themselves, and by their own nature?   *Dialogues*, 162

'It were, therefore, wise in us, to limit all our enquiries to the present world, without looking farther' is Philo's typically Humean conclusion.

But it is the contention of Swinburne (p. 204) and others that we have alternatives. Either we can take the regular workings of the universe as brute facts, ultimately unexplainable by reference to anything. Or we can explain the regular workings of the universe by reference to 'the rational choice of a free agent'. Of these alternatives Swinburne prefers the latter because 'we can explain some few regularities of succession as produced by rational agents and the other regularities cannot be explained except in this way'. Hume would seem to prefer the former because no more general understanding of the universe is achieved by postulating an agent as its cause. But the preference for an agent explanation may be an

anthropocentric prejudice. In what sense is the rational choice of a
free agent an ultimate explanation, while behaviour in accordance
with some high order principle of nature (e.g. gravitational
attraction) is a mere brute fact or a less than ultimate explanation?

There certainly are things in the universe – for example the framed
copy of the *Oxford Almanack* for 1750 which hangs on the wall in front
of my desk now – which lack a sufficient explanation if mention is
not made of the rational choices of a free agent (mine in this
instance). But I do not see in what way, for example, the regular
workings of the solar system lack a sufficient explanation if they are
not referred to the free choice of a rational agent. What is supposed
to be insufficient in the Newtonian story given with suitable
footnotes by Einstein etc? If the answer is 'the existence of the
regularities themselves' then the answer may be retorted back on
agent explanation in the way Hume suggests. What lacks a
sufficient explanation in the account of the almanack on the wall is
the wholly unexplained existence of this odd corner of nature called
'the free choice of a rational agent'. *That* is in itself no better
understood than the brute fact order in nature and if, as Hume
remarks, we are to give a preference to one sort of order above the
other it had better be to the brute fact order which we observe giving
rise to rational agents. It is the orderly process of animal generation
which gives rise to reason, not the other way about.[24] (See *Dialogues*,
180.)

(I)   '*Is there a system, an order, an economy of things, by which matter can
preserve that perpetual agitation, which seems essential to it, and yet
maintain a constancy in the forms, which it produces?*' (*Dialogues*, 183)

Hume's answer is that there is such an economy, both in general
in the orderly processes of the inanimate universe (which provide
the starting point for the regularity argument) and in particular in
the orderly structures of living organisms (which provide a starting
point for the teleological argument). In his discussion in Part VIII of
the *Dialogues* Hume makes the latter a particular case of the former,
but since the subsequent development of the theory of evolution has
given the particular case a strength and content which the
generalisation still lacks, I shall consider the particular case first.

Philo's argument is this. If matter is finite in quantity but exists
in infinite time, then there will be a chaos, 'till finite, though
innumerable revolutions produce at last some forms, whose parts

and organs are so adjusted as to support the forms amidst a continued succession of matter' (*Dialogues*, 184). In Hume's unamended manuscript the following paragraph then occurs without the two additional paragraphs which now intervene:

> It is in vain, therefore, to insist upon the uses of the parts in animals and vegetables, and in their curious adjustment to each other. I would fain know how an animal could subsist, unless its parts were so adjusted? Do we not find, that it immediately perishes whenever this adjustment ceases, and that its matter corrupting tried some new form? *Dialogues*, 185

From the idea that a living organism would not remain in existence as a living organism unless its parts were working in such a way as to preserve it there is only a small step to the idea of natural selection: that organisms, individuals and species, ill-adapted to their surroundings do not survive. Now both the theory of natural selection and Hume's anticipation of it have two consequences for the design argument. In the first place they provide an explanation for the structural order in living organisms. The order need not be related to the activities of an agent but could be the outcome of random variations occurring in conditions which have the effect of selecting some of the variations for preservation. In the second place the teleological argument is fatally weakened. If the appearance of purpose, the apparent adjustment of means to ends in animate nature, is only the satisfying of conditions which have to be satisfied if the organism is to survive, then the analogy in the teleological argument between human purposive contrivances and the seemingly purposive parts of nature altogether disappears.

An objection to all this is that what we can *now* see as a daring anticipation by Hume of the very well-evidenced theory of natural selection was *for him* merely a logical possibility. As Pearl remarks 'The possibility, if it is to undermine the design argument, must be grounded like the design argument on experience' (op. cit. p. 287). Now while it is obvious that Hume did not have at hand collected data of the sort Darwin provided in 1859, nevertheless he does present his suggestion as grounded on experience: 'Do we not find . . .' etc. The experience is of individuals, not species, but it is experience all the same. But the significance of Hume's suggestion lies not so much in the evidence with which he could support it as in the way in which it stands on its head traditional thinking about purpose in nature. The *same* evidence which could be read, for example, as 'how wonderfully the circulation of the blood is contrived in order to feed and warm the human body' could *also* be read 'the human body exists in its present form only because and as long as there is circulation of the blood'. The first reading, from which the teleological argument gathers all its strength, is no *better* grounded on experience than the second reading. They are both possible ways of interpreting experience. The particular contribution of the theory of natural selection has been to give enormously greater scope and content to the second reading. But this does not show that Hume's suggestion was not, in its time, a brilliant insight into the possible nature of things, nor does it show that because Hume preceded Darwin, therefore the design argument at the time Hume wrote was better grounded in experience than the non-teleological possibility he suggests. Design and natural adaption were of equal status as far as experience could decide since they were both ways of interpreting the same experience. This equality is in itself sufficient to upset the exclusive claims of design as a way of accounting for the order, in particular the purposive structure, of living things.

The case of order in living things is however just a special application of a more general thesis which Hume introduces as a possible way of accounting for the existence of order in the universe at large. His general thesis is that the present world actually is a system in which enduring order has arisen out of chaos,[25] and in which relatively permanent forms are produced by the undirected movements of a vast but finite quantity of matter operating over a limitless period of time: 'The continual motion of matter, therefore, in less than infinite transpositions, must produce this economy or order; and by its very nature, that order, when once established, supports itself, for many ages, if not to eternity' (*Dialogues*, 185).

In an article on the *Dialogues*, G. J. Nathan remarks that this is Philo again 'merely repeating the principle of internal causes of order' under 'the guise of presenting a particular system of cosmology'.[26] Philo certainly is again saying that 'the beginning of motion in matter itself is as conceivable *a priori* as its communication from mind and intelligence' but he is not 'merely' saying this. He is also saying how 'unguided matter' could *develop* the order we observe:

Thus the universe goes on for many ages in a continued

succession of chaos and disorder. But is it not possible that it may settle at last, so as not to lose its motion and active force (for that we have supposed inherent in it), yet so as to preserve an uniformity of appearance, amidst the continual motion and fluctuation of its parts? This we find to be the case with the universe at present. Every individual is perpetually changing, and every part of every individual, and yet the whole remains, in appearance, the same. May we not hope for such a position, or rather be assured of it, from the eternal revolutions of unguided matter, and may not this account for all the appearing wisdom and contrivance which is in the universe?   *Dialogues*, 184

There are two difficulties here. In the first place, if the universe continued for ages in chaos and disorder, why should it *ever* 'settle at last' into the regular appearances there now are? This difficulty does not occur if the account of order is confined to the origin of settled structures – fixed objects like the moon or a lump of meteoric iron or a living organism. These could, and almost certainly have, come about from 'void and formless' matter formed and reformed in the sort of processes described in fundamental chemical and physical laws. But the difficulty becomes acute if we ask of the processes themselves how they could have evolved out of a state in which there was neither mechanical nor statistical order. However in Part VIII of the *Dialogues* Hume seems to be thinking not of a world of total disorder, but of one comprising matter behaving in accordance with fundamental physical laws though having no fixed or semi-permanent structures: That is to say of a world possessing regularities of succession but not of copresence. I say this because he speaks of 'a continued succession of matter', of 'the eternal revolutions of unguided matter', of 'a perpetual revolution or motion of parts' and he always contrasts this with permanent forms rather than attributes to it absolute lawlessness. In this weak interpretation, his hypothesis would account for the development of structures but not for the regular processes or fundamental regularities of succession which give rise to them.

The second difficulty is that if Hume is, after all, suggesting a genesis of the *processes* which give rise to the structures we have, then there should, according to his theory, be evidence that at some remote time the most general laws of nature known to us did not hold, or held with a different range of application than they have now. As far as I know there is no such evidence. Hume's account of the origin of order is then either wrong or else it should be understood in the weaker version I suggested above; namely as an account of orderly structures, in particular 'those very artificial parts of animals', not of orderly processes. These will be either inherent in the nature of matter as such or must be accounted for by the creative activity of an intelligent agent in the manner of the regularity argument. As Hume remarks 'The beginning of motion in matter itself is as conceivable *a priori* as its communication from mind and intelligence' and faced with these alternatives the only reasonable response is 'a total suspense of judgement'.

(J) *'Our line is too short to fathom such immense abysses'* (*Enquiry*, 72: 83).

There is at least one other criticism of the design argument implicit in much of what Hume says. It is that 'Our experience, so imperfect in itself, and so limited both in extent and duration, can afford us no probable conjecture concerning the whole of things' (*Dialogues*, 177). This final objection to the design argument is far wider in its aim than the present mark. It is one of Hume's most general and most persistently urged arguments that there are areas of traditional thinking 'of divinity or school metaphysics, for instance' in which a proper appraisal of human understanding will show that the whole subject-matter is as nearly incomprehensible as makes no difference: 'We are got into a fairy land, long ere we have reached the last steps in our theory; and *there* we have no reason to trust our common methods of argument, or to think that our usual analogies and probabilities have any authority. Our line is too short to fathom such immense abysses' (*Enquiry*, 72: 83). Because this objection is so general and applies just as much to the ontological argument or to theology in general as to the design argument in particular, I shall reserve it for discussion in a later chapter.

'PRINCIPLES OF ORDER' AND 'IRREGULAR ARGUMENTS'

The foregoing interrelated objections to the design argument do not exhaust the details of Hume's criticisms although they do, I believe, indicate all the main lines of his objections to the 'formal and regular' argument he devised for Cleanthes both in its teleological and nomological forms.

Do Hume's criticisms invalidate the design argument? If a traditional theistic conclusion (that there is a single, body-less, infinitely powerful agent, possessing moral and intellectual qualities) is drawn from it, then Hume's objection that we cannot infer a moral designer from a non-moral design is very damaging indeed. I shall discuss the full implications of this particular objection in the next chapter. If a similar conclusion is drawn, but omitting reference to moral qualities, then his objections are slightly less clear-cut. Their effect is cumulative, and this particularly applies to his erosion of the plausibility of the analogy. At the very least he has fragmented a once brief and dominant argument into a large number of minute philosophical discussions, few of which seem capable of decisive resolution either way. In this process he has damaged beyond repair the design argument as an easy way to rational belief in anything the religious man might want to call god,[27] although perhaps not as the remote possibility Philo allows at the conclusion of the *Dialogues*.

But two important issues remain for Hume despite his critical damage to the 'formal and regular' design argument. These are (1) whether Philo's contention that there is a 'principle of order' in nature represents any significant movement towards the conclusion of the design argument, and (2) whether an 'irregular' argument in fact carries conviction despite the 'regular' argument resulting in no more than a weak and remote probability.

(1) 'I esteem none more plausible than that which ascribes an eternal, *inherent principle of order* to the world' says Philo (*Dialogues*, 174: my italics).

Philo professes to adopt this suggestion as the most plausible among a group of theories which he rejects, namely, those which depend upon the principle 'What we see in the parts, we may infer in the whole'. But in the present instance his rejection is less than complete. He observes that 'all the changes and corruptions, of which we have had experience, are but passages from one state of order to another: nor can matter ever rest in total deformity and confusion' . . . 'How could things have been as they are, were there not an original, inherent principle of order somewhere, in thought or in matter?' He adds 'Chance has no place, on any hypothesis, sceptical or religious. Every thing is surely governed by steady inviolable laws' (ibid.).

Philo's suggestions contain both a confusion and an insight. Let us note the confusion first. It arises from his use of 'chance' as a synonym for the phrase 'total deformity and confusion'. Very briefly: there are at least two degrees of order known to us. There is the mechanistic order in systems of a conveniently observable size in which the fixing of parameters at one time enables the state of the system at any other time to be calculated. One of the most obvious examples is the solar system. In such a system neither 'chance' nor 'total disorder' has any place. But there is also the much more widely found statistical order in which the concept of chance, or of randomness, has a place, while that of total disorder has not. This is the sort of order in which the predictable outcome is the statistical resultant of a collective in which the individual events, frequently unobservable, are, or are taken to be, chance or random results. For example, the uniform pressure upon the surface of a gas jar is the statistical resultant of the random movements of molecules contained within it. Total disorder, on the other hand, would give no predictable result of any sort: the gas jar might just as well dissolve or become a hedgehog or *anything*. Now the confusion which starts in Philo's reference to matter in total 'deformity and confusion' can be made clearer. While we could perhaps formulate a concept of 'total disorder' and then agree that it was not satisfied by anything in nature (which is what Philo wants to do), this agreement would *not* imply that in nature 'chance has no place' nor would it imply that 'every thing is surely governed by steady inviolable laws'. Philo reaches these two conclusions by assuming that the notion of mechanical order must apply to the random events which make up statistical order. This assumption is made possible by illicitly conflating the notion of 'chance' with that of 'total disorder' and then ruling out the former on the grounds that the latter is never found in nature.

The insight is in opening up the possibility that in the design argument we arrive ultimately, not at an object – a being or agent who has attributes – but at what Hume calls a 'general cause' or *'principle'*. Hume's account of 'ultimate springs and principles' (very different from, and frequently obscured by, his better-known account of causally related objects) has to do with the most general regularities of succession which objects obey and in virtue of which they can be observed to be causally related. He gives us a list of such principles: 'Elasticity, gravity, cohesion of parts, communication of motion by impulse' (*Enquiry*, 30: 45). Another list is provided by Philo (*Dialogues*, 178) for a different purpose. But of course if the design argument does lead to an 'original, inherent principle of order' this would make the argument quite useless to religion. Such a principle could no more be good or compassionate than gravity could be angry or greedy. Principles, in the senses in which Hume uses the term, cannot carry agent-predicates. But even if this difficulty could be skirted, Philo had earlier pointed out a consequence of identifying god with a principle of order: a consequence which no theist could accept. In *Dialogues* IV, in the course of a discussion of what could be meant by god being or having a mind, Philo remarks.

> It were better . . . never to look beyond the present material world. By supposing it to contain the principle of its order within itself, we really assert it to be god; and the sooner we arrive at that divine Being so much the better.   *Dialogues*, 162

This is no sort of a move towards the conclusion of the design argument; it is not even something remotely acceptable to theism. In the first place it identifies the divine agent with the material world in the manner of pantheism. Secondly it makes it possible for atheist and theist to agree that there is a god, but at the cost of making the word 'god' shorthand for the readily acknowledged fact that the universe is orderly. But this fact was never in dispute in the argument. What is in dispute is whether the order is a brute fact or whether it could be, or, more strongly, on rational grounds *ought* to be attributed to the activity of a divine agent.

(2) *The irregular argument.* In *Dialogues* III, Cleanthes appears to commit himself to a new presentation of the design argument which leaves Philo 'a little embarrassed and confounded' and is left unanswered by him. Cleanthes' says:

> Consider, anatomize the eye: Survey its structure and contrivance; and tell me, from your own feeling, if the idea of a contriver does not immediately flow in upon you with a force like that of sensation. . . . And if the argument for theism be, as you pretend, contrary to the principles of logic: its universal, its irresistible influence proves clearly, that there may be arguments of a like irregular nature.   *Dialogues*, 154f

In his edition of the *Dialogues*, pp. 224–35, (see note 15) Nelson Pike points out that what is being said here is that the perception that structure and contrivance come from a designing agent is not an inference drawn from an empirically established analogy between classes of objects, but a *direct* awareness akin to sensation. The process is specifically compared by Cleanthes to being aware of the existence of another mind from the evidence of articulate and intelligent speech.

There are three questions to be asked. Is this irregular argument a form of reasoning? If it is a form of reasoning, is it in any important respect different from the reasoning employed in Cleanthes' earlier 'formal and regular argument'? If it is not a form of reasoning, does it nevertheless recommend itself to us as a direct perception of how things are, or in some other way yet to be analysed?

The problem with the first question is that two positions seem to exist side by side in Cleanthes' remarks. There is the suggestion that 'the idea of a contriver' flows in upon us 'with a force like that of sensation'. Then there is the *argument* that recognising the contriver is just like recognising an intelligent mind behind a voice. Now as P. S. Wadia has pointed out,[28] as an argument the 'irregular argument' is of the same form as Cleanthes' earlier statement of the design argument, and subject to similar criticisms: we unfailingly associated articulate voices with intelligent minds, but how analogous is this to associating design with order, *and so on*. All Cleanthes is doing is to assert that the conclusion in the case of the design argument is so close to our perception of order or means/ ends in nature, that we do not have to think about it; the conclusion comes to us with the force of sensation (not *as* sensation), and as naturally as associating an articulate voice with another mind. So what Cleanthes offers is not a new argument or a new form of reasoning. He is saying, and here is perhaps the cause of Philo's confusion, that there is something very specially and obviously natural in transferring our thoughts from order and purposive contrivance to a designer. It is almost irresistible *despite* the way in which the sceptic can show that it is 'contradictory to the principles of logic'.

I shall return in Chapter 7 to the all important question whether our feeling that there is design has, in Hume's view, the *acceptable* status of a natural belief, i.e. of an essential belief neither arrived at nor permanently removable by any process of reasoning. But first there are other arguments concerning the reasonableness of belief in God or any god. One of these is the problem of evil.

3

Evil, Freedom and the Religious Hypothesis

I returned, and saw under the sun, that the race
is not to the swift, nor the battle to the strong,
neither yet bread to the wise, nor yet riches to
men of understanding, nor yet favour to men of skill;
but time and chance happeneth to them all.

Ecclesiastes, IX

Hume's main discussion of what is usually termed the problem of evil (or the problem of suffering) is in Parts X and XI of the *Dialogues* and in Section XI of the *Enquiry*. Section VIII of the *Enquiry* contains some remarks on freedom and necessity which are relevant to what, following Flew and Plantinga, I shall call the 'Free Will Defence'. But these form an argument in their own right and I shall deal with them separately in the final section of this chapter.

Hume's main argument is that the existence of various forms of evil in the world places a highly significant restriction upon the inference which can be drawn from the order in the world to the character of the orderer. I shall call this the inference problem of evil. It is for Hume just a special case of the general illegitimacy (already discussed, see above p. 17) of inferring more power, more goodness – more anything – in the cause than is actually manifest in the effect, the Universe itself. But as so often in Hume's critical discussion of sensitive religious positions his overt discussion of a 'philosophical' problem lightly conceals his real discussion of a crucial religious issue. In the present case his discussion of the inference problem of evil barely conceals what he has to say about the much more vexing aspect of evil which simply is the traditional problem of evil: the problem of showing that the evil appearances of the world are *consistent* with the existence of a god whom we already believe, from a mistaken estimation of the design argument or on other grounds, to be limitlessly powerful and good.

In this chapter I shall consider first the problem of evil as an objection to the design argument (the inference problem); secondly evil as an objection to belief in a benevolent and powerful god however such belief is arrived at (the consistency problem). I shall conclude with a look at Hume's contribution to the Free Will Defence.

THE INFERENCE PROBLEM OF EVIL

It seems probable that to a disinterested observer the existence of evil in the world would merely suggest a restricted inference: if an agent could be inferred from the phenomena then no moral characteristics could be inferred in the agent. But of course the inference from world to god is seldom disinterested. It is biased by preconceived ideas about what god is or should be like. One of the most dominant of these is the idea that god has moral qualities. He is concerned with the good, or so we suppose, and evil forms no part of him. Now Hume's position is simply that of the disinterested observer. The position is argued with great confidence by Philo in the *Dialogues* and again, more briefly, by the sceptical friend in *Enquiry* XI. The position is that the design argument does not establish the existence of a god with moral characteristics: 'there is no view of human life, or of the conditions of mankind, from which, without the greatest violence, we can infer the moral attributes' (*Dialogues*, 202). But if this is so, then to the theist the design argument will be of much reduced value. He may even sense, as I think Hume intends, that if the phenomena of the world do not allow us to infer the existence of a god who is morally concerned with the world, then the phenomena may well be actually inconsistent with the existence of any such god. In other words, if evil restricts the inference in the design argument it may also restrict what sort of god there could be.

The crux of Hume's position rests upon showing – what to many people is only too painfully obvious – that evil of one sort or another does exist in the world in sufficient measure to obstruct the inference to an omnipotent and benevolent god. Thus the first half of Part X of the *Dialogues* is occupied by Philo and Demea pointing out just how much misery there is in the world. There is in abundance both *natural evil* (or 'physical evil' as Hume is inclined to call it), in other words, evil brought upon us by nature quite apart from our own actions or omissions, and *moral evil*, or evil brought upon ourselves by our own actions or omissions. Men are tormented by diseases and insanity. There is perpetual war amongst all living creatures which embitters life. Storms destroy. War, famine and pestilence maim and kill. At worst our lives are nasty, brutish and short; at best we never reach contentment or true felicity: 'All the goods of life united would not make a very happy man: But all the ills united would make a wretch indeed'. According to Hume, but in this he misrepresents Leibniz (see below, p. 62), Leibniz and Dr King (*De Origine Mali*, 1702) alone have denied the reality of evil but their theories are unacceptable to suffering humanity (and, Hume could have added, lack 'all force for anyone who is not convinced that God's existence can be firmly established despite actual evil[1]). Cleanthes demurs a little at the exaggeration of misery: 'I can observe something like what you mention in some others'. But his protest is brushed aside: He is a fortunate man indeed who is able merely to 'observe' it in others. The first half of Section X culminates in Philo's classic statement of the problems of evil:

And is it possible . . . that after all these reflections, and infinitely more, which might be suggested, you can still persevere in your anthropomorphism, and assert the moral attributes of the Deity, his justice, benevolence, mercy, and rectitude, to be of the same nature with these virtues in human creatures? His power we allow infinite: Whatever he wills is executed: But neither man nor any other animal are happy: Therefore he does not will their happiness. His wisdom is infinite: He is never mistaken in choosing the means to any end: But the course of nature tends not to human or animal felicity: Therefore it is not established for that purpose . . . In what respect, then, do his benevolence and mercy resemble the benevolence and mercy of men?

Epicurus's old questions are yet unanswered. Is he willing to prevent evil, but not able? then he is impotent. Is he able, but not willing? then he is malevolent. Is he both able and willing? whence then evil? *Dialogues*, 198

The application of this to the inference problem is obvious and is stated no less than four times by Philo in the course of *Dialogues* X and XI, and once by the sceptical friend in *Enquiry* XI. If a man is 'not antecedently convinced of a supreme intelligence, benevolent, and powerful, but is left to gather such a belief from the appearance of things' then he will never infer perfect power and benevolence in the cause. But – an escape clause for the consistency problem – if a man already takes for granted the absolute power and benevolence of the cause then it is not *impossible* that in some way the appearance of things may be shown to be consistent with such an assumption: 'however consistent the world may be, allowing certain suppositions and conjectures, with the idea of such a Deity, it can never afford us an inference concerning his existence. The consistency is not absolutely denied, only the inference' (*Dialogues*, 205).

This observation, I think most people would agree, is correct. But Cleanthes does try the only obvious way of disputing it:

> The only method of supporting divine benevolence . . . is to deny absolutely the misery and wickedness of man. Your representations are exaggerated: Your melancholy views mostly fictitious: your inferences contrary to fact and experience. Health is more common than sickness: Pleasure than pain: Happiness than misery.   *Dialogues*, 200

But as Philo is quick to point out, even if his representations are exaggerated, the mere *preponderance* of health over sickness is not sufficient to let us infer *infinite* power and wisdom and goodness in the designer. For that inference *all* apparent evil would have in reality to be an illusion or a misunderstanding by us of what is necessary for the best possible world, and we have no reason to believe, as disinterested observers, that evil is an illusion or is necessary in the world. But supposing, as Cleanthes suggests at the beginning of Part XI, we drop all talk about infinite attributes which 'savour more of panegyric than philosophy' and talk instead of '*admirable, excellent, superlatively great, wise and holy*' (*Dialogues*, 203). Surely 'a satisfactory account may then be given of natural and moral evil'? Philo's reply is again that a disinterested observer would not infer from the given world even a limited but very great degree of benevolence in the cause. But why not?

Suppose that our cosmic isolation from any other possible habitable world were less absolute than it is. Suppose that a moon of Jupiter were found to be a world entirely similar to New Zealand before colonisation, save that it contained no men-like creatures. Would not the human space traveller find it very good indeed? And if he later discovered that some few individuals among the species which he found or implanted upon this fertile Ganymede perished miserably in occasionable tempests or plagues, would he not *still* say that his new discovered world was very good for such creatures as men? And if he followed the design argument to its conclusion would he not infer a benevolent intention, great power and wisdom, in the designer of Ganymede?

There are at least two difficulties with these agreeable speculations. In the first place, by parity of reasoning, they invite questions about the benevolence or otherwise of the intentions of the designer when he (or it) produced those vastly greater areas of the known universe which are alien to human or any other sort of life (even the Earth contains a Sahara and a Gobi desert). It is only by concentrating attention upon a very partial selection of worlds and then ignoring parts of those worlds that benevolence can be *inferred* in the designer. In the second place, it could be argued, from this scarcity of habitable worlds we should not infer that the designer is occasionally benevolent enough to permit life. Instead we should infer that the Earth (and Ganymede) have achieved one of those cosmically unusual states in which the existence of living things is possible.

These states are allowed for by the designer, if there is one, but are of no particular concern to him (or it) and the individuals in any species which happen to evolve are likewise of no concern. Thus, although to someone already believing that the designer has a moral interest in mankind the numbers of uninhabitable planets will provide no positive evidence against this belief, Philo's conclusion that the original cause, *as inferred from the phenomena*, is non-moral (that is, lacks any concern with or interest in the existence, let alone the happiness, of men) is the correct inference from a non-selective and impartial view of the universe. The original cause 'has no more regard to good above ill than to heat above cold, or to drought above moisture':

> There may *four* hypotheses be framed concerning the first causes of the universe: *that* they are endowed with perfect goodness, *that* they have perfect malice, *that* they are opposite and have both goodness and malice, *that* they have neither goodness nor malice. Mixed phenomena can never prove the two former unmixed principles. And the uniformity and steadiness of general laws seem to oppose the third. The fourth, therefore, seems by far the most probable.   *Dialogues*, 212

But the most probable inference from the phenomena (and I now take it that Hume's fourth possibility is the most probable) is the one which is most radically different from the assumption of virtually all religious belief, namely, the assumption that the gods are *concerned* with the affairs of men. If the cause or causes of the universe are in no way bothered about the existence, let alone the good or ill, of living things in general and of men in particular, then these causes are not the gods which religions have worshipped. The only favourable thing to be said for theism by way of the design argument would then be that the very modest inference which the design argument does permit, although amounting to vastly less than a theistic god, is not actually inconsistent with the existence of a theistic god. Or is it?

Since the inference from the phenomena is to a non-moral cause, if the cause is alleged to be limitlessly or even very very powerful and good, then the appearance will be that the phenomena are inconsistent with this. Consider a parallel example. There is a large and representative collection of paintings by one Fiasco. Nothing is known about Fiasco except that he painted all the pictures in the collection. The collection contains no dominant group of subjects. There are portraits, still lifes, Arcadian landscapes, street scenes, well-known buildings, seascapes, mythological subjects, biblical scenes etc. The most straightforward inference from the collection is that Fiasco was very catholic in his taste and painted whatever took his fancy. But a certain group of critics believe, on the basis of an unsubstantiated anecdote, that the only subjects Fiasco really took any delight in painting were seascapes. Now the fact that the paintings are of many subjects and that seascapes form an insignificant proportion of the whole is prima facie evidence that the critics are wrong. At least it is much simpler, much less intellectual fuss, to accept the obvious inference from the pictures – that Fiasco did not particularly care what he painted – than to contort and complicate the inference in order to accommodate the critic's belief.

Now although Hume, through Philo, repeatedly allows the *possibility* that the phenomena of the world could be shown to be consistent with the existence of an intelligent, good and powerful god if we already have other grounds for believing in such a god, he also implies that the search for such consistency (like trying to interpret the artist's manifest indifference to subject-matter as a real preference for seascapes) is an intellectual fuss which the more obvious inference to a non-moral cause renders quite unnecessary. The point is put most vigorously in the *Enquiry*, 139: 148.

> But still I ask; Why take these attributes [power and benevolence] for granted, or why ascribe to the cause any qualities but what actually appear in the effect? Why torture your brain to justify the course of nature upon suppositions, which, for ought you know, may be entirely imaginary, and of which there are to be found no traces in the course of nature?

The answer to the second question is of course that traditional religious beliefs have seldom been regarded as merely suppositions or hypotheses which form one 'method of accounting for the visible phenomena of the universe'. To those who hold them, religious beliefs form an ultimate metaphysic of existence. Those who torture their brains to reconcile the facts of evil in the world with the existence of a good and powerful God do so because their belief in such a God is strong enough to withstand the prima-facie simplicity and force of the inference that the original source of all things does not care an iota about any individual living thing or even about life as opposed to non-life in the universe.

THE CONSISTENCY PROBLEM OF EVIL

The consistency problem of evil, for someone who believes in the existence of an infinitely powerful and loving God, is the familiar problem of accounting for the existence in the world of moral and physical evil which should apparently have no place in the creation of such a God: 'Why is there any misery at all in the world? Not by chance surely. From some cause then. Is it from the intention of the Deity? But he is perfectly benevolent. Is it contrary to his intention? But he is almighty' (*Dialogues*, 201). Philo adds that 'nothing can shake the solidity of this reasoning, so short, so clear, so decisive'. But if someone already claims to know (in any commonly recognised sense of 'know' such as 'to be sure and have a right to be sure') that a God exists who is all-powerful and concerned with living things, then for him some view of the world (not necessarily any which Hume considers) *must* shake Philo's reasoning. The mixed phenomena of the world *must* be consistent with the existence of a good and all-powerful God. But Hume nowhere allows the legitimacy of such claims to knowledge of God – knowledge which could be strong enough to overrule the problem of evil without solving it. The most he allows is confident belief in a God which the believer struggles to reconcile with the apparently contrary phenomena of the world. Four of the possible moves in this struggle for reconciliation attract Hume's comments. These moves are:

(A)   *The Porch Argument: that distributive justice is executed elsewhere and anon.*

The argument is touched upon by the 'sceptical friend' in *Enquiry* XI only to be quickly dismissed:

> *Are there any marks of a distributive justice in the world?* If you answer in the affirmative, I conclude, that, since justice here exerts itself, it is satisfied. If you reply in the negative, I conclude, that you have then no reason to ascribe justice, in our sense of it, to the gods. If you hold a medium between affirmation and negation, by saying, that the justice of the gods, at present, exerts itself in part, but not in its full extent; I answer, that you have no reason to give it any particular extent, but only so far as you can see it, *at present,* exerts itself.   *Enquiry*, 141f: 150f

The contention is not that life *could not* be 'a porch which leads to a greater and vastly different building' but that no evidence exists to show that it is. To attempt to reconcile the ways of god to man in this manner is mere possibility and hypothesis (cf. *Dialogues*, 200). Hume leaves the argument here. The suggested reconciliation is entirely speculative. But it is worse than that. It is no reconciliation at all. If one person organises or condones a brutal assault upon another person, the evil of that assault is never justified, although it may be atoned for, by the aggressor organising the ultimate felicity of the sufferer. This situation is not altered if we attribute omnipotence or omniscience to the aggressor; indeed it is made worse. The human person may be excused by sickness or ignorance. But the divine person knows what he is about and no deficiency in him obliged *him* to construct a faulty porch to his great building. This was something he chose and such a choice would be inconsistent with *our* ideas of moral excellence.

In *Dialogues*, 199, Demea makes a suggestion to account for natural evil which is in part similar to the Porch Argument but which turns out to be something much more interesting.

(B)　*The General Laws Argument: that evil results from the observance of general laws in the universe.*

> This world is but a point in comparison of the universe: This life but a moment in comparison of eternity. The present evil phenomena, therefore, are rectified in other regions, and in some further period of existence. And the eyes of men, being then opened to larger views of things, see the whole connection of general laws, and trace, with adoration, the benevolence and rectitude of the Deity, through all the mazes and intricacies of his providence.　　　　　　　　　　　　　　　　*Dialogues*, 199

The point is made more succinctly in the *Enquiry*. 'The obstinate and intractable qualities of matter, we are told, or the observance of general laws, or some such reason, is the sole cause, which controlled the power and benevolence of Jupiter, and obliged him to create mankind and every sensible creature so imperfect and so unhappy' (*Enquiry*, 139: 148). In both contexts the argument elicits the same reply. *If* we already believe that god is both vastly powerful and completely good then 'such conjectures [as the observance of general laws] may, perhaps, be admitted as plausible solutions to the ill phenomena'. But, Hume replies (*Enquiry*, 139: 148), such a belief about god's nature lacks sufficient independent justification for us to need to clutch at the operation of general laws as a possible way of protecting the belief.

But this reply will not quite do. Those who believe in a powerful and good god usually hold (whether justly or unjustly does not matter at the moment) either that they do have sufficient independent evidence for their belief or that no evidence is needed. The real question is then: given the belief in such a god, could the good resulting from the observance of general laws account for the evil which sometimes results from their operation in particular circumstances?

In *Dialogues* XI Philo considers four circumstances upon which the occurrence of evil depends: 'none of them appear to human reason in the least degree, necessary or unavoidable'. One of these is 'the conducting of the world by general laws' (*Dialogues*, 206). Philo has two suggestions. The first is that the deity might conduct everything by particular volitions, preventing evil and producing good in all cases. The second is that the deity might at least turn to good effect all issues which we now call chance.

Professor John Hick describes the world which would result from Philo's first suggestion: 'In such a world, animal organisms would not have to learn to move about circumspectly, because all serious hazards would be obviated by a complex system of avoidance or transformation. . . .'.[2]

Hume too is aware of the oddity of such a world: 'the course of nature would be perpetually broken, and no man could employ his reason in the conduct of life'. But would this really matter? Hick points out that at least it would make a great deal of difference. Evolutionary selection would become impossible. Exact sciences could never be formulated. Effort and strife against difficulty would be obviated. The world would be very different, but would it be worse? Hick's answer, which I accept, is that such a world would be worse from the point of view of the characteristically Christian notion of good: 'the kind of goodness which according to Christian faith, God desires in His creatures, could not in fact be created except through a long process of creaturely experience in response to challenges and disciplines of various kinds' (op. cit., p. 344). But even if we accept that the kind of goodness which the Christian God desires is the best possible kind of goodness, Hick's point does not touch Philo's second suggestion for the remedy of evils which result from the operation of general laws:

> Health and sickness, calm and tempest, with an infinite number of other accidents, whose causes are unknown and variable, have a great influence both on the fortunes of particular persons and on the prosperity of public societies: And indeed all human life, in a manner, depends on such accidents. A Being, therefore, who knows the secret springs of the universe, might easily, by particular volitions, turn all these accidents to the good of mankind, and render the whole world happy, without discovering himself in any operation.   *Dialogues*, 206

It does not appear to me that if the deity were to decide chance events in favour of the good and against evil that this would in any important or even noticeable way upset the structure of the world we know or produce a race of lotus-eaters; but it *would* make the world a lot safer to live in. The rotten building would still fall down but at a moment when no one was in it. The flu virus would still mutate but not to produce a new and deadly infection. The defective sperm would still exist but would fail to reach the ovary. There seems to be no reason why a benevolent god armed with great power and wisdom could not do these things and yet still leave a world in which the Christian ideal of good was possible. In order to dismiss Philo's second suggestion it would have to be established that every evil accident is unavoidably necessary in order to maintain, on the one hand, our knowledge of the sciences, and on the other hand, the possibility of the good life as understood by Christians. I do not see how such a position could possibly be established. Hick's comment on Philo's second suggestion is that 'evils are exceptional only in relation to other evils which are routine', *therefore*, however many evil chances are made good, others would remain (op. cit., p. 363). But this should not present any difficulty for the deity. The precise points at which chance outcomes should be directed by divine benevolence is a problem of discrimination and judgement, not a logical antinomy which it would be irrational to expect divine wisdom to solve.

(C)   *The Optimum World Argument: that evil (moral and physical) is a logically necessary component in the best of all possible worlds.*

> There are many philosophers who, after an exact scrutiny of all the phenomena of nature, conclude, that the WHOLE, considered as one system, is, in every period of its existence, ordered with perfect benevolence; and that the utmost possible happiness will, in the end, result to all created beings, without any mixture of positive or absolute ill or misery. Every physical ill, say they, makes an essential part of this benevolent system, and could not possibly be removed, even by the Deity himself, considered as a wise agent, without giving entrance to general ill, or excluding greater good, which will result from it.   *Enquiry*, 101: 109f

This argument is much closer to part of Leibniz' position than the denial of the reality of suffering which Hume attributes to him in *Dialogues*, 194 (see above p. 54). Hume's reply is that when the argument is confronted by real suffering it is simply not acceptable as an explanation of the suffering. It may please a speculative man placed in ease and security but would 'more irritate than appease' a man subject to some painful disease or other apparently unnecessary physical evil. The same consideration, according to

Hume, applies to moral evil. There is no practical plausibility in saying that 'everything is right with regard to the *whole*, and that the qualities, which disturb society, are, in the main, as beneficial, and are as suitable to the primary intention of nature as those which more directly promote its happiness and welfare' (*Enquiry*, 102: 111).

There can be little doubt that in these remarks Hume has put his finger on the objection which in fact leads very many people to reject the Optimum World Argument out of hand. The rejection is not for logically coherent reasons but from the heart. Job, we feel, would dismiss Dr Pangloss as a fool who had no comprehension of what real suffering is, and Job would be right to dismiss Dr Pangloss in this way.

But let us consider the logical possibilities opened up by the Optimum World Argument rather than merely its existential implausibility. Nelson Pike suggests[3] that it formally cracks the consistency problem. He points out, as I have done, that within a religion which takes the existence of an omnipotent and benevolent God as given, the existence of evil in the world *must* somehow be consistent with the existence of such a God. Now, 'If instances of suffering were necessary components of the best of all possible worlds, then an omnipotent and omniscient being would have a morally sufficient reason for permitting instances of suffering.' Hence the existence of God would be consistent with the existence of evil. But it is at least *possible* 'that instances of suffering are necessary components of the best of all possible worlds', and this possibility means that the world we have could indeed be the best of all possible worlds as created by a being at once infinitely wise, powerful and good.

As a purely formal possibility I do not think Hume would have found fault with this reasoning. As Philo remarks with respect to the consistency problem in general 'The consistence is not absolutely denied, only the inference. Conjectures, especially where infinity is excluded from the divine attributes, may, perhaps, be sufficient to prove a consistence; but can never be foundations for any inference' (*Dialogues*, 205). But the formal possibility opened up by the Optimum World Argument is not a plausible or valuable defence of theistic belief for four reasons. The first has already been noted. It is that Job would not be comforted by Dr Pangloss. The second is that it is arguable whether instances of suffering are *logically necessary* components in the best of possible worlds. Although this is arguable, Hume does not argue it; neither shall I. The third reason why the formal possibility of the Optimum World Argument is not convincing is one dear to Hume's whole philosophical outlooks. In Chapter 5, I shall examine what he has to say about the division between matters which are comprehensible and those which are beyond our understanding, but to anticipate: notions of possible worlds may well be incomprehensible. The point is this. We cannot know how the system we have compares with the best of all possible systems. Being finite men, not omniscient gods, we have no idea what the best of all possible systems would be like. We do not even know what would count as a 'possible' system and we do not know what the word 'best' is the superlative of in such a context. Best for whom? For what? With respect to what? All we can intelligibly do, in theory or practice, is to examine the system we have and make such improvements as we can. For the system we have it certainly does not *look* as though every evil is necessary and the successes of medicine, it might be argued, have already shown that *not* every evil is necessary. So the crucial premise in the Optimum World Argument appears to be not so much contradictory as unusable, because the language in which it is expressed has no relation to the only world we know. In short, the meaning of the phrase 'best of all possible worlds' is so obscure that no reliable argument can be formulated to show that it is (or is not) logically possible that the world we have is the best of all possible worlds. We do not even get as far as Demea's slightly less high-flown theodicy to which Cleanthes objects: 'To establish one hypothesis upon another is building entirely in the air; and the utmost we ever attain, but these conjectures and fictions, is to ascertain the bare possibility of our opinion; but never can we, upon such terms, establish its reality' (*Dialogues*, 200).

The fourth, and crucial, reason for rejecting the form possibility of the Optimum World Argument is that if we do try to make sense of the notion of 'the best of possible worlds', it does *not* look as if the world we have is in fact the best of possible worlds. Why? Because we can imagine how it could be improved, and in certain respects we actually can improve it. The denial of this practical possibility is the last theodicy Hume considers.

(D)   *That no better world than the present could be imagined or devised.*

This way of dealing with the consistency problem of evil altogether escapes the logical and linguistic perplexities of the

Optimum World Argument. It simply offers a challenge to devise a world better than the one we have. Hume takes up this challenge in *Dialogues* XI. He points out that there are four circumstances which produce most of the evil in the world and these do not appear to be necessary circumstances.

One is the mechanism of animal creation 'by which pains, as well as pleasures, are employed to excite all creatures to action, and make them vigilant in the great work of self-preservation' (*Dialogues*, 205). Why, Hume asks, could not men have been so constructed as to be activated exclusively by pursuit of pleasure rather than by pursuit of pleasure *and* avoidance of pain.

Professor Hick (op. cit., p. 339) finds a flaw in this suggestion. Since 'pleasant' and 'unpleasant' are the limits of a continuous hedonic scale, abolishing the unpleasant would merely remove the bottom half of the existing scale, re-establishing the new 'unpleasant' at what had been the middle of the old scale. The continuation of such a process would either abolish all contrast in the scale as new 'unpleasants' were successively removed, or would reduce to a semantic recommendation 'that we describe the unpleasant as a lower degree of the pleasant'.

While this is a fair objection to any suggestion that the unpleasant should be abolished, it does not appear to me a conclusive objection to what Hume is actually suggesting. He is suggesting that the particular sensation called 'pain', which makes up *some* of the unpleasant experiences on the hedonic scale, should be abolished. He is also recommending that, in situations in which pain would have been felt, a diminution of pleasure should be experienced instead. Now this is not to say that the unpleasant should be abolished nor does it imply a shortening of the hedonic scale (for example, acute thirst may well be more unpleasant than acute pain). Plenty of unpleasant experiences would be left: pinching and crushing kinesthetic sensations, blinding light, heat and cold which fall short of causing pain, thirst, hunger, the need to urinate or get out of a stuffy atmosphere into fresh air. What is more, Hume might say, if the human need for water can be adequately regulated by the (at first) mildly unpleasant sense of thirst, why cannot the human need to visit a dentist be regulated by an itching in the tooth rather than by raging toothache. And why, if pain *must* be retained in some warning systems, should it so often remain or become blazing agony when all possible corrective action has been taken?[4] Hume's suggestion is not 'I wish no living thing to experience unpleasantness' but rather, with Shelley, 'I wish no living thing to suffer pain', a sentiment which it would not seem unreasonable to expect a powerful and benevolent god to share and act upon.

Another circumstance of the world which produces great and, according to Hume, unnecessary ill, is the conducting of the world by general laws. As he remarks, the mere capacity to feel pain (the first circumstance) would not matter if the world had been so constituted that the capacity was very seldom activated. I have already considered what Hume has to say about this and offered some comments on Hick's reply. In summary: a world ruled by particular benevolent volitions of the deity would be different from the present world in ways which might well appear unattractive to most men and which would be unacceptable to Christians; but this objection does not seem to hold against a world in which evil chances were turned to the good by divine volitions.

The *third* circumstance is 'the great frugality with which all powers and faculties are distributed to every particular being' (*Dialogues*, 207f). The complaint is general but Hume gives a particular illustration of it. How much better life would be if men were 'endowed wth a greater propensity to industry and labour'. I am in full agreement with Hick's objection here: 'If all men were endowed with, let us say, twice as much industry and perseverance as at present, this would mean not only that good men would work twice as hard for good ends but also that evil men would work twice as hard for evil ends. And the resulting state of the world would be proportionately the same' (op. cit., p. 365). And an objection of this character would apply not only to Hume's rather dour preference for industry and labour but to the amplification of almost any faculty or combination of faculties possessed by men. The result would not be more secure or happy men, but more powerful men; *physical* evil might be fractionally diminished but at the cost of an enormous potential increase in *moral* evil.

But it is the final circumstance which provides Hume with an almost unanswerable occasion for suggesting that benevolence armed with great power could have produced a better world:

> It must be acknowledged, that there are few parts of the universe which seem not to serve some purpose, and whose removal would not produce a visible defect and disorder in the whole. But at the same time, it must be observed, that none of these parts or principles, however useful, are so accurately adjusted, as to keep

precisely within those bounds in which their utility consists. . . .
The irregularity is never, perhaps, so great as to destroy any
species; but it is often sufficient to involve the individuals in ruin
and misery.   *Dialogues*, 209f

The sort of thing Hume is thinking of is the wind which becomes a
destroying tempest, the rain which becomes a flood, the heat which
becomes a drought, the multiplying cell which breaks free of its
proper bounds and becomes a cancer. These things, and many
others like them, cause an immense amount of individual suffering
and death and there appears to be no reason why they should ever
have been allowed into the contrivance of the universe.

Hick's concession at this point to a view which can hardly be
congenial to him is very generous: '. . . when such things happen
we can see no gain to the soul, whether of the victim or of others, but
on the contrary only a ruthlessly destructive process which is utterly
inimical to human values'. He then considers and rejects the
traditional view that nature is corrupted by the fallen angels (op.
cit., pp. 367–8) before concluding:

Our 'solution', then, to this baffling problem of excessive and
undeserved suffering is a frank appeal to the positive value of
mystery. Such suffering remains unjust and inexplicable,
haphazard and cruelly excessive. The mystery of dysteleological
suffering is a real mystery, impenetrable to the rationalizing
human mind.   op. cit., p. 371

At an earlier point in his discussion of evil Philo appears to advocate
a somewhat similar conclusion: 'How then does the divine
benevolence display itself, in the sense of you anthropomorphites?
None but we mystics, as you were pleased to call us, can account for
this strange mixture of phenomena, by deriving it from attributes
infinitely perfect, but incomprehensible' (*Dialogues*, 199; see also
and compare the reference to 'sublime mysteries' in *Enquiry*, 103:
111). But the intention here is very different from Hick's. *His*
intention is to commend the mystery as a thing of religious worth in
itself: the suffering may be a part of the divine process of
soul-making; mystery as such may be part of this process. *Hume's*
intention is to argue that we should not find an inconsistency
between the fact of evil in the world and the nature we suppose god
to have because we do not know what nature god has. God's

attributes are incomprehensible. With Hick, the mystery is the fact of evil. With Hume, the mystery is the nature of god. But of course from the point of view of Christian theism Hume's location of the mystery will not do. It shoots out the baby with the bath water (the gently tongue-in-cheek tone of the passage indicates Hume was well aware of this). There is no problem of evil for 'we mystics' because 'we' have refused to say that god is good and *that* refusal is more distasteful to the Christian theist than a frank acknowledgement that he cannot account for the evil which his compassionate God permits in the world.

Of Hume's four circumstances which produce evil in the world – and in each case he is clearly thinking about physical evil – the abolition of pain as an activating mechanism for the preservation of living species seems, at least in part, possible. Total government of the world by particular benevolent volitions of the deity would produce a world of beings unattractively like Tennyson's lotus-eaters, and quite unlike the men we know, but benevolent direction of evil chances would have no such obvious disadvantages. An increased capacity in man for industry (or whatever) would be no improvement at all and might well prove a disaster. But circumscribing nature at the points where orderly processes appear to break down or become overwrought would greatly mitigate suffering without producing any apparent compensating disadvantage. Thus it does seem possible to devise a world more agreeable to mankind than the world we have, and if it is possible to devise such a world, the question remains: if god is benevolent and powerful, how is it that the world contains the physical evil it does?

Although Hume does not accept any of the four 'solutions' to the problem of evil that we have been considering, and although he twice presents the problem in a very categorical form (*Dialogues*, 198 and 201) – 'Nothing can shake the solidity of this reasoning' – it does not seem to be part of his final purpose to argue the absolute or logical incompatibility between the facts of evil in the world and the existence of a very good and very powerful god. On the one hand he shows, conclusively I think, that a theistic God cannot be inferred from the phenomena. On the other hand he argues that the facts of physical evil make the existence of such a God very improbable. His existence is *improbable* because the simplest and most obvious construction which can be put upon the phenomena is inconsistent with it. But his existence remains *possible* because there may yet be some way (so far undiscovered) of showing how God's benevolence could be consistent with the facts of evil. The case is similar to that of Fiasco the painter with his supposed predilection for seascapes. It is possible, but, in the face of the evidence, implausible to say that his only real love was painting seascapes. Likewise it is possible, but highly implausible, to say that god is vastly powerful and wholly good. In each case the implausibility tells against the assumption which generates the implausibility. The critics are therefore probably wrong in attending to the unsubstantiated anecdote about Fiasco and the sea. The theologians are probably wrong in accepting God's omnipotence and benevolence as axiomatic.

THE FREE WILL PROBLEM

So far Hume's discussion of evil has been largely confined to physical evil. But in Section VIII of the *Enquiry*, after he has been discussing the meaning which can be given to 'freedom' and 'necessity' as these terms are applied to human agents, he suddenly presents a theological dilemma which results from his conclusions and which is highly relevant to one possible explanation of the existence of moral evil. The explanation in question is the one which says that a good and powerful god permits evil of the sort introduced into the world by the free actions of men (everything from the mischief of tipping rubbish in public places to the infamies of a Stalin can be included) because *not* to permit this would so circumscribe the freedom of men as to reduce them to mere automata quite different from the free moral agents they are assumed to be at present. Following convention, let us call this the Free Will Defence. Now Hume's arguments in Section VIII give rise to two answers to the Free Will Defence. One is the answer he himself suggests in the theological coda to the chapter. The other is the answer which Flew and Mackie developed independently in 1955 and which has given rise to a protracted controversy in the journals.[5]

Hume's argument in Section VIII is that men are free or have liberty of action in the sense that 'liberty' is taken to mean *'a power of acting or not acting, according to the determination of the will; that is, if we choose to remain at rest, we may; if we choose to move, we also may'* (*Enquiry*, 95: 104). In this sense a man has freedom or liberty if he is not subject to constraint. But a man is also subject to necessity, or is determined in his actions, in the only sense Hume ever allows for 'necessity', namely, 'the constant *conjunction* of similar objects, and the consequent *inferences* from one to the other'. Thus it is generally true among men that similar motives produce similar actions and it is true of individual men that each acts according to his character. Such action in character is voluntary action for which a man is responsible and morally accountable. Random or motiveless action on the other hand is the involuntary work of a lunatic, not of a responsible agent. Thus, according to Hume, a normal man in normal conditions is both free *and* determined since Hume attaches a sense to these terms which makes them compatible. It will be noticed that in effect Hume debars talk about freedom of the will and directs us to talk instead about freedom of actions. The point is underlined in a footnote: 'We feel, that our actions are subject to our will, on most occasions; and imagine we feel, that the will itself is subject to nothing' (*Enquiry*, 94n: 103n). But the will just *is* our character with its motives, store of information etc.

Flew's attack on the Free Will Defence begins by defining a free action as an action which follows from the character of the agent and is free from external constraint (op. cit., p. 150). He then points out that acting freely in this sense is not merely compatible with being caused to act in the way in which one does act but actually presupposes that our actions are causally related to our characters. If they were not so related our actions would be random not free. But this being so it would seem that god could have made us in such a way that we always freely choose to do the right thing. Hence the Free Will Defence is broken-backed.[6]

The similarity between Hume's account of liberty and the account which Flew gives in developing his argument is too obvious for comment. But there is nothing to show that Hume ever noticed that his account of liberty and necessity could be appled to the Free Will Defence in the way Flew (and Mackie) were to apply it, nor do his remarks anticipate in any interesting way the controversy which followed from the Flew-Mackie argument. But Hume does follow up in detail another and equally important answer to the Free Will Defence. This is the theological dilemma with which Section VIII concludes. Hume presents it, with an affection of self-depreciating modesty, as an objection to his own account of liberty and necessity. But it is more than that. It is a crucial impasse in the traditional Christian account of God's character and foreknowledge:

if voluntary actions be subjected to the same laws of necessity with the operations of matter, there is a continued chain of necessary causes, pre-ordained and pre-determined, reaching from the original cause of all to every single volition of every human creature. . . . The ultimate Author of all our volitions is the Creator of the world, who first bestowed motion on this immense machine, and placed all beings in that particular position whence every subsequent event, by an inevitable necessity, must result.   *Enquiry*, 99: 108

But, it might be objected, this is denying the fundamental (and reasonable) assumption of the Free Will Defence that we have in fact got free will. The illicit denial is then being used as a means of foisting responsibility for our actions onto god. Nothing of the sort! Hume is simply pointing out that if we *are* free in the sense required for moral responsibility, in other words, if we act in character and without external constraint, then the moral responsibility transfers to him in whom we live and move and have our being because *he* set in motion the necessary causes which give us the characters he foresaw we would have. Hume appears to develop the problem from his own theory but it occurs in most Christian theology and was particularly clearly seen by Calvin. From it the dilemma follows:

First, that, if human actions can be traced up, by a necessary chain, to the Deity [i.e. 'He foresaw, he ordained, he intended all those actions of men which we so rashly pronounce criminal'], they can never be criminal; on account of the infinite perfection of that Being from whom they are derived, and who can intend nothing but what is altogether good and laudable. Or, *Secondly*, if they be criminal, we must retract the attribute of perfection, which we ascribe to the Deity, and must acknowledge him to be the ultimate author of guilt and moral turpitude in all his creatures.   *Enquiry*, 100: 109

Hume answers the first horn of the dilemma firmly. Even if some philosophers (Hume only cites the Stoics but in a similar context in the *Dialogues* Leibniz is mentioned by name) do adopt what I have called the Optimum World Argument, this will not induce us to regard either physical or moral evil as things which should properly be viewed as goods. Evil is what it is and no speculative system of philosophy will make us think otherwise. So it is no use saying that if god is responsible for what appears as evil it must really be good.

But Hume does not reject the second horn of the dilemma with the same vigour. Indeed he does not reject it at all. He simply says it is not possible 'to explain distinctly, how the Deity can be the immediate cause of all the actions of men, without being the author of sin and moral turpitude. These are mysteries, which mere natural and unassisted reason is very unfit to handle' (*Enquiry*, 104: 111). Flew has pointed out[7] that earlier commentators have almost entirely failed to spot that Hume is not sincerely attempting to resolve the dilemma he presents. Flew himself describes the reference to 'sublime mysteries' as 'a smirking genuflexion of piety' and I do not doubt it is just that. But the significant point is surely that Hume's lack of enthusiasm for resolving the dilemma as a whole is biased against one horn of it. He *does* reject the suggestion that evil acts are not really evil. He does *not* reject the possibility that 'we must retract the attribute of perfection, which we ascribe to the Deity' and this possibility is just the one which Philo positively advocates in the *Dialogues*.

When Philo winds up his argument towards the end of Part XI he contends vigorously and at length (pp. 211f) that all the appearances point to an original cause which is blind to all moral or personal concern with living things: 'The true conclusion is, that the original source of all things is entirely indifferent to all these principles, and has no more regard to good above ill than to heat above cold, or to drought above moisture, or to light above heavy'. Nelson Pike (op. cit.) comments here: 'Philo claims that *there is* an 'original Source of all things' and that this source is indifferent with respect to matters of good and evil. He pretends to be inferring this conclusion from observed data. This represents a departure from Philo's much professed skepticism in the *Dialogues*.' Pike goes on to say that 'the point is not, I think, that Philo's new hypothesis is true, or even probable' but that Cleanthes' hypothesis (of a benevolent god) is very improbable. I agree that Cleanthes' hypothesis is improbable and that Philo is saying so, but I can see no evidence at all in the *Dialogues* or in any other Hume text to show either that the inference to a non-moral original source of things is inconsistent with Philo's scepticism or that he does not really mean what he says when he speaks of 'the true conclusion' from the observed data. Philo's inference to a non-moral origin of things simply makes an explicit affirmation of the horn of the theological dilemma which

Hume significantly fails to reject in the *Enquiry*. His position would then be that the Free Will Defence is broken-backed, not merely because it could entangle God in man's moral depravity, but because if the regress of determining causes goes back to anything then it goes back to a non-moral original source (which could be called 'god' if we feel so disposed).

*   *   *

Hume does not argue that there is a logical incompatibility between the belief in an omnipotent and perfectly good god and the facts of evil in the world. He says, on the one hand, that the facts of the world could never be used to infer the existence of such a god, and, on the other hand, that the facts of the world make the existence of such a god highly improbable. He considers and rejects four possible ways of reconciling the goodness of god with the facts of natural evil, and he rejects one possible way of reconciling the goodness of god with moral evil. If he concludes anything about the nature of god, then his conclusion is that god – the origin of things we may dimly and uncertainly discern – has no moral nature. This is the appearance of things and, as we shall see in subsequent chapters, Hume is unable to find any rational ground for any other belief about the *nature* of god. But the claim is sometimes made that our knowledge of the *existence* of god is not the dim discerning of some faintly probable origin of natural order but the *a priori* knowledge that all contingent things have their being in a necessarily existent being. I shall now examine Hume's intended total rejection of this claim.

4

Being and Necessity

Mr Panscope: You seem desirous, by the futile process of analytical dialectics, to subvert the pyramidal structure of synthetically deduced opinions, which have withstood the secular revolutions of physiological disquisition, and which I maintain to be transcendentally self-evident, categorically certain and syllogistically demonstrable.

Squire Headlong: Bravo! Pass the bottle. The very best speech that ever was made.

Mr Escot: It has only the slight disadvantage of being unintelligible.

Peacock, Headlong Hall

The terms 'ontological argument' and 'cosmological argument' are anachronistic when applied to Hume and tend to set one in search of more sharply differentiated subject-matter than is to be found in his work. As such he never discusses the ontological argument. But he has things to say, particularly of the sort 'Whatever *is* may *not be*' (*Enquiry*, 164: 171; *Dialogues*, 189 *et al.*) which are highly relevant to it. These convey the idea that he must have had in mind something like Descartes' ontological argument in *Meditations* V[1] (if not actually Anselm's original in the *Proslogion*). It is, however much more likely that in these passages he is concerned with the 'necessarily existent being' which *also* figures in the cosmological argument: that 'simple and sublime argument *a priori*' set out by Demea in *Dialogues* IX.

In the section of the *Treatise* called 'Why a Cause is always Necessary?' Hume questions the supposed *a priori* truth 'that every thing whose existence has a beginning, should also have a cause'. The focus of his attack here (*Treatise*, 80), and again in *A Letter* 23 (and finally, and most extensively, in *Dialogues*, 190), is explicitly Dr Samuel Clarke. Clarke's Boyle Lectures for 1704, later published as *A Demonstration of the Being and Attributes of God*,[2] had set out at length, and with considerable sophistication, an *a priori* argument for the existence of god. It is what we would now call a cosmological argument. As reported by Demea in the *Dialogues* it is as follows. I shall subsequently refer to it as Clarke's *a priori* argument, although it is really Clarke's argument as understood (and partly misunderstood) by Hume.

> Whatever exists must have a cause or reason of its existence; it being absolutely impossible for any thing to produce itself, or be the cause of its own existence. In mounting up, therefore, from effects to causes, we must either go on in tracing an infinite succession, without any ultimate cause at all, or must at last have recourse to some ultimate cause, that is *necessarily* existent: . . . [the first supposition provides no reason why the whole chain of causes is what it is or is at all]. . . . What was it, then, which determined something to exist rather than nothing, and bestowed being on a particular possibility, exclusive of the rest? *External causes*, there are supposed to be none. *Chance* is a word without a meaning. Was it *nothing*? But that can never produce any thing. We must, therefore, have recourse to a necessarily existent Being, who carries the REASON of his existence in himself; and who cannot be supposed not to exist without an express contradiction. There is consequently such a Being, that is, there is a Deity.
>
> *Dialogues*, 188f

Hume's unequivocal rejection of this argument occupies only four pages in the *Dialogues* and a few lines elsewhere in his work, and it would be foolish to expect from him the subtlety and scope which characterise some recent discussions of the cosmological arguments. Nevertheless, what he has to say contains in outline three seminal objections to either the ontological or cosmological arguments (or both *a priori* arguments). The first objection concerns the notion of a necessarily existent being; the second that of a sufficient reason; the third the notion of existence as it alters or does not alter our conception of an object. I shall devote one section of this chapter to each of these in turn. But there is a preliminary matter concerning the way in which Hume's arguments should be approached.

Demea's paraphrase of Clarke's arguments is, as M. A. Stewart has pointed out,[3] a botched job. Not only does it try to compress Clarke's original into too brief a compass, but it contains wording which shows that Hume failed to grasp the import of some of what Clarke says. For example, Demea's statement *'External causes*, there are supposed to be none' gives away the very possibility of a 'higher' or 'metaphysically different' cause to which Clarke's argument (in company with most Thomistic cosmological argument) tries to direct us. The question thus arises: should we examine and assess Hume's arguments in relation to their historical objectives alone, *or* should we do what he clearly failed to do and discuss Clarke's important argument accurately and in detail, *or* should we forget about the historical context altogether and consider what Hume has to say as if he were contributing to a modern philosophical journal? The first enterprise is not within the main scope of this book. It has anyway been undertaken so thoroughly and so ruthlessly by Stewart that further investigation is unlikely to be rewarding. The second enterprise has recently been carried out for Clarke by W. L. Rowe in *The Cosmological Argument* (Princeton 1975. This is one of the best works on the argument as a whole). The third, although followed with some distinction by D. C. Stove,[4] affords too much scope for anachronistic cleverness at the expense of the original author. My own purpose in this book is to make clear the scale and importance of Hume's critique of religion. In that critique what he says about the *a priori* argument is seminal, even if it is neither as decisive as he supposed nor as attentive to Clarke *et al.* as we would wish.

NECESSARY BEINGS

Hume's first and 'decisive' objection to Clarke's *a priori* argument is in form an objection to any argument (such as Descartes' in *Meditations* IV and V) which sets out to deduce the existence of a thing from the thing's necessary or 'demonstrable' existence:

I shall begin with observing, that there is an evident absurdity in pretending to demonstrate a matter of fact, or to prove it by any arguments *a priori*. Nothing is demonstrable, unless the contrary implies a contradiction. Nothing, that is distinctly conceivable, implies a contradiction. Whatever we [can distinctly] conceive as existent, we can also conceive as non-existent. There is no Being [i.e. thing we can distinctly conceive as existent], therefore, whose non-existence implies a contradiction. Consequently there is no Being [i.e. as before], whose existence is demonstrable.

Dialogues, 189

In the paragraph which follows this it becomes clear that Hume regards 'necessary' and 'demonstrable' as interchangeable words and his final conclusion is that the words 'necessary existence' or 'demonstrable existence' have no meaning.

Let us allow that with pedantic explication (indicated above in square brackets) of the terms used, Hume's argument is formally valid. The faults lie in the premises.

In the first place, even given that 'necessary' and 'demonstrable' are interchangeable, there remains a serious ambiguity in the premise 'Nothing is demonstrable, unless the contrary implies a contradiction'. To say that some proposition is 'demonstrable' could mean that it is merely the conclusion of a valid argument. In this sense its contrary would *only* be a contradiction if one accepted all the premises as true. On the other hand, to say that some proposition is demonstrable could mean that it is a necessary truth – one whose negation makes no sense, whatever the premises. Now D. C. Stove suggests here, rightly I believe, that what Hume means by a 'demonstrative argument' is a valid argument from necessarily true premises: 'Similarly, by calling a proposition "demonstrable", [Hume] means that it is deducible from necessarily true premises; and by the verb "to demonstrate" [a certain proposition] he means, to construct a valid argument from necessary truths to that proposition as conclusion.'[5]

Having taken this on board, we can move back to Hume's rather bland assertion that there is an 'evident absurdity' in demonstrating a matter of fact. Although such an assumption is fundamental to virtually all empiricist epistemology, it is not quite so evident that it can be taken without explanation. Hume's explanation is in the *Treatise* and, more succinctly, in the *Enquiry*, 25f: 40f and 163f: 171f.

The fundamental epistemological distinction, which I shall follow Flew in calling 'Hume's Fork' and from which the assumption is drawn, is between 'relations of ideas' or 'demonstrations' on the one hand and 'matters of fact' on the other. The former 'are discoverable by the mere operation of thought, without dependence on what is anywhere existent in the universe'; the latter are only discoverable by experience of the way things are. The former comprise parts of pure mathematics and formal logic; the latter comprise all statements about the way the world works and all statements about what things do or do not exist. The negation of any demonstration (i.e. necessary truth) is contradictory and cannot be clearly conceived. The negation of any true matter of fact is merely false, not contradictory, and can be conceived as clearly as the true state of affairs: '*That the sun will not rise to-morrow* is no less intelligible a proposition, and implies no more contradiction, than the affirmation, *that it will rise*'. The same with statements of existence; 'that Caesar, or the angel Gabriel, or any being never existed may be a false proposition, but still is perfectly conceivable and implies no contradiction' (*Enquiry*, 25: 40 and 164: 172).

Now from this it is quite clear that the conclusion 'there is no being whose existence is demonstrable' is already built into Hume's epistemology. The possibility that any thing could necessarily exist is ruled out at source by Hume's Fork. But Clarke might reply that he is questioning this epistemology. There is at least one being, god, whose non-existence would be contradictory. *He* necessarily exists. The epistemology which rules this out could be an arbitrary stipulation. If so, then it can be disregarded. Alternatively the epistemology could be a non-universal generalisation about types of knowledge. In this case god is an exception. Possibly the only exception, to the generalisation.

The sheer weight of authority and usage in favour of *something* like Hume's distinction between demonstrations and matters of fact sheds doubt on the suggestion that the distinction is arbitrary. If it is arbitrary the onus of showing it to be so must rest upon those who maintain such an unconventional position. On what grounds could it be said to be arbitrary? What should be put in its place? How else than by means of such a distinction could we advise people of the silliness of trying to prove by pure mathematics that there is a yew hedge in my garden or of trying to establish Taylor's Theorem by careful observation of the segments of a chocolate cake? It is just not feasible to say that the demonstration/matter-of-fact dichotomy is arbitrary. But one *exceptional* being whose existence is necessary is an altogether different matter. The possibility of such an exception has been canvassed in several different ways. Let us consider four of these.

(1)   To begin with, the existential propositions in mathematics, it is said, are necessarily true; therefore the entities whose existence they assert necessarily exist. If an exception to empiricist epistemology can be made in order to admit these, why not a like exception to admit the necessary existence of the Supreme Being? But, *per contra*, wherever sort of existence a mathematical entity might be supposed to have, the existence of the Supreme Being can hardly be similar. The one (arguably)

depends upon human convenience, convention and stipulation; the other (supposedly) is absolutely independent and self-subsistent. The existence of a mathematical entity, one is tempted to say, could no more be like the existence of the Supreme Being than a quaterion could be like a smut on the chimneypiece. Moreover it seems to be in keeping with the intentions of Hume's epistemology *not* to include among matters of fact – since these are specified by reference to experience – those somewhat esoteric existential statements which occur, for example, in mathematics: note, for example, that he speaks twice in the *Enquiry* Section IV of '*real* existence and matter of fact' (my italics). Thus, whatever grounds there may be for asserting 'there is a prime number between 13 and 29', appeals to observation and experience are not among them. But perhaps, someone will insist, god's existence *is* just like this – in no way related to observation and experience – and therefore not subject to the categorical prohibition on necessary existence among matter of fact existences. But if this is insisted upon it will permit god's necessary existence only at the expense of giving up what makes god's existence the most gigantic matter of fact we can apprehend. The devotee of the *a priori* arguments cannot have it both ways. He cannot give to god the conventionalist necessity of an entity in a logical system *and* avoid the triviality of such conventions. He cannot make god's existence necessary in this sense, and at the same time preserve his god's awesome consequence in all matters of fact.

(2)   Another way in which the necessary existence of the Supreme Being could be understood is as the existence of a Being which always has existed and never will go out of existence. In this sense the indestructible atoms spoken of in Lucretius[6] are necessary. If they exist, then they have always existed and always will exist. But use of the word 'necessary' (or Hume's homologue for it, 'demonstrable') to mean 'always existed and always will exist' is exceedingly misleading. If it is asserted that god necessarily exists in this sense it will still be an open question whether he does in fact exist – whether there is in reality anything satisfying the concept of necessary existence thus understood – and for the *a priori* arguments this question cannot be left open. The converse does of course hold. If god, as spoken of in the great theistic religions, does in fact exist,

doubtless he always has and always will exist. But this is an elucidation, not an *a priori* demonstration, of what is believed.

(3) Again, god's existence is 'factually' necessary, it is sometimes said, while Hume's rejection of necessary existence refers to logical necessity. The notion of factual necessity is one which has been much canvassed in its own right apart from arguments for the existence of god. Suffice to say in the present context that accounts of factual necessity, as applied to the existence of an entity, always seem to appeal to notions like 'uncaused', 'independent' or 'eternal'. As before, it remains an open question whether *in fact* there exists anything which is factually necessary in the sense specified, whether that thing could be identified with god, and whether the notions employed make sense.

(4) Finally, as Jerome Shaffer points out[7] there are tautologous existential statements other than those considered above. Examples are: 'Fictitious objects do not exist'; 'Members of extinct species existed once but no longer exist'. But these, it appears to me, are not of the same kind as the statement 'god exists'. Their wording analytically entails the non-existence of their subject-class and no one need to be worried by or question this obvious entailment. It is as straightforward as the tautology in 'non-existent wasps do not exist'. I therefore find Shaffer's position somewhat strange when he remarks: 'Just as the tautology, "Fictitious objects do not exist", leaves open the question whether there are any fictitious objects, so the tautology "God exists" leaves open the question whether there is a God' (op. cit., p. 240). I would have thought that the first tautology does *not* leave open any question about the existence of fictitious objects just because 'do not exist' is a repetition of the sense of the word 'fictitious': the tautology shows that to assert the existence of fictitious objects would be self-contradictory. But the second (alleged) tautology *does* leave open questions about the existence of god since the meaning of the word 'exists' does not analytically repeat the meaning of the word 'god': to assert that god does not exist may be false, but it is not self-contradictory in any obvious way.

These four, together with the suggestion that god's existence is necessary by contrast with the contingency of all other things (see next section), do not provide an exhaustive survey of the ways in which Hume's Fork might be defied in the interest of giving meaning to the phrase 'necessary existence'. But they do seem to indicate that there is no obvious or overwhelmingly powerful reason to admit the sort of necessary existence which the Deity might be supposed to have as an exception to Hume's 'Whatever *is* may *not be*'. The exceptions pitched upon turn out to be either mathematical entities which it is at least arguable that Hume never thought of as matters of fact and existence, or tautologous existential statements, or cases where the meaning given to the word 'necessary' leaves open the question whether the necessarily existent object *in fact* exists. (Just such an example is provided by Geach's suggestion that god should be spoken of as having an 'imperishable existence that has no liability to cease'.[8]) In short, Hume's general comment 'there is an evident absurdity in pretending to demonstrate a matter of fact' leading to his conclusion 'the words, *necessary existence*, have no meaning' is still a defensible position even if I have not here fully defended it.

Hume's objection to *demonstrating* the existence of a thing does however suffer from a disadvantage not yet discussed. This is the way in which he conflates (in the *Enquiry*) the psychological notion of inconceivability with the logical notion of (self) contradictory and, in like manner, the notion of 'perfectly conceivable' with the notion of 'implies no (self) contradiction'. This mixing of the logical and psychological shows itself in the premises of his objection to Clarke's *a priori* argument, particularly in the premise 'Nothing, that is distinctly conceivable, implies a contradiction'. After some preliminary prodding at this area, Jonathan Barnes thrusts home an objection which he makes a cause for totally rejecting Hume's position:

> Although Hume gives no satisfactory account of what he means by 'conceive', what little he does say is enough for our purposes: his analysis of belief shows that '*P* is believed' entails '*P* is conceived' and hence '*P* is conceivable'. But it is certainly possible to *believe* propositions which are logically impossible (everyone who makes a genuine mistake in mathematics or logic does so); and so it is possible to *conceive* propositions which are logically impossible.[9]

Hence on this interpretation the premise in Hume's argument 'Nothing that is distinctly conceivable, implies a contradiction' is false. I disagree with Barnes here because I can find nothing in Hume's account of belief which nails him without possibility of escape to the position '*P* is believed' entails '*P* is *distinctly* conceived' and *distinct* conception is the term being used in Hume's argument. Certainly the converse is not Hume's position. As he says 'We conceive many things, which we do not believe' (*Treatise*, 94).

But what happens when someone believes '37 + 58 = 85'? Is he not distinctly conceiving something which implies a contradiction? No. What I think Hume would say he is doing is entertaining a confused conception in such a way that the false arithmetical proposition is conceivable to the person just as long as the confused conception is retained. Thus when he spots that he added 7 and 8, made 15, put down the 5, and then in his excitement forgot to 'carry' 1, his distinct conception will be '37 + 58 = 95', i.e. as soon as the conception becomes distinct it will be realised that '37 + 58 = 85' was not a distinct conception. As a result of such indistinct conception it is possible to believe something which is a contradiction. The contradiction has not been recognised. But of course spoken of in this way, Hume's 'distinctly conceived' can practically be replaced by the phrase 'properly understood'. This, however, transfers the difficulty to matters of fact. While one may get away with saying that the negation of any matter of fact is 'conceivable' it is very doubtful if the negation of certain matters of fact can be 'properly understood', particularly some of those matters of fact which are concerned with existence. For example, although I can imagine my own non-existence after my death, I do not think I can properly understand what such non-existence would be since *my* understanding something always presumes a *me* who is doing the understanding and the case I am imagining presumes the non-existence of me.

The point is that Hume's 'conceivable' seems to hang fire between 'understand' and 'imagine', tending to the one or the other according to the convenience of the context, and it is not unequivocally certain that in all contexts these two words can be replaced by 'possible' (i.e. non-contradictory). This, I think, is part of what Robert Adams is saying when he argues that the 'method of distinct conception' cannot establish 'that *everything* which can be conceived to exist can also (without logical impropriety) be conceived not to exist'[10] since this would involve conceiving one by one the non-existence of *every* thing and 'everything' is (presumably) an infinite class of objects. Adams goes on to say

I think probably the only way in which the method of distinct conception could yield a general proof that non-existence is logically possible in *every* case would be by providing a proof that a state of affairs is logically possible in which nothing would exist at all. And it does not seem to me likely that such a state of affairs can be conceived in such a way as to exclude all rational doubt of its logical possibility.

The difficulty is a compounded version of my conceiving my own non-existence and I would reply again that the problem is not in *imagining* the non-existence of everything (every *thing* going out of existence leaving only empty space and Newton's absolute duration) but in *understanding* this situation. Likewise in the case of the Supreme Being I can conceive (imagine) a universe just like this one in which, or in relation to which, no such Being is to be found. But I cannot conceive (understand) what such failure to find would be like nor, for that matter, can I conceive (understand) what finding such a Being would be like. But if I can understand neither the existence nor the non-existence of such a Being this suggests a difficulty more general than merely 'The words *necessary existence* have no meaning'. The difficulty will now be the meaning of *any* talk about such a Being. I shall return to Hume's treatment of this problem at the end of Chapter 5.

But Hume's original 'decisive' objection to Clarke's *a priori* argument would certainly have stood on firmer ground could it have been expressed without reference to conceivability. Can it be so expressed while still retaining the main features of Hume's objection? If we bring together *Dialogues* 189 and *Enquiry*, 25: 40 and 163: 171, and read 'conceivable' as 'negation not contradictory' we get:

No assertion is demonstrable unless its negation is contradictory. No negation of a matter of fact is contradictory. All assertions about the existence of *things* are matters of fact. Therefore no negation of an assertion that some *thing* exists is contradictory. Hence there is no thing whose existence is demonstrable.

The emphasis given to the word *thing* is an attempt to indicate that the scope of the argument does not extend to tautological existential statements or the entities of mathematics. In this form Hume's argument makes an appeal to the same epistemological distinctions as before but without some of the bother inherent in relating the conceivable and the possible. It will be questioned at the same points, to wit, whether it is true that 'No negation of a matter of fact is contradictory' and whether the Supreme Being's existence should be regarded as a matter of fact (how else it could be regarded and the Supreme Being still be regarded as an adequate object of worship is obscure to me).

Before leaving Hume's remarks about 'necessary existence' it is worth noting the striking similarity between his contention 'The words, *necessary existence*, have no meaning; or, which is the same thing, none that is consistent' and Russell's very characteristic remark 'The word "necessary" I should maintain, can only be applied significantly to propositions. And, in fact, only to such as are analytic – that is to say – such as it is self-contradictory to deny.'[11] In short, Hume's objections to proving *a priori* the existence of anything derive from his empiricist epistemology. Similar objections will be raised by anyone, such as Russell, who adopts a similar epistemology. In our own century these will include the logical atomists, the logical positivists, and all those lesser empiricists who owe a significant part of their theory of knowledge to the Hume/Russell tradition. For them, as for Hume, the *a priori* arguments for god's necessary existence are, and will remain, totally vacuous.

THE INFINITE CHAIN OF INSUFFICIENT REASONS

Hume's second seminal objection to his representation of Clarke's *a priori* argument focuses upon the argument's insistent demand for a sufficient explanation, not merely of each item in any causal chain, but for the causal chain considered *either* as a whole, *or* as having a terminus in that ultimate cause which contains within itself the sufficient reason for its own existence.

To the demand for explanation of any causal chain considered as whole Hume replies that the uniting of its parts into a whole is an 'act of the mind', an artificial concept which 'has no influence on the nature of things': 'Did I show you the particular causes of each individual in a collection of twenty particles of matter, I should think it very unreasonable, should you afterwards ask me, what was the cause of the whole twenty. This is sufficiently explained in explaining the cause of the parts' (*Dialogues*, 190). The fundamental assumption in this objection is one which almost totally dominates all modern scientific and secular thinking. It is that there is no need to go beyond the world and its contents in explaining either the world or any of its contents and no intelligible possibility of doing so. Is this assumption justified?

If I explain that the flood in the lane outside my house is caused by a collapsed conduit under the old railway, I have explained the cause of the flood. If I am asked why the conduit collapsed, I can explain that it was broken by the heavy lorries taking timber away from the wood. If I am asked why this broke the conduit, I can talk about the crushing load on salt-glazed six-inch pipes and *so on*. The 'so on' will indicate a series of causal explanations which will terminate at a point where I run out of information, or just have to say 'that's the way things are' (or lose my temper). If my questioner then asks me the cause of the whole series of causes, and if I do not know he is fishing for the answer 'god', I would be entirely at a loss to know what manner of answer he could possibly expect since all available causal explanations have already been given and these are all the explanations that are needed or possible. There is no call for an explanation of everything considered as a whole. My response is not unlike Russell's answer to Copleston's question 'Why shouldn't one raise the question of the cause of the existence of all particular objects?' – 'Because I see no reason to think there is any. The whole concept of cause is one we derive from our observation of particular things; I see no reason whatsoever to suppose that the total has any cause whatsoever' (op. cit. p. 179).

Hume's objection to asking for the cause of causal sequences is, however, not so much Russell's, that there is none, but that the question is incoherent. It is a request for an explanation of an illicit causal category. The request is akin to finding that Benjamin is the parent of Harry, Harry is the parent of John, and John is the parent of Rupert, then asking who is the parent of all four people 'considered as a whole'.

But the assumption that there is no need to go beyond the world and its contents in explaining the world or any of its contents, and no intelligent possibility of doing so, may be challenged in another way. My questioner about the broken conduit could have finished up asking me why things are as they are (or why the world is as the most sophisticated science finds it to be). Now clearly this question cannot be answered by reference to the world and its contents. These are already bypassed in the way the question has been formulated. The question is not looking for an answer – an explanation – which is any longer of the same *kind* as answers to all scientific and secular questions. It is a *meta*physical question which may be asked in two ways. Why are things as they are? Why is there anything at all? Both, it is claimed in the *a priori* arguments, can only be given an answer by reference to something self-causing or self-explaining which is *external* to, or of a different order of reality from, the universe of physical caused causes. Hume does not discuss this position as such, but he comes near to doing so.

Hume's comment in the *Dialogues* on the demand that all causal sequences should have a beginning in that ultimate cause which contains within itself the cause of its own existence is brisk but incomplete: 'it seems absurd to enquire for a general cause or first Author' of an eternal succession of objects since a cause 'implies a priority in time and a beginning of existence'. Perhaps it does, but surely in the case of god what is being supposed is a being which has priority in time to all else but has no beginning of existence. The succession of objects is not eternal but their metaphysical cause or explanation must be. If this account of god as necessary cause (and creator of things *ex nihilo*) is to be rejected then one or other of two alternatives have to be viable. Either (a) at some time things just came into existence uncaused and out of nothing, or (b) the succession of causes is infinite, i.e. the universe of things in space had no beginning. If neither (a) nor (b) is viable, then we will be left with the conclusion that there is some necessary being which exists independently and self-caused and in which all other causal sequences began. I shall call this being 'the first cause'.

In the *Treatise*, (I, iii, 3) Hume argues a point which implies the possibility of (a). As in the *Dialogues*, Clarke is specifically mentioned, and in *A Letter*, 23, Hume points out that it is Clarke's *a priori* argument for the existence of god (not Descartes') which is threatened. The point is this. If it can be shown that it is not necessarily true that *'whatever begins to exist must have a Cause of Existence'* (*A Letter*, 22; *Treatise*, 78), then the possibility that the totality of things exists without a cause becomes viable, and the logical pressure exerted by the demand for a first cause is relaxed.

Hume's argument in the *Treatise* is essentially an application of the epistemology already described in the first section of this chapter. The proposition is 'neither intuitively nor demonstrably certain'; an uncaused event is conceivable; it is no good objecting that an uncaused event would produce itself, i.e. exist before it existed, or would be produced by nothing:

> 'Tis sufficient only to observe, that when we exclude all causes we really do exclude them, and neither suppose nothing nor the object itself to be the causes of the existence; . . . If every thing must have a cause, it follows, that upon the exclusion of other causes we must accept of the object itself or of nothing as causes. But 'tis the very point in question, whether every thing must have a cause or not.
> *Treatise*, 81

If an uncaused event – one that follows a preceding state of affairs but is in *no* way related to preceding states of affairs – is possible, then there is at least a *possibility* that the things in the universe came into existence uncaused and out of nothing. Because Hume allows such a possibility, Anthony Kenny[12] couples Hume with 'big bang' cosmologies, and Aquinas with Hoyle and 'steady state' cosmologies. Hume admits the possibility of something coming 'into existence not only from nothing, but also by nothing; not only without matter, but also without a cause'. Aquinas and Hoyle on the other hand think 'that the origination of matter calls for a cause'. This may be so, but I would have thought that Hoyle's cause of matter – a sort of void into which other matter has decayed – comes much closer to a universe of things in space which has no beginning (that is, (b) above) than to a beginning in any Being 'quod omnes dicunt Deum', and alternative (b) is just as damaging to the *a priori* arguments (Aquinas' 'Third Way' included) as alternative (a).

Alternative (b) has in fact always seemed more plausible than (a), presumably because even the great 'atheistical' systems of antiquity accepted the maxim 'Nil posse creari de nilo'.[13] But if the first cause argument is to have logical force, the possibility of an infinite regress of causes having no explanation has to be ruled out. Leibniz tries to do just this: 'And so, however far you go back to earlier states, you will never find in those states a full reason why there should be any world rather than none, and why it should be such as it is'.[14] The same thought is in Hume's paraphrase of Clarke's *a priori* argument: 'What was it, then, which determined something to exist rather than nothing, and bestowed being on a particular possibility exclusive of the rest?' (*Dialogues*, 189). The inference in each case is that a temporally infinite regress gives no answer to questions: Why this? Why anything?

I myself can see no stronger commendation of the possibility of a self-subsisting infinite temporal regress than that provided by John Hick when he observes that the modern mind 'sees no *a priori* impossibility in the idea of a temporally as well as a spatially unbounded universe'.[15] In this sense Hume is a 'modern mind' (see, for example, *Dialogues*, 183) and any appeal to the need for a first cause will fall on deaf ears with Hume as it will with us. But *should* Hume and a 'modern mind' see any impossibility, not in an infinite regress of caused causes, but in an infinite regress of things whose existence is contingent upon other things?

In the last analysis the objections to such a regress seem to depend upon the sort of assumptions made by Aquinas in the 'Third Way': the argument which begins with caused contingent beings (i.e. ourselves and every observable thing in the universe) and concludes with an uncaused necessary Being (quod est per se necessarium non habens causam suae necessitatis aliunde). This Being is supposed to answer the questions: Why this? Why anything? But does the contingency of everything give any logical or rational force to the demand for such a necessary being?

A short answer (which might very well have been given by Hume) is once again provided by Russell: 'The difficulty of this argument is that I don't admit the idea of a necessary being and I don't admit that there is any particular meaning in calling other beings "contingent". . . . The word "necessary", it seems to me, is a useless word, except as applied to analytic propositions, not to things' (Russell and Copleston, op. cit., p. 170). But this, it may be said, is an appeal to an empiricist theory of knowledge which Clarke and Leibniz certainly, and Aquinas possibly, would have rejected. Very well. Let us try to put the point another way. Why should there be a contradiction or even rational difficulty in holding that no being exists which is necessary by contrast with the contingency of everything else? There is no logical need for such a being precisely because it seems coherent to suppose that all things exist contingently in an infinite temporal regress. The only difficulty with such a regress comes from supposing that the regress is not really infinite. This supposition then allows an insistent question about the end and origin of the regress. But in an *infinite* temporal regress of events the question of ends and origins could literally *never* arise. The contingent existence of every thing would *always* be explainable in terms of other contingent things. The pseudo-logical demand that contingency should terminate in necessity is a demand which gathers its force from presuming the impossibility of an infinite regress, not from demonstrating such an impossibility, and *demonstration* of the impossibility that things could exist from eternity is what the *a priori* argument requires to arrive at a necessarily existent first cause. If we are left with competing possibilities – possibly an infinite temporal regress (and this is the possibility Hume takes to be obviously true – *Dialogues*, 190); possibly a finite temporal regress terminating in a first cause – then this is no good. For the *a priori* argument to be good the second possibility has to logically exclude the first. Then and only then would the necessary existence of such a first cause entail the existence of such a first cause.

But if there is no contradiction in supposing the universe to be spatially and temporally limitless, what happens to the question 'why anything?' It becomes simply unanswerable, not because of our lack of information, but, in Hume's terms, because in general we lack any possibility of understanding how we should settle questions about 'the origin of worlds'. Thus the question 'why anything?', far from necessitating the answer 'god', is not even comprehensible and what is more (Hume might have added), if the universe had been empty, would the question 'why nothing?' have been supposed to necessitate the same answer which the question 'why anything?' is supposed to necessitate in the universe of things?

The question 'why this?' will still be answerable in a spatially and temporally limitless universe in the same ways in which such a question is usually answered. If I ask what causes the stars to shine, old port to give me evil dreams, and the ewes to go to the tups at the right moment, I would normally expect three distinct answers. But if I got an answer of the form: that which contains within itself the cause of its own necessity – 'quod omnes dicunt Deum' – then I would have no answer at all to my questions in the sense in which I had asked them. Even the psalmist asking similar questions is not speering for a logically necessary answer about some being which is the cause of its own necessity. He is commending men to the mystery and majesty of the things done by his God. He is affirming that a certain answer is appropriate to the cosmic question 'why these things?' He is not using the question as a logical lever to force some remote semblance to that answer out of the intellectually unpersuaded.

There are thus three candidates for the ultimate origination of things. In the beginning things appeared from nothing and by nothing. In the *Treatise* Hume allows us to infer that this is at least a possibility. Secondly: In the beginning was the being which contains within itself the cause of its own necessity. This is the candidate which has to logically exclude the other two if it is to succeed in the cosmological argument or in Clarke's *a priori* argument. Thirdly: There never was a beginning. The universe is spatially and temporally limitless. In the *Dialogues* Hume does not argue but rather assumes this to be the case (as many of us now would). If it is the case, or even possibly could be the case, then the demand for 'some ultimate cause, that is necessarily existent' loses its compulsive force. There may be such a being. But the *possibility* is not enough for the *a priori* argument.

EXISTENCE AND THE CONCEPTION OF A THING

Although Hume's few and brief remarks on the subject of *existence* were the catalyst which produced Kant's celebrated refutation of the ontological argument, it would now be a little ridiculous to use what Hume has to say as an excuse for entering full scale into the modern discussion of the subject. There is much to commend Hartshorne's remark 'we must do our own thinking, and not expect Kant or Hume to have done it for us'.[16] But let us at least get one thing straight. Hume did not say 'existence is not a predicate' nor does he so much as hint at such an expression. What he speaks about is 'ideas' and 'conceptions', and I think his main point can be discussed in these terms without indulging in the very questionable translation to talk about predicates. What he says is 'that the idea of existence is nothing different from the idea of any object, and that when after the simple conception of any thing we wou'd conceive it as existent, we in reality make no addition to or alteration on our first idea'. He continues with the particular case: 'Thus when we affirm, that God is existent, we simply form the idea of such a being, as he is represented to us; nor is the existence, which we attribute to him, conceived by a particular idea, which we join to the idea of his other qualities, and can again separate and distinguish from them' (*Treatise*, 94).

Jerome Shaffer (op. cit., p. 235f) points out that in *Treatise*, 66, Hume appears to say something different from the above: 'To reflect on any thing simply, and to reflect on it as existent, are nothing different from each other. That idea, when conjoined with the idea of any object, makes no addition to it. *Whatever we conceive, we conceive to be existent'* (my italics). The final sentence is the trouble. This view, Shaffer remarks, 'is a most embarrassing one for Hume to hold' since it is entirely at variance with what else Hume has to say on existence. But when Shaffer has finished his chastisement he generously concedes 'Perhaps Hume was writing carelessly.' I can see no other credible interpretation of the sentence in italics. It concludes a passage in which Hume has said in a variety of ways that existence makes no difference to our idea of an object and the sentence has every appearance of intending to say this in yet another way rather than make a new, uncharacteristic and divergent point which is nowhere followed up.

Ignoring for the moment the trouble already identified, namely that a conception wavers between an imagination and an understanding, what Hume seems to be saying is this. When I form a conception of a thing what I am doing is bringing together a number of ideas. These form a 'complex idea' (*Treatise*, 2f). But when I say 'the complex idea exists' I am not really saying anything more about the *idea*. I am not adding to or subtracting from my idea of the thing. Instead, I am saying that my idea has an instance in the real world, or that what I am forming an idea of can actually be found somewhere or in some way. For example: I have a very well-developed idea of a hobbit. But whether I say 'hobbits exist' or 'hobbits do not exist' makes no difference to my idea of a hobbit. Or again: I have an idea of a democracy but my idea is not altered by knowing whether there are or are not any democracies. Hume's own example on p. 94 of the *Treatise* (quoted above) is that the idea which we have of god does not alter in any way when we think of him as existent. In the footnote on p. 96 he underlines the point: 'in that proposition, *God is*, or indeed any other, which regards existence, the idea of existence is no distinct idea, which we unite with that of the object, and which is capable of forming a compound idea by the union'. But in the *Meditations*, when Descartes unearths his vision of the ontological argument, he finds that existence is implied by the idea which he has of a Perfect Being. Hence the existence of that Perfect Being, God is as certain as a demonstration in geometry. But if Hume is right, no analysis of any compound idea could yield the idea of existence. Hence Descartes' ontological argument must be invalid or contain a false assumption.

To put it another way: what would be the result if existence were to be regarded as part of the idea of an object ('object' being used in the widest possible sense)? The first result would be that existence would cease to be a relation between my idea and the object of which it is an idea, and would become instead merely part of my idea. But surely, Hume might have said, if I enquire whether hobbits exist, my enquiry does not concern the *idea* of a hobbit but the *exemplification* of that idea in the real world. If the notion of existence has been incorporated into the idea of a hobbit, and I know that it has, I still have no answer to the exemplification question, and the exemplification question is the fundamental existence question which survives after the notion of existence has supposedly been taken somewhere else, namely, into the idea of the object. So if Descartes insists that the idea of existence is contained in the compound idea we can form of the Perfect Being this is quite all right (Descartes, if not Hume, might comprehend how existence could be part of a compound idea). But it does not settle the question whether the idea of a Perfect (existent) Being is exemplified in the real world and *that* is the question which people are asking when they ask if god exists.

So at the very least, when followed out in their own terminology, Hume's observations suggest some sort of clarification of the verbal legerdemain which the ordinary man senses in Descartes' ontological argument. Even Samuel Clarke, although he could not quite bring himself to dismiss the Cartesian version out of hand, does complain of '*This* Obscurity and Defect' that 'it seems to extend only to the *Nominal Idea* or *mere Definition* of a Self-Existent Being' and does not clearly refer that definition 'to any *Real* particular Being *actually existing without us*' (op. cit., p. 20).

*   *   *

Clarke's *a priori* argument concludes with a being which 'cannot be supposed not to exist without an express contradiction'. Clarke derives this necessity from the cosmic demand for a first cause which contains within itself the sufficient reason for its own existence. Hume will have nothing to do with this notion or with *any* way of arriving *a priori* at a necessarily existent being: 'The existence, therefore, of any being can only be proved by arguments from its cause or its effect; and these arguments are founded entirely on experience' (*Enquiry*, 164: 172). Not all his reasons for this conclusion are sound, but I have tried to show that a number of them are seminal.

In the *Dialogues* Hume's concluding comment on the *a priori* proof of god's existence is characteristic of his ability to lift his head from philosophical minutiae and put the issue in proportion:

> The argument *a priori* has seldom been found very convincing, except to people of a metaphysical head, who have accustomed themselves to abstract reasoning, and who finding from mathematics that the understanding frequently leads to truth, through obscurity, and contrary to first appearances, have transferred the same habit of thinking to subjects where it ought not to have place. Other people, even of good sense and the best inclined to religion, feel always some deficiency in such arguments, though they are not perhaps able to explain distinctly where it lies. A certain proof, that men ever did, and ever will, derive their religion from other sources than from this species of reasoning.   *Dialogues*, 191f

Whether or not Hume's reasons for rejecting 'the argument *a priori*' are as decisive as he took them to be, his rejection of it (and his discerning identification of a similar rejection among others 'the best inclined to religion') is of central importance in his critique of religion. As I shall argue later, his final assessment is that the design argument establishes a very weak probability that the cause or causes of order in the universe could bear some remote analogy to human intelligence. To this position nothing more can be added either by pure reason ('the argument *a priori*' is a failure) *or*, as we shall now see, by any exercise of the understanding ('Our line is too short to fathom such immense abysses').

5
Meaning, School Metaphysics and Divinity

> I suppose it may be of use, to prevail with the busy mind of man to be more cautious in meddling with things exceeding its comprehension . . . and to sit down in a quiet ignorance of those things which, upon examination, are found to be beyond the reach of our capacities.
>
> Locke, Essay

One of Hume's conclusions in the *Enquiry* is that divinity and school metaphysics are 'sophistry and illusion' unless they are found to contain matters of fact or abstract demonstrations. Elsewhere he observes that arguments about god's nature or the origin of worlds carry us 'quite beyond the reach of our faculties', that we have 'no idea' of certain theological positions and that if we predicate such a term as 'good' of the deity it can only have the normal or anthropomorphic sense 'for we know no other'. These and many other apparent strictures on the comprehensibility of theology invite the questions whether, to what extent, and on what grounds Hume regarded religious belief as incomprehensible and the language in which it is expressed as meaningless. In this chapter I shall consider these questions under three heads. First, the use Hume makes of his impression/idea dichotomy as a criterion of meaning. Secondly, his requirement that if ordinary language predicates are to be used meaningfully in theology then they must be kept reasonably close to their normal meanings. Finally, but more important of all, Hume's general thesis, which he shares with Locke, that certain subjects lie beyond the limits of human understanding and therefore we cannot have any rational confidence about the truth concerning them.

WORDS AND IDEAS

In the manifesto at the beginning of the *Enquiry* Hume is very emphatic about his purpose. It is 'to enquire seriously into the

94

nature of human understanding, and show, from an exact analysis of its powers and capacity, that it is by no means fitted for such remote and abstruse subjects' (such subjects as a considerable part of metaphysics and metaphysics used to give 'popular superstition' an air 'of science and wisdom'). One of the principal mechanisms for executing this purpose is the impression/idea dichotomy which Hume set out at the beginning of the *Treatise* and which he repeats, with slightly different emphasis, in Section II of the *Enquiry*. In brief, his position is as follows.

By 'impressions' are meant all our sensations, passions, emotions and feelings 'as they make their first appearance in the soul' or as they are actually experienced. By 'ideas' are meant (*Treatise*, 1) 'the faint images of these in thinking and reasoning'. (Hume never uses the word 'image' again in the first chapter of the *Treatise*, and in Section II of the *Enquiry* he seems to go out of his way to avoid its use, speaking merely of 'ideas or thoughts'. I shall try to indicate the importance of this later on.) Thus, for example, the origin of our idea of a man or of our idea of the colour red is in each case a previous experience – an 'impression' of a man or an 'impression' of red. The idea, together with the impression which is its origin, may be 'simple' as in the case of red (i.e. not capable of being analysed into other impressions or ideas) or 'complex' as in the case of man (i.e. capable of being analysed into other complex and/or simple impressions or ideas). Every *simple* idea takes its origin from a simple impression but some *complex* ideas may be formed which are not derived from complex impressions. Thus: 'I can imagine to myself such a city as the New Jerusalem, whose pavement is gold and walls are rubies, tho' I never saw any such' (*Treatise*, 3). I can do this because I have ideas (derived from impressions) of walls, gold, rubies, streets and cities, and I can put these together and form the complex idea of the New Jerusalem without ever having had actual experience of it. An impression and an idea 'differ only in degree, not in nature' (*Treatise*, 3) and the difference is the same as that between an experience and an experience recalled in a thought: the former is more lively, vivid and intense than the latter.

But this would mean, if we adopt the usual interpretation of Hume (namely, that by 'idea' he means 'mental image'), that the challenge which he throws down (*Treatise*, 4; *Enquiry*, 19: 28) to 'show' or 'produce' a simple idea which is not derived from an impression is not capable of being taken up. This is not for the usually cited reason which Flew calls the Conventionalist Sulk (roughly, that the proposition 'ideas are copies of impressions' is presented by Hume as a contingent generalisation but becomes true by definition when needed to rule out apparent counter-instances[1]). It is because in no ordinary sense of the words is it possible to 'show' or 'produce' an idea when 'idea' is understood as a mental image which differs from an actual experience merely by being less lively or vivid. Such a mental image of a lively experience is private and unproducible as far as other people are concerned. What then could Hume have intended by his apparently absurd challenge to 'produce' or 'show' an idea?

The question admits no satisfactory answer if we stick to the conventional misinterpretation of Hume that 'all ideas are for him (mental) images'. I say *mis*interpretation because even if such an interpretation could be made to stick to the *Treatise* on the evidence of its first page and of his occasional talk about ideas 'copying' impressions, it will not stick in any consistent way to his recharacterisation of the same doctrine in Section II of the *Enquiry*. In that Section the contrast between ideas and impressions is never presented as one between mental images and that which is imaged. Instead it is regularly presented as the contrast between thoughts and experiences. The word 'thought' or its cognates occurs nine times in the chapter. In six of these it could apparently be replaced by the word 'idea' while in the remaining three (and again at the beginning of Section III) it is explicitly allowed as an alternative to the word 'idea' *as Hume intends the word 'idea' to be used*. Thus on p. 18: 27 he remarks 'The less forcible and lively [perceptions] are commonly denominated *Thoughts* or *Ideas*' (Hume's italics). On p. 19: 28 he speaks about what happens 'when we analyse our thoughts or ideas' and in the important footnote which appears at the end of the chapter in all the editions he firmly contrasts his use of the word 'idea' meaning 'thought' with Locke's different use of the term: 'Again, the word *idea* seems to be commonly taken in a very loose sense, by Locke and others; as standing for any of our perceptions, our sensations and passions, as well as thoughts'. The only evidence which Section II provides for the view that Hume thinks of an idea as a mental image is his occasional use of the phrase: ideas *copied* from a precedent feeling or sentiment. But there is also evidence to show – quite apart from his consistent choice of 'thought' rather than 'image' as an alternative to 'idea' – that he is not using the word 'copy' in anything like the sense 'mental photocopy' or 'preserved image', but rather as a philosophically familiar gloss of a notion which does not involve images at all: 'In short, all the materials of thinking are derived either from our outward or inward sentiment: the mixture and composition of these belongs alone to the mind and will. Or, to express myself in philosophical language, all our ideas or more feeble perceptions are copies of our impressions or more lively ones' (*Enquiry*, 19: 28). In the context of a chapter where 'ideas' and 'thoughts' are used as freely interchangeable terms it is difficult not to conclude that the 'philosophical language' of 'ideas' and 'copies' should be interpreted by means of the layman's gloss of 'materials of thinking' and 'derived' rather than the other way round.

A remarkable example of the staying power of the conventional generalisation that for Hume ideas are mental images is to be found in E. J. Furlong's *Imagination*[2] where the author absorbs both the generalisation and a part of the contrary evidence into the same expository paragraph

> First, to think is, for Hume, to have ideas. But all ideas are for him images. Hence to think is to have images, i.e. to imagine. A theory of thinking will be a theory of imagining. We therefore find Hume using 'imagination' where another man, uncommitted to the view that all ideas are images, would employ 'thought' or 'mind'. Sometimes, of course, Hume forgets, and we find him using 'mind' in a context where his theory would require 'imagination' . . . (p. 96f).

Of course Hume will 'forget' to live up to a generalisation if, as I have argued, he does not hold it. It is only fair to point out that in the context from which I have quoted, Furlong is mostly concerned with the *Treatise* and, if the tradition that for Hume all ideas are mental images can find support, it can be found there, not in the *Enquiry*. I am not arguing that Hume is unequivocally consistent in what he says even in the *Enquiry*. But I am saying that if his position can be summarised at all, the summary is that ideas are thoughts, not that ideas are images.[3]

Now if this is so, it makes a great deal of difference both to his challenge to produce a simple idea which is not derived from an impression and to the use which he makes of his impression/idea dichotomy as a criterion of meaning. Let us take the challenge first. Although I cannot 'produce' or 'show' a mental image I *can* produce a thought or 'the materials of thinking' because these are usually (perhaps always) words and I *can* show (or significantly fail to show) whether I am able to apply the words correctly in the public sensible world. That ideas are thoughts or the materials of thinking, and that these are either identical with words or at the very least become identical with words when the thought is articulated, is something which Hume takes as understood when he speaks of 'words expressive of ideas' (*Enquiry*, 21: 32). But 'thoughts' and 'the materials of thinking' are not interchangeable terms. So is an idea a thought or a material used in thinking? From Hume's insistent use of 'thoughts' and 'ideas' (always the plural) as synonyms, together with the words or phrases he actually instances as 'expressive of ideas', it would appear that by 'ideas' he means the phrases or single words which form the distinguishable parts of whole thoughts (much as words form the distinguishable parts of sentences). Thus ideas are thoughts in the sense that a thought is *composed* of ideas, not in the sense that a thought is *identical* with an idea: ideas are the materials of thinking. If this is so, then Hume's challenge to produce a simple idea which is not derived from an impression is no longer an invitation to perform an absurdity. It is an invitation to produce a word or phrase which expresses an idea where the idea is not derived from experience. But how, according to Hume, can we show that a word or phrase expresses an idea? Only by pointing out the experiential situation – the impression – from which the idea, and hence the word which expresses the idea, derives its origin or use: 'To give a child an idea of scarlet or orange, of sweet or bitter, I present the objects, or in other words, convey to him these impressions' (*Treatise*, 5). There is an obvious difficulty here. Ideas *not* derived from impressions appear to be ruled out at source since Hume allows only one way in which an idea can be acquired. I shall return to this point shortly.

But if words express ideas, what happens when the idea expressed is in some way confused or altogether lacking? In the former case the words are employed 'without a distinct meaning' (but the meaning could be made distinct if a determinate idea could be formed); in the latter case the words are employed 'without any meaning' at all (*Enquiry*, 22: 30). Thus with any word or phrase ('term' in Hume's usage) there are three possibilities. First, that the term expresses a determinate idea and has a distinct meaning. Examples Hume gives are 'fear', 'sweet', 'orange' and 'golden mountain' among others. Secondly, that the term expresses an idea which is in some way confused or obscure and has no distinct meaning. Hume is not very forthcoming with examples, but possibly 'freedom of the will' would do. Finally, that the term expresses no idea at all and is employed without any meaning. Examples to which Hume argues in the body of his work are 'power' and 'substance'. Thus in brief, ideas can be determinate, confused or lacking. Terms can have a distinct meaning, an unclear meaning or no meaning at all.

It is obvious that this trichotomy provides Hume with a very vigorous form of meaning empiricism with which to attack crucial philosophical and theological terms, and he uses it to good effect: we have no idea of a necessarily existent being; we have only a confused idea of a first cause; we have no idea of the general origin of worlds or of an immaterial substance; we have no idea of the best of possible worlds. But Hume does not say that we have no idea of god. We have no idea of 'power' or 'efficacy' in him any more than we have an idea of these in anyone else (*Treatise*, 160). Our 'idea of that supreme Being is derived from particular impressions' (*Treatise*, 248). More explicitly in the *Enquiry* we are told 'The idea of God, as meaning an infinitely intelligent, wise, and good Being, arises from reflecting on the operations of our own mind, and augmenting, without limit, those qualities of goodness and wisdom' (p. 19: 28). This is to say that in Hume's view the meaning of the word 'god' at least *starts* its life in experience despite the confusions and obscurities which later appear (see *Dialogues*, 159). But supposing Hume were to say that some cherished phrase or formulation in a religion lacked meaning. For example, it is said that God is 'three persons in one *substance*'. What reply can be made when Hume argues that we have no idea of substance?

The reply could be, as Bennett[4] and others have pointed out, that 'substance' is one of the class of words to which Hume's meaning empiricism is inapplicable. The word does express an idea but the idea is not derived from experience. To this Hume has a number of possible counters. He can say there is no such class of immune words. It is true by definition that *every* idea is derived from impressions. But this invites the stalemate situation where his opponent simply refuses to allow the definitional truth. Hume can then say that the class of words for which immunity is claimed is so small and so peculiar (being almost entirely metaphysical or philosophical terms) that the authority which meaning empiricism gains elsewhere gives it authority as a normative generalisation to legislate for these few words as well. Again a determined rejection of the authoritarian claims would be hard to overrule. But Hume can also say that if immunity from meaning empiricism is claimed for 'substance' or 'necessary connection' or 'necessarily existent being' (all suspiciously out-of-the-ordinary terms) then the whole weight of showing that these terms do have meaning is thrown onto those who wish to use the terms. *They* have to provide a convincing account of what these terms mean since the presumption engendered by the wide applicability of the empiricist criterion of meaning is that the terms mean nothing. If our understanding of the idea of substance cannot be located in an experienced situation, where is it located? In general, if someone claims to employ a word with a distinct meaning but cannot locate the empirical situation in which its meaning could be displayed ('cashed' in Ian Ramsey's useful metaphor), it is at the very least a reasonable question to ask whether and how he understands the word, or, in Hume's more usual terms, whether he has a confused idea or has in fact got any idea at all. It is a reasonable question because of the very large number of terms for which empirical 'cashability' *does* count as success in a quest for meaning. This 'prove yourself!' challenge to alleged ideas which lack empirical 'cashability' is weaker than one might at first have been led to expect from Hume's meaning empiricism, but it is in accord with what he says at the end of his discussion of the matter in Section II of the *Enquiry*. He is there saying in effect that some language has a special clarity because it can show 'how it connects to the empirical world'[5] and this is a situation which sets up a suspicion about philosophical language which cannot in any way show this:

> All ideas, especially abstract ones, are naturally faint and obscure: the mind has but a slender hold of them: they are apt to be confounded with other resembling ideas; and when we have often employed any term, though without a distinct meaning, we are apt to imagine it has a determinate idea annexed to it. On the contrary, all impressions, that is, all sensations, either outward or inward, are strong and vivid: the limits between them are more exactly determined: nor is it easy to fall into any error or mistake with regard to them. When we entertain, therefore, any suspicion that a philosophical term is employed without any meaning or idea (as is but too frequent), we need but enquire, *from what impression is that supposed idea derived?* And if it be impossible to assign any, this will serve to confirm our suspicion.
>
> *Enquiry*, 21f: 30

It is in part from his meaning empiricism that Hume derives his *general* presumption against claims to determinate understanding of matters which lie beyond possible experience. But before I turn to this subject I wish to look at another general aspect of what Hume has to say about meaning. It is an aspect which is particularly relevant to the claimed (but remote) 'analogical' use of language in religious formulations.

A MEANING WHICH CONFOUNDS EVERYTHING

Once stated, Hume's point is obvious. It is that if someone uses an ordinary language word in contexts which do not satisfy the commonly accepted range of application of the word then the result will be confusion or dishonesty. In religious language, according to Hume, such confusion or dishonesty results when the theologian insists upon applying such anthropomorphic attributes as 'good' and 'intelligent' to a god whose apparent nature is incompatible with the normal meanings of these words.

Suppose it is said that in the country of Ruritania the government allows complete political freedom. But a visitor to Ruritania discovers that the law only recognises one political party in the state; that political dissentients are confined in corrective labour camps; that press, wireless and television are controlled by the one Party; that public criticism of the government is punishable by loss of job, pension and home and that private criticism is suppressed by a secret police. Suppose all these things. Now what is the visitor to say to Comrade Rassendyll when he insists that the Ruritanians have political freedom? The visitor can either say that on the evidence produced it is just false that they have freedom, or he can say that they do not understand the word 'freedom' in the way in which he does. Perhaps they are afraid to acknowledge the real position. Perhaps they have adopted a political Newspeak in which 'freedom' *is* slavery, 'industrial action' *is* industrial inaction, 'health centres' *are* ill health centres, and so on.

Now it is Hume's contention in more than one of his writings on religion that dishonesty through fear, or confusion through a religious version of Newspeak, is characteristic of much of the language used to talk about god or to address him. This is the case because we speak of God as good and merciful and yet we (Christians and Mohammedans alike) say *both* that he does not prevent the suffering in the world which he could prevent *and* that he countenances and employs the everlasting torments of Hell. Concerning the former I have already pointed out (Chapter 3) that in the *Dialogues* Hume's (at least Philo's) suggestion for overcoming the dishonesty or double talk is that we should rescind the attribute good or benevolent and acknowledge that from the phenomena alone (and revelation apart) it appears that god has no moral attributes. Concerning the latter Hume says very explicitly in the essay 'Of the Immortality of the Soul' that god's sanction and use of eternal punishments for man's transient offences 'is inconsistent with *our* ideas of goodness and justice', and (*Dialogues*) 'we know no other' idea which the word 'good' can express than the idea it expresses in our ordinary use. To say a man is good (ordinary sense) but god is 'good' (special sense) confounds everything because the second 'good' has the *appearance* of meaning the same as the first without the reality of doing so[6] (just like the confusion in saying that in Scotland we are free while in Ruritania they are 'free'). The traditional Christian (although partly extricated by the doctrine of a Purgatory) is guilty of just this sort of unwitting dishonesty or double talk about his loving and merciful God who also casts into the fires of Hell those who displease him.[7] Likewise the Koran can threaten that 'Those whose scales are heavy shall triumph, but those whose scales are light shall forfeit their souls and abide in Hell for ever. Its flames will scorch their faces and they will writhe in pain' (ch. 'The Believers') and all this 'in the name of Allah, the Compassionate, the Merciful'. In each case the believer thanks God for 'mercies' which if performed by a man would constitute unimaginable vindictiveness (*N.H.R.*, 67) and the effect, according to Hume, is either to stand the meaning of words on their heads or to misrepresent the nature of the deity.

In the *Dialogues* Hume, through Demea and Philo, considers a way of escape from this misapplication of anthropomorphic language: 'How then does the divine benevolence display itself, in the sense of you anthropomorphites? None but we mystics, as you were pleased to call us, can account for this strange mixture of phenomena, by deriving it from attributes, infinitely perfect, but incomprehensible' (*Dialogues*, 199). But as has already been pointed out by Cleanthes (*Dialogues*, 157–9) this will not do. Incomprehensible attributes are no more informative than sublime mysteries. They are both an excuse for saying nothing about god, and being able to say nothing about god is, as Cleanthes points out, not readily distinguishable from atheism. The silence (holy or sceptical) prevents the theist from saying that his god is intelligent, wise and good, and these things *must* be said if the god is to be anything of concern to mankind. But as soon as these things *are* said then the god has to satisfy the requirements of character and performance which would warrant use of these terms. According to Hume the theistic god does not satisfy the requirements for moral attributes because he permits natural evil and, according to various revelations, sanctions and employs the torments of Hell. Since the god does not warrant use of these terms their continued use (like saying Ruritanians have freedom) is either false praise or misleading use of language. God, Hume might have said, is either good or not good or partly good or beyond good and evil. But he cannot be 'good' (outside a theological *Nineteen Eighty-Four*) without introducing a misuse of language which confounds everything.

At the end of Part III of the *Dialogues* Hume argues in similar vein about attributing to the deity intelligence as *we* understand the term:

> we may conclude, that none of the *materials* of thought [ideas] are in any respect similar in the human and in the divine intelligence [nor the *manner* of thinking] . . . it would, in such a case, be an abuse of terms to apply to it the name of thought or reason. At least, if it appear more pious and respectful (as it really is) still to retain these terms, when we mention the supreme Being, we ought to acknowledge, that their meaning, in that case, is totally incomprehensible; and that the infirmities of our nature do not permit us to reach any ideas, which in the least correspond to the ineffable sublimity of the divine attributes. (*Dialogues*, 157 Demea speaking.)

As before, Cleanthes insists this is no good. To attribute incomprehensible intelligence is to attribute 'intelligence' with no meaning in the word and such 'intelligence' is not worth insisting upon.

It will be noticed that none of this is an application of Hume's meaning empiricism. It is simply an appeal to the obvious fact about language that if you wish words to carry their common meanings (or even something like their common meanings) then you cannot insist that they be used regardless of their appropriateness. If you do insist that they be used regardless of appropriateness then you can take your pick between the unacceptable consequences: either the word means what it commonly means and what you say by means of it is false, or the word does not mean what it commonly means and either you convey nothing by its use or you convey something different from what you intended. In the case of the moral attributes of the deity this meaning-dilemma is acute. I shall investigate its implications later.

THE IMMENSE ABYSS

In the very last sentence of the *Treatise* Hume writes in a manner which recalls Locke's words quoted as motto to this chapter: 'Nothing is more suitable to that philosophy, than a modest scepticism to a certain degree, and a fair confession of ignorance in subjects, that exceed all human capacity'. In the Introduction to the *Treatise* he had already given a strong indication how subjects exceeding human capacity will be recognised: ''tis still certain we cannot go beyond experience; and any hypothesis, that pretends to discover the ultimate original qualities of human nature, ought at first to be rejected as presumptuous and chimerical'. In the *Enquiry* the most frequently repeated refrain in the book is that we must be content to limit our enquiries to what is intelligible to us, and what is intelligible to us is marked out by the limits of our experience. See *Enquiry*, 6: 16, 72: 73, 81: 90, 103: 111, 142: 151, 162: 170, *et al*. In the *Dialogues* the same sort of thinking pervades Philo's remarks. A very characteristic passage occurs in Part I:

> But when we look beyond human affairs and the properties of the surrounding bodies: When we carry our speculations into the two eternities, before and after the present state of things; into the creation and formation of the universe; the existence and prop-erties of spirits; the powers and operations of one universal spirit, existing without beginning and without end; omnipotent, omniscient, infinite, and incomprehensible: we must be far removed from the smallest tendency to scepticism not to be apprehensive, that we have here got quite beyond the reach of our faculties.   *Dialogues*, 135; see also 177, 201 *et al*.

Hume is particularly disparaging about arguments and disputes concerning the ultimate origination of things: 'Our experience, so imperfect in itself, and so limited both in extent and duration, can afford us no probable conjecture concerning the whole of things'

(*Dialogues*, 177; see also *Enquiry*, 162: 170 for a very forceful repetition of this contention).

Hume's position is thus: (1) that our understanding is limited; (2) that the limits are drawn in some way by our experience; (3) that we can and should recognise and accept these limits; and (4) that conclusions about the nature of the universal spirit and the ultimate origination of things are characteristic of subjects which lie beyond our understanding. How does Hume reach this position? How judicious is it? What are its consequences for religious belief?

Of the four propositions by means of which I have characterised Hume's position, (1) and (2) are fundamental. They are arrived at by several routes. The first, most obvious and least interesting is via Locke. Hume shares with Locke the basic assumption that in some form or other experience is the source of all that can be known. I shall not dwell upon the Lockean origins of Hume's position since these do not constitute any philosophically arguable reason in favour of it or against it.

The second route to propositions (1) and (2), and to the link between them, is Hume's theory of the meaning of terms: that for a word or phrase to have a meaning it must express an idea; that ideas are the materials of thinking (*Enquiry*, 19: 28; *Dialogues*, 156); that ideas are got from experience. Hence thought – that which can be constructed from the materials of thinking – is limited by experience. But wait a minute – proposition (1) was that our *understanding* is limited, not that our *thought* is limited. So how does thought relate to understanding in Hume's scheme of things? I am inclined to answer that when we have clear and determinate thoughts (the words which comprise the thoughts express determinate ideas; see p. 98 above), thought and understanding are the same. When we have confused thoughts (the words which compose the thoughts express confused ideas or no ideas at all), then we do not have understanding. In short, understanding is clear and determinate thought. Thus in terms of (1) and (2), understanding or determinate thought is limited by experience. Proposition (3) merely says that we can recognise the truth of (1) and (2) – presumably when we note the experiential source of determinate ideas. It then commends the attitude of mind which accepts that our understanding has limits beyond which no certain or dogmatic conclusions can be justified. Hume sometimes says that conclusions are uncertain if they go beyond our experience (e.g. *Enquiry*, 142: 151); sometimes that we should confine our enquiries to our experience (e.g. *Enquiry*, 160: 170). There is no inclination that he thinks these injunctions are materially different from each other.

Hume's idea/impression dichotomy is thus one route to his typically empiricist limitation upon what we can understand or clearly think. Another route is his distinction between demonstrations and matters of fact (see above, p. 77). Demonstrations are not only contrasted with matters of fact in the degree of certainty which attaches to them (negation self-contradictory *v.* negation false) but also in point of origin. The demonstration is 'discoverable by the mere operation of thought'. The matter of fact depends upon 'the present testimony of our senses' and 'the relation of *Cause and Effect*' and this relation 'is not, in any instance, attained by reasonings *a priori*; but arises entirely from experience, when we find that any particular objects are constantly conjoined with each other' (*Enquiry*, 27: 42f). Thus the source of matters of fact is experience and no allowance is made for matters of fact from any other source. But Hume is by no means eccentric or perverse in what he calls a matter of fact. It would be quite hard to find an example of what the layman would call a matter of fact whose source was altogether *other* than experience. The sort of positive pronouncements in 'school metaphysics and divinity' to which Hume objects are rational attempts to prove 'the existence of a Deity and the immortality of souls' in which the conclusions are presented as having demonstrable *or* matter-of-fact certainty. They do not have demonstrable certainty (their denial is not self-contradictory) nor do they come within the scope of matter of fact certainly because these – Hume would say we all agree and probably most of us do – are related to experience.

The conclusion so far is that propositions (1) and (2) are suggested to Hume by his acceptance of Lockean presuppositions and recommended to us by his theory of meaning and by his account of the different 'objects of enquiry'. But it must not be thought that Hume's contrast between what we can understand and what is beyond our understanding is the same as the positivist contrast between verifiable propositions and all other propositions. What Hume is saying is that when we can relate our thoughts to experience we are thinking clearly and are able to give some sort of grounds for being sure about our conclusions. When we cannot so relate our thoughts 'we are got into a fairyland'. Hence, in Sections I and XII of the *Enquiry*, he contrasts the conclusions of common life and experience with those of abstruse philosophy and metaphysics which serve 'only as a shelter to superstition and a cover to absurdity and error'. We are entitled to be confident about the conclusions of common life because these relate to experience. But nothing entitles us to be confident about the conclusions of abstruse philosophy. Doubts about the former are impractical and foolish. Doubts about the latter are nothing worse than the proper hesitations of a reasonable man aware that he has no grounds for rational confidence about matters altogether outside all possibility of experience. He cannot be confident in his arguments and conclusions about the origination of worlds, the nature of god, the ultimate destiny of things or the constitution of spirits. At least as a *rational* man he cannot be confident and dogmatic about such things. He can be and, as Hume observes, often is dogmatic about such subjects if he is a man subject to the 'miracle' of religious faith. But this dogmatism is of quite a different kind to the pseudo-rationalistic dogmatism in theology and metaphysics which Hume is so anxious to condemn and which he constantly contrasts with '*faith* and divine revelation': the true foundations of religion.

*   *   *

What Hume has to say about meaning and understanding has three applications to religious language and dogma. In the first place his impressions/ideas dichotomy allows him to say that certain terms, for example, 'spiritual substance' and 'necessary being' are meaningless. Secondly, he has the no-Newspeak-in-theology argument to limit use of anthropomorphic language in stating god's attributes. Thirdly, he has the general prescription that rational confidence in matters which run wide of common life and experience is unjustified because such matters are beyond the limits of our understanding. 'Our line is too short to fathom such immense abysses'.

6

Scepticism and Natural Belief

'Tis happy, therefore, that nature breaks the force of all sceptical arguments in time, and keeps them from having any considerable influence on the understanding . . .
Tho' the *common* opinion concerning the continu'd and distinct existence of body be false, 'tis the most natural of any, and has alone any primary recommendation to the fancy . . .

Treatise, 187 & 213

Hume's total rejection of the *a priori* arguments for god's existence, his damaging critique of the design arguments, his use of the problem of evil to question the probability of god having moral attributes, the doubts which he sheds on the meaning and comprehensibility of the language of 'divinity and school metaphysics'; all these lead to the question: If there are no good and sufficient grounds for a reasoned belief in god, why is the belief so widely held? A number of distinct answers to this question are discussed by Hume.

In the first place it could be that we have evidence of God's existence and activity from a particular historical revelation, and that the evidence bears marks of authority and authenticity which no reasonable man could reject if he became aware of them. I shall examine Hume's highly provocative rejection of this 'argument from revealed religion' in Chapter 8. On the other hand there could be (and according to Hume there undoubtedly is) a 'natural history' of religion which establishes that there are causes in human nature (psychological, anthropoligical, or sociological) which account for the existence of belief in a god or gods quite apart from any reasons or evidence which might substantiate such a belief. I shall return in Chapter 10 to this non-rational origin of belief in the divine.

There is, however, a further possible answer within Hume's philosophy to the question why belief in god is so widely and tenaciously held. It is that belief in god is one of a small group of beliefs which have to survive philosophical scepticism because they are, in the final analysis, indispensable. The group is usually identified by commentators on Hume as 'natural beliefs' – although the phrase is not to be found in his own writings. The doctrine of natural beliefs is a response by Hume to some of the unacceptably sceptical positions which he finds himself driven to by philosophical considerations taken in isolation from the inescapable demands of common life. I shall first show how Hume's various subdivisions of scepticism lead to natural belief as a check on *excessive* scepticism, and then how his theory of belief leads to a category of non-rational beliefs which include *both* unacceptable irrational beliefs *and* acceptable natural beliefs. I shall then use the results of these investigations to ask what the defining characteristics of natural beliefs are. In the following chapter I shall apply these results to the much disputed question whether belief in god is a natural belief. I shall argue that it is not, but that there is an understandable inclination to identify it as one because belief in god unites the feeble rational datum surviving from the design argument with the insistent *feeling* in most of us that the world is ordered.

But first a word of caution: the phrase 'natural belief' is not in all instances synonymous with Hume's own phrases 'natural instinct' and 'original instinct'. In *some* contexts (e.g. *Enquiry*, 151: 160) Hume's 'natural instinct' is the psychological mechanism with parallels the epistemological category 'natural belief', and the denotation of the two terms is insignificantly different. But in other contexts (e.g. the 'Author's Introduction' to the *Natural History of Religion*) Hume's usage is much closer to Cicero's 'innate concept' (of gods) as in *De Natura Deorum*, I, xvi. Whether we have in fact an innate concept (or 'preconception') of god and, if we do, whether it has any evidential value, will be considered later. But whether we have or have not such a concept is quite a different question to whether belief in god is or is not 'natural' in the sense used by Hume's commentators. Because that sense is not in all respects uniform, it will perhaps clarify the direction of my argument if I anticipate a summary of what I shall mean by the phrase. An *essential natural belief* is one which is (a) an ordinary belief of common life, (b) in the final analysis incapable of rational justification, (c) a belief in whose absence the activities of normal life become impossible, and which is, as a consequence, (d) universally held. ('Essential' does not qualify 'natural belief' but emphasizes (c).)

VARIETIES OF SCEPTICISM

Most of what Hume has to say about scepticism is to be found in Section XII of the *Enquiry* and in the Sections on 'Scepticism with Regard to Reason' and 'Scepticism with Regard to the Senses' in the *Treatise*. There is a mild difference of emphasis on these subjects in the two works but no conflict. Hume returns to the subject of scepticism in Part I of the *Dialogues* in order to apply to religion his distinction between excessive and mitigated scepticism.

In the *Enquiry* he rejects extreme Cartesian doubt as a desirable or even possible antecedent to doing philosophy. Such doubt cannot be achieved, and if it were, no one could ever rid himself of it. But there is a more modest version of antecedent scepticism which is of value:

> It must, however, be confessed, that this species of scepticism, when more moderate, may be understood in a very reasonable sense, and is a necessary preparative to the study of philosophy, by preserving a proper impartiality in our judgements, and weaning our mind from all those prejudices, which we may have imbibed from education or rash opinion.   *Enquiry*, 150: 159

This account of *antecedent* scepticism presents no philosophical problems and Hume has little more to say about it. But there is, according to Hume, another species of scepticism which is *consequent* upon the pursuit of philosophy (*Enquiry*, 150: 159). This has both an acceptable and an unacceptable form. The acceptable form is *mitigated* scepticism. The unacceptable form is *excessive* scepticism.

Mitigated scepticism is the due recognition that certain conclusions are altogether beyond our grasp: 'Our line is too short to fathom such immense abysses'. In the very last sentence of the Appendix to the *Treatise* Hume indicates his approval of this sort of scepticism: 'Nothing is more suitable to that philosophy than a modest scepticism to a certain degree and a fair confession of ignorance in subjects, that exceed all human capacity'.[1] Similarly in the *Enquiry*, 162: 170, having just contrasted mitigated scepticism with violent and obstinate dogmatism, Hume remarks: 'Another species of *mitigated* scepticism, which may be of advantage to mankind, and which may be the natural result of Pyrrhonian doubts and scruples [i.e. excessive scepticism], is the limitation of our enquiries to such subjects as are best adapted to the narrow capacity of human understanding.' I have already indicated in Chapter 5 by what means Hume hoped to mark out those areas which are beyond the capacity of human understanding. Certainly dogmatic theology (but not necessarily belief in god) is one of them: 'The whole is a riddle, an enigma, an inexplicable mystery. Doubt, uncertainty, suspense of judgement appear the only result of our most accurate scrutiny, concerning this subject' (*N.H.R.*, 76). The reference of 'this subject' is not absolutely clear but must be something like the theological disputes he had just been talking about.

Mitigated scepticism is thus the wise and apt recognition that in certain metaphysical and theological disputes no conclusion is possible because the whole subject-matter lies outside the range of our understanding. For example: 'It seems to me, that this theory of the universal energy and operation of the Supreme Being, is too bold ever to carry conviction with it to a man, sufficiently apprized of the weakness of human reason, and the narrow limits to which it is confined in all its operations' (*Enquiry*, 72: 83). But these areas of futile dispute in metaphysics and theology are perfectly remote from all common life and experience (*Enquiry*, 72: 83). We may be sceptical with regard to *them* without undermining any of our knowledge of 'matters of fact' or 'relations of ideas'.

Excessive or *Pyrrhonian scepticism* on the other hand is the extravagant and inappropriate despair which not only acknowledges the limitations of human understanding but also abandons all confidence in even the most commonsense beliefs about the world:

> There is another species of scepticism, *consequent* to science and enquiry, when men are supposed to have discovered, either the absolute fallaciousness of their mental faculties, or their unfitness to reach any fixed determination in all those curious subjects of speculation, about which they are commonly employed. Even our very senses are brought into dispute, by a certain species of philosophers; and the maxims of common life are subjected to the same doubt as the most profound principles or conclusions of metaphysics and theology.   *Enquiry*, 150: 159

At one stage Hume had been a victim of such excessive scepticism:

> The *intense* view of these manifold contradictions and imperfections in human reason has so wrought upon me, and

heated my brain, that I am ready to reject all belief and reasoning, and can look upon no opinion even as more probable or likely than another . . . I begin to fancy myself in the most deplorable condition imaginable, inviron'd with the deepest darkness, and utterly depriv'd of the use of every member and faculty.

Treatise, 268–9

The psychological antidote to this anguish and confusion is simple. Since philosophy cannot dispel the doubts, practical life must. Hume recommends the treatment thus: 'I dine, I play a game of back-gammon, I converse, and am merry with my friends; and when after three or four hours' amusement, I wou'd return to these speculations, they appear so cold, and strain'd and ridiculous, that I cannot find in my heart to enter into them farther' (*Treatise*, 269). In the *Enquiry* the same antidote is recommended more succinctly: 'The great subverter of *Pyrrhonism* or the excessive principles of scepticism, is action, and employment, and the occupations of common life' (p. 158: 167).

The philosophical antidote on the other hand involves a robust practical check to the pretensions of metaphysical and sceptical argument. It is the doctrine of natural belief. A natural belief is one which in practical life cannot be abandoned and which we *all* hold and are absolutely justified in holding (*Dialogues*, 134) irrespective of philosophical objections. An example is belief in the continuous existence of an external world independent of my perceptions. If, on analysis, it appears that neither reason nor sense experience can confirm this belief, then this does not mean that the belief should or even could be abandoned since without it practical life in the ordinary world would be impossible. Though the belief be false, ''tis the most natural of any, and has alone any primary recommendation to the fancy'. It must be emphasised that a natural belief can only be a check to *excessive* scepticism – which is just that sort of scepticism which threatens to destroy our most fundamental, practical, commonsense beliefs about the world, (i.e. our natural beliefs). These specially sacrosanct beliefs cannot check, would indeed have nothing to say about, *mitigated* scepticism – scepticism which says in effect that some subjects are too abstruse and remote from common life and experience for us to form any view of them. Thus excessive scepticism *is* doubting natural belief. Natural belief cannot be doubted in practice. Hence excessive scepticism is untenable both for the ordinary man *and* for the philosopher (except for brief and uneasy periods).

REASONABLE BELIEF

Hume's remarks on belief are scattered throughout his philosophical writings but major clusters of them occur in *Treatise*, 94–106, *Treatise*, 628–9 (the Appendix) and *Enquiry*, 47–55: 61–8. A passage from the *Treatise* (which he repeats verbatim in the *Enquiry*) contains the main outline of his final[2] theory:

> . . . 'tis evident, that belief consists not in the nature and order of our ideas, but in the manner of their conception, and in their feeling to the mind. I confess, that 'tis impossible to explain perfectly this feeling or manner of conception. We may make use of words, that express something near it. But its true and proper name is *belief*, which is a term that every one sufficiently understands in common life.[3] And in philosophy we can go no farther, than assert, that it is some thing *felt* by the mind, which distinguishes the ideas of the judgement from the fictions of the imagination. It gives them more force and influence; makes them appear of greater importance; infixes them in the mind; and renders them the governing principles of all our actions.
>
> *Treatise*, 629; *Enquiry*, 49: 63

And again: 'It follows, therefore, that the difference between *fiction* and *belief* lies in some sentiment or feeling, which is annexed to the latter, not to the former, and which depends not on the will, nor can be commanded[4] at pleasure'. It is axiomatic for Hume that while I may *imagine* what I please, I cannot *believe* something at will: 'We can, in our conception, join the head of a man to the body of a horse; but it is not in our power to believe that such an animal has ever really existed' (*Enquiry*, 48: 61).

In his account of belief Hume thus adopts a position characterised by the following points: (a) The word 'belief' signifies an attitude to or feeling about what is believed. This attitude or feeling can be recognised (introspectively) but is difficult to characterise further. (b) The belief-feeling or attitude influences action. (c) The belief-feeling or attitude cannot be commanded at will.

Leaving aside most of the usual criticisms of this position, it remains clear that there are problems in it for anyone wishing to distinguish between *reasonable* beliefs on the one hand and *irrational* or *unreasonable* beliefs on the other: a distinction of great importance in any account of natural beliefs since such beliefs are in a certain sense non-rational. (I shall use the term 'non-rational' whenever it is unnecessary to draw attention to sub-distinctions of the non-rational implied by the words 'irrational', 'unreasonable' etc.).

Problem A. If believing P consists in having a belief-feeling for P, this belief-feeling will presumably be the same whether the belief is reasonable or non-rational. How then should reasonable and non-rational beliefs be distinguished?

Problem B. If belief is some attitude which cannot be given or withheld at will, 'Hume seems to be leaving no room for the possibilities either of legitimately criticising people for holding irrational beliefs, or of altering our own beliefs or those of others with the help of argument'.[5]

Some of the teeth of problem A can be drawn by admitting that for the believer there is *no* difference between the belief-feeling for a reasonable belief and the belief-feeling for a non-rational one. Both are his beliefs and their rationality depends upon something other than the manner in which they are entertained. Upon what does it depend? Hume does not say, but he does not *prevent* us from saying (unoriginally) that the rationality of a belief depends (a) upon the person's ability to justify his belief that P (the justification involving the production of reasons or evidence that P is the case, or the pleading of successful action undertaken on the presumption that P is the case) and (b) upon the person's ability to *modify* the belief-feeling for P in the face of fresh evidence. But according to problem B this modification is just what the believer cannot undertake at will. Now there is no doubt Hume, like everyone else, does wish to distinguish between reasonable and non-rational beliefs, 'weaning our mind from all those prejudices, which we may have imbibed from education or rash opinion' (*Enquiry*, 150: 159). What account then can be given, within Hume's theory of belief, of a reasonable man altering his beliefs in the light of fresh evidence?

Consider an example: if I truly announce 'I believe I shall be killed if I enter an aeroplane', then Hume is *right* in saying I cannot at will abandon my belief-feeling about this proposition. The belief stole in on me over a longish period, unnoticed and unreasoned, and I cannot shake it off when it suits me to do so. Nor can I decide to adopt a belief (say, belief in god) in the way in which I could decide to *think* about the existence of god. But what can happen (and this is the part of the story which Hume does not specifically mention although what he says allows for it) is that various considerations such as accident statistics can be put before me which might be expected to result in a modification of my belief about the danger of flying. I do not at this stage *decide* to change my belief-feeling, but I attend to the evidence which tells against what I believe and if my belief satisfies the conditions for what is called 'reasonable' belief, my belief-feeling will be found to alter. The situation is exactly parallel in Hume's account of ethical disputes. If I say 'X is wrong' and you say 'X is right' this means that I approve of X and you disapprove. I cannot decide to change my approval, but on hearing and agreeing with your account of the misery produced by X, my feeling of approval may wear off and become one of disapproval *provided* that my ethical view is reasonably based. (See, for example, *Moral Enquiry*, 180: 13).

Likewise my belief-feeling cannot be changed at will but if it has as its object a reasonable belief it can change as a result of my attention to and assessment of the evidence, and such attention is voluntary. There are of course numerous well-tried methods of preventing modification of the belief-feeling – for example, giving attention to a partial selection of evidence or by 'forgetting' that one's reasons for the belief are insufficient – but these do not alter the general case that with reasonable belief the belief-feeling occurs or fails to occur or is modified as the involuntary accompaniment of an honest assessment of the evidence. If we wish to call this assessment 'deciding to believe' (or 'deciding not to believe') this would probably be in conformity with ordinary usage, but it would also, according to Hume, muddle an important distinction between the evidence which I can review at will and the belief-feeling which I cannot.

There are however a number of beliefs, according to Hume, which are *not* the resultant of a conscious rational assessment of evidence and which are *not* upset by such an assessment except in brief moments of 'philosophical melancholy and delirium' (*Treatise*, 260).

It seems evident, that men are carried, by a natural instinct or prepossession, to repose faith in their senses; and that, without any reasoning, or even almost before the use of reason, we always suppose an external universe, which depends not on our perception, but would exist, though we and every sensible creature were absent or annihilated.   *Enquiry*, 151: 160

They are, as he says, 'a species of natural instincts, which no reasoning or process of the thought and understanding is able either to produce or prevent' (*Enquiry*, 47: 60). Nevertheless one does not wish to call these beliefs either irrational or unreasonable although they may be non-rational. They belong to the class of beliefs which Hume *sometimes* speaks of as 'original instincts' – that is, the class of natural beliefs which have already been encountered as Hume's philosophical check to excessive scepticism.

NATURAL BELIEF

Hume distinguishes at least three[6] 'species of natural instincts' or essential natural beliefs:

(1) Belief in the continuous existence of an external world independent of our perception of that world (*Enquiry*, 151: 160, etc.)
(2) Belief that the regularities which have occurred in our experience form a reliable guide to those which will occur (many locations).
(3) Belief in the reliability of our senses qualified to take account of acknowledged and isolatable areas of deception and confusion (many locations).

Professor R. J. Butler[7] would add a fourth belief: Belief in an orderly universe stemming from an agent designer commonly called god. I do not think this belief is an essential natural belief nor that Hume regarded it as one, but these points will be discussed later. Now what is it that makes beliefs (1) to (3) essential natural beliefs?

According to Butler (p. 78) 'Hume indicates that natural beliefs are non-rational, that they have a certain degree of force, and that they are unavoidable.' In the subsequent discussion he points out that the first of these considerations does not separate natural beliefs from irrational beliefs while the second is not a distinguishing mark because according to Hume it is a characteristic of all beliefs. The third on the other hand is one which Hume never abandons although he might be forced into the position of admitting that not all natural beliefs are true. Unfortunately Butler does not explain in what sense natural beliefs are unavoidable, nor, it appears to me, does he state all their characteristics. This I shall now try to do.

If we examine what Hume has to say about the natural beliefs listed above we find that they have four distinctive characteristics, namely:

Firstly, they are ordinary beliefs of common life. Hume would argue that philosophical conclusions must therefore keep close to them: 'philosophical decisions are nothing but the reflections of common life, methodized and corrected' (*Enquiry*, 162: 170, see also *Dialogues*, 134, and *Treatise*, 181–218 *passim*). But the 'common life' here appealed to is not merely the common life of a particular culture or of a learned or unlearned population. It is the common life of mankind in general. And the 'ordinary beliefs' are not merely widely accepted but revisable persuasions (such as that the earth is still and the sun moves round it). They are beliefs with a very special character which makes them *unrevisable* for any rational being who lives in a coherent relation to the given appearances of things.

Secondly, these 'instincts and propensities of nature', as Hume sometimes calls them, are arrived at without reasoning, and cannot for long be suspended as a consequence of any sort of reasoning. But their indispensability is not merely a quirk of our irrational psychological natures. Our practical experience is such as to leave no other epistemic possibility open. These beliefs are non-rational but not irrational (*Enquiry*, 153: 162) and they are unrevisable. Why? Because:

Thirdly, neither the excessively sceptical philosopher, nor anyone else, can act in the world unless he has these beliefs of common life. This is the vital point which makes these beliefs 'unavoidable' and it is their absolute justification. Hume is very emphatic about it in more than one of his works: 'Here I find myself absolutely and necessarily determined to live, and talk, and act like other people in the common affairs of life' (*Treatise*, 269; see also *Treatise* 183, 184, 187, 193, 197, 213, 216, 273, etc.). The same point is made in the *Enquiry* with the conciseness usually displayed in the later work:

> Nature is always too strong for principle . . . And [Pyrrhonian scepticism] can have no other tendency than to show the whimsical condition of mankind, who must *act and reason and believe*; though they are not able, by their most diligent enquiry, to satisfy themselves concerning the foundation of these operations,

or to remove the objections, which may be raised against them
[my italics].   *Enquiry*, 160: 168–9; see also *A Letter*, 19

Significantly this same point is brought out very forcibly by Philo at
the beginning of the *Dialogues* and is never controverted by any
other speaker: 'To whatever length any one may push his
speculative principles of scepticism, he must act, I own, and live,
and converse like other men; and for this conduct he is not obliged to
give any other reason than the absolute necessity he lies under of so
doing' (*Dialogues*, 134). If, in a moment of 'philosophical melancholy
and delirium', one loses these beliefs then one can only remain in a
state of paralysed non-communication with the world, 'utterly
depriv'd of the use of every member and faculty' (*Treatise*, 269).
Again it must be emphasised that this paralysis is not a consequence
of the particular psychological natures we have but might not have
had. It is a consequence of our epistemic situation.

Fourthly, and this is a consequence of the third, these beliefs are
universally, i.e. always and everywhere, held. Thus *everyone*,
always acts as if there were an independent, continuous physical
world, even if this belief is in most cases unarticulated.

In short, natural beliefs are ordinary beliefs of common life. They
are non-rational in being neither established by nor destroyable by
reason. They are necessary as a precondition of action, and they are
universally held. Which of these criteria distinguish natural beliefs
from irrational or unreasonable beliefs?

(a) As with irrational beliefs there is inability to produce good
evidence that the belief is true. *But*, unlike irrational beliefs, there is
no evidence which makes it more reasonable to adopt any
alternative set of beliefs. The sceptical criticism of natural beliefs
establishes no others in their place (*Enquiry*, Section XII). In saying
this I differ sharply from D. F. Norton when he observes 'All in all,
our natural beliefs or inclinations are not particularly reliable.'[8]
Certainly our common *persuasions* are not particularly reliable (for
example, that the sun moves round the earth[9]). But common
persuasions are not essential beliefs, and although we cannot
(according to Hume) show natural beliefs to be true, this gives us no
reason to presume them unreliable *per se*, or by comparison with *any*
alternative. Why? Because unlike a common persuasion (e.g. that
the sun moves) there is *no* alternative to them.

(b) Unlike irrational beliefs there *is* justification for *acting* as if they
are true. The justification is the discovery that there is no other

course open to us. If we do not act as if these beliefs are true, we do not act at all. As Hume remarks in the *Abstract* '. . . upon the whole [our author] concludes, that we assent to our faculties, and employ our reason only because we cannot help it'.[10] This is why excessive scepticism – scepticism with regard to natural belief – cannot be maintained: 'the first and most trivial Accident of Life must immediately disconcert and destroy [it]' (*A Letter*, 19). Excessive scepticism does not just subvert some *special* system of life such as Christianity or Idealism or Anarchism. It subverts the practical ways of encountering and understanding the world and ourselves which form the bases for *all* systems of life; a special system of life may be subverted, but not *all* systems. Thus one may opt to disregard the thoughts of Chairman Mao. But surely disregard of the thoughts of Chairman Mao could have upset life rather badly for some people? Precisely! For *some* people in *certain* societies it may. But consistently believing that the future will not be like the past and trying to act on this belief would totally disrupt anyone's life in any society. To disregard Chairman Mao might have been political heroism (or obscurantism); to disregard a natural belief would be more like madness. I labour this point because when we consider the case of belief in god it will be vital that the universality and practical inevitability of natural beliefs should have been noted.

*   *   *

In summary: a natural belief is in a certain sense 'non-rational' but it is *not* irrational or unreasonable and it *does* have the very important practical justification that things 'work out well' if I have the belief and *cannot work out* if I do not have the belief.[11]

I now come to the intricate and controversial questions which relate natural beliefs, belief in god, and the *feeling* about the significance of natural order which seems to survive rational criticism of the design argument.

7

God and Natural Order

> The existence of God is not self-evident. For if God impressed us automatically, the Dogmatists would have agreed together regarding his essence, his character, and his place; whereas their interminable disagreement has made him seem to us non-evident and needing demonstration.   Sextus Empiricus, *Outlines*, III

If belief in god can be shown to be an essential natural belief, then something will have been established which is both of enormous importance in understanding Hume's philosophy of religion as a whole, and of enormous general importance in justifying what could be used as a basis for theistic religion. My contention is that belief in god is not a natural belief. I shall first attempt to establish this by contrast with the opposite thesis urged by R. J. Butler. In doing so I shall argue that for Hume belief in god is a vestigial *rational* belief which has no religious significance. In the second part of the chapter I shall argue that the propensity to believe in god, which we are half inclined to regard as a natural belief, comes in main part from our *feeling* (reported in Cleanthes' 'irregular' design argument) that cosmic order originates in an intelligent agent.

BELIEF IN GOD AS A NATURAL BELIEF

Professor Butler's thesis[1] is that since Hume speaks in several of his works as if the existence of god could never be doubted, since the question in the *Dialogues* concerns god's attributes and not his existence, and since each of the participants in the *Dialogues* appears to assent to belief in god as something natural and unavoidable, then this belief *is* a natural belief. Philo's criticism of the argument from design 'should be viewed as an attempt, not to deny that God exists, but to break down Cleanthes' initial opinion that theological beliefs may find rational support in the recognition of evidence' (Butler, p. 87). Up to and including *Dialogues* XI Hume's argument takes the form: no evidence either *a priori* or *a posteriori* justifies belief in god, 'but we commonly act in accordance with belief in design. Therefore belief in design must be a natural rather than a rational belief' (p. 88). In the final section of *Dialogues* XII Philo explains just how little this natural belief involves. It amounts only to acknowledging 'the fact of design' which is unavoidably impressed upon us by 'our belief in an ultimate principle of order in the universe, and this belief, like our belief in causation, is unavoidable: nobody behaves as if the universe were ultimately a chaos!' (p. 98). Belief in design is equivalent to belief in a designer, and this belief 'would make no sense if God lacked intelligence; . . . But nothing can be said *about* God's intelligence as contrasted with man's' (p. 90).

Butler's thesis has striking merits. It makes Hume's theory of belief and his account of religious belief into a connected whole. It makes Philo's apparent confession of belief in god in Section XII of the *Dialogues* into a comprehensible development of his own argument instead of something apparently at variance with his earlier utterances. It makes Hume's repeated assertions[2] that there is a god into honest reports of his belief rather than prudential insincerities calculated to keep him clear of the charge of atheism.

But these and other advantages of interpretation also attach to a quite different understanding of Hume's thought, namely that:

(1) Belief in god does not satisfy all the criteria for an essential natural belief.
(2) Hume knows that it does not satisfy the criteria and Philo admits by implication that it does not: yet both assent to the existence of god in the highly attenuated sense explained by Philo at the end of the *Dialogues*. This assent is therefore to a reasonable belief and not to a natural belief.
(3) This rational assent is given to a proposition so limited that it is of no significance to religion.

I shall now try to substantiate this understanding: item (1) in isolation, items (2) and (3) conjointly.

(1) Examined under the criteria for an essential natural belief, belief in god fails at least two of the four tests. In the first place, is belief in god an ordinary belief of common life? The criterion is difficult to apply. Quite clearly belief in god often is just such a belief. But it is arguable that the belief is usually inculcated by education or cultural background, that is, by factors which could be

absent, rather than by factors present in the experience of all men as such. This would mean that it is more like a common persuasion than the sort of belief of common life which could be a natural belief. But by itself, the criterion is indecisive.

Secondly, is it the case that belief in god lacks rational foundation? Without begging the question of a very large area of philosophy no general answer can be given and even Hume's answer is, at first sight, equivocal. He seems to say in different places that theological reasoning is 'too sublime for our understanding' or 'sophistry', *and* that the Christian religion is founded on faith not on reason *and* that every reasonable man will believe in god. These positions are, I think, compatible, but for the moment their complexity forestalls an answer to the question 'does Hume think that belief in god is reasonable?'

Thirdly, is belief in god unavoidable in the crucial sense (which Butler does not point out) that no one can *act* in the world if he lacks this belief? Surely not. Only too clearly men can and do live in a coherent and successful manner without belief in god. In some rather deep sense they may not live as satisfactorily as those who have the belief but they *can* function in the world and in society without it or any form of it. Thus scepticism with regard to belief in god would be mitigated scepticism: more like disregarding the thoughts of Chairman Mao than the excessive scepticism of refusing to believe that the past is a guide to the future. One very important system of life would not be possible if one were sceptical about god's existence; but other systems of life would still be practical, even if psychologically difficult. In the *Dialogues* Philo brings out this point very clearly right at the beginning. If the philosophical sceptic discovers no rational justification for believing, say in an external world, he still 'must act, and live, and converse like other men' (*Dialogues*, 134). The sceptic is under an 'absolute necessity' to do so, and his excessive philosophical scepticism must give way whenever he attends to the ordinary world of his experience. But the religious sceptic is not in this situation. His mitigated scepticism is not rendered academic and unrealistic when he attends to the ordinary world of his experience. Quite the reverse. Such is the remoteness of theological speculation by contrast with our normal experience that 'We must be far removed from the smallest tendency to scepticism not to be apprehensive, that we have here got quite beyond the reach our faculties' (*Dialogues*: 135; Philo speaking).

The fourth criterion of a natural belief is that it is universally, even if inarticulately, held. Hume sometimes speaks as though a shadowy form of belief in god were almost universal, but he is careful not to commit himself: 'The belief of invisible, intelligent power has been very generally diffused over the human race, in all places and in all ages; but it has neither perhaps been so universal as to admit of no exception; nor has it been, in any degree, uniform in the ideas, which it has suggested' (*N.H.R.*, 21). The lack of uniformity has always been evident. The lack of universality is much more evident to us than it could have been to Hume. But apart from suggesting that belief in god is not universal, Hume also provides an account of the causes of belief in god (to which I shall return in Chapter 10) which explains *why* it is not, and need not be, universal. Terence Penelhum nicely formulates Hume's position:

> The forces that impel us to adopt the beliefs of common life are found in all men, whereas those that lead us into metaphysics or into religion are found only in *some* men. Metaphysics is a relative rarity, indulged in only by philosophers. Religion is not a rarity in the same way, but the forces that produce it are *pathological* forces, such as the superstitious fear of the unknown, and fortunate men in civilized communities can be free of them.[3]

In summary: the first criterion for a natural belief is indecisive. The second cannot be applied as yet. But the third and fourth rule out belief in god as an essential natural belief.

(2) & (3) In the *Dialogues*, Cleanthes, Philo's opponent, does indeed express himself in a manner which suggests that belief in god, via the argument from design, could be a natural belief: 'Consider, anatomize the eye, survey its structure and contrivance, and tell me, from your own feeling, if the idea of a contriver does not immediately flow in upon you with a force like that of sensation' (*Dialogues*, 134). But this part of Cleanthes' case is not endorsed by Philo, and in a letter, unequivocally in his own person, Hume admits that he cannot establish via the design argument that belief in god is unavoidably forced upon us like belief in our senses:

> The Propensity of the Mind towards it [the design argument], unless that Propensity were as strong & universal as that to believe in our Senses & Experience, will still, I am afraid, be esteem'd a suspicious Foundation. Tis here I wish for your Assistance. We must endeavour to prove that this Propensity is

somewhat different from our Inclination to find our own Figures
in the Clouds, our Face in the Moon, our Passions & Sentiments
even in inanimate Matter. Such an Inclination may, & ought to be
control'd, & can never be a legitimate Ground of Assent.

Letters, I, 155

The most straightforward reading of the conditional 'unless that
Propensity were as strong and universal as that to believe in our
Senses and Experience' would suggest that Hume thinks the
condition is not satisfied. This reading is confirmed elsewhere. In
the *N.H.R.* he comes close to speaking of belief in god as a natural
belief but shies off it: 'The universal propensity to believe in
invisible, intelligent power, if not an original instinct, is at least a
general attendant of human nature' (*N.H.R.*, 75). In the 'Author's
Introduction' to the same work he had already admitted that belief
in god is not universal and is not an original instinct: 'Some nations
have been discovered, who entertained no sentiments of Religion, if
travellers and historians may be credited;' (*N.H.R.*, 21).

Elsewhere (but notably in the *Enquiry*) Hume maintains that it is a
mistake to try to establish religion (but he does not say belief in
god) upon good reasons and arguments (see for example, *Enquiry*,
130: 140 and 135: 145). Thus he appears to conclude that belief in god
is not an original instinct; that it is not universal; that it does not
'flow in upon you with a force like that of sensation', that religion *in*
general cannot be established by reason.

The difficulty with the last item in this summary of his views is
that in several of his writings he affirms belief in a deity by way of
the design argument: 'The whole frame of nature bespeaks an
intelligent author' (*N.H.R.*, 21). At the end of the *Dialogues* Philo also
affirms his reasoned belief in a divine Being: 'No one has a deeper
sense of religion impressed on his mind, or pays more profound
adoration to the divine Being, as he discovers himself to reason, in
the inexplicable contrivance and artifice of nature. A purpose, an
intention or design strikes everywhere the most careless, the most
stupid thinker' (*Dialogues*, 214; see also 202). This is puzzling,
particularly the phrase 'as he discovers himself to reason', since the
whole burden of Philo's argument appears to have been that he does
not discover himself to reason. But this crucial phrase is repeated by
Philo three pages later: 'Here then the existence of a Deity is plainly
ascertained by *reason*' (my italics). If we adopt Kemp Smith's
arguments that Philo very largely speaks for Hume in the *Dialogues*,[4]

it might appear that Hume is here admitting that belief in god, like belief in an external world, survives the destruction of its supporting arguments: his continued use of the word 'reason' being merely perverse and confusing. He should have used the phrase 'natural instinct'. But this appearance is misleading.

In the first place, Philo has already asserted in his discussion with Cleanthes concerning scepticism that 'If we distrust human reason, we have now no other principle to lead us into religion' (*Dialogues*, 193). This assertion is never disputed by Cleanthes despite his attempt to argue the fact of design as something unavoidably obvious. It is surely as clear a warning as could be given by Philo that it is not part of his programme to allow that belief in god is a natural belief or 'original instinct'. In other words it is not a belief which must survive, after the supporting philosophical arguments collapse, because it is a universal requirement for living in the world.[5] In the second place, as Kemp Smith and Butler both point out, Philo's profession of belief, qualified as it is by the phrase 'as he discovers himself to reason', amounts to exceedingly little. Just how little is emphasised by Hume in an addition to the text dating from 1776 (the year of his death). The paragraph is given to Philo and is the last in the book:

> If the whole of natural theology, as some people seem to maintain, resolves itself into one simple, though somewhat ambiguous, at least undefined proposition, *that the cause or causes of order in the universe probably bear some remote analogy to human intelligence*: If this proposition be not capable of extension, variation, or more particular explication: If it afford no inference that affects human life, or can be the source of any action or forbearance: And if the analogy, imperfect as it is, can be carried no farther than to the human intelligence; . . . what can [a man] do more than give a plain, philosophical assent to the proposition, as often as it occurs (Hume's italics). *Dialogues*, 227

I would thus argue that Philo does not concede that belief in design (as Butler maintains) 'must be a natural rather than a rational belief'. Instead he concedes that belief in a designer is after all a *rational* belief: one to which the mind has a strong propensity but which is 'somewhat ambiguous', probable rather than certain, incapable of rational development or extension, dependent upon an imperfect and very limited analogy, and which commits the believer neither to action nor forbearance from action. This is the substance of the existential assent to belief in god which is found so frequently in Hume's writings and which Philo reserves for himself despite his arguments. As Hume says in an early letter: He has an objection 'to every thing we commonly call Religion, except the Practice of Morality & the Assent of the Understanding to the Proposition *that God exists*' (*New Letters*, 13).

It is this assent of the understanding to the very limited proposition 'there is a god' together with the 'propensity' of the mind to give the assent when it contemplates the orderliness of nature, which might suggest that Hume considers belief in god a natural belief. But it is not. The assent is not universal and, unlike a normal religious belief in god, it does not even influence action, let alone form a prerequisite of action. Assent to the existence of god in this sense carries no duties, invites no action, allows no inferences, and involves no devotion. It is, as Hume argues through Philo in *Dialogues* XII, and as Lysicles the sceptic in Berkeley's *Alciphron* had argued in strikingly similar terms,[6] a proposition so hedged by doubts, restrictions and ambiguities that by suitable prompting both the religious man and the speculative atheist can be brought to give their assent to it. But the assent is *not* a natural belief.

THE FEELING OF DESIGN

A difficulty for the position I have been advocating (that belief in god is a vestigial rational belief not a natural belief) is put succinctly by Penelhum in one of the important essays he has contributed to Humeian exegesis.[7] The difficulty is the enthusiasm with which Philo, in Part XII of the *Dialogues*, abandons his sceptical case – 'A purpose, an intention, or design strikes everywhere the most careless, the most stupid thinker . . . no stupidity could mistake them . . : the existence of a Deity is plainly ascertained by reason' and so on. Even when we find that this enthusiasm is finally watered down into the almost contentless deism of Philo's (and Hume's) final speech on the subject, a problem remains. Penelhum puts it thus:

> If we read Philo's speeches (especially paragraphs 6 and 8 of Part XII) we find that the reasoning to which he says he is assenting is the analogical reasoning he has attacked all the way through . . . I

suggest that the minimal deism of Part XII is accepted by Philo as the inescapable conclusion of an argument which he has shown, and knows he has shown, to be a complete philosophical failure – except in the one respect that when we encounter it we cannot help assenting to its conclusion! In this respect minimal deism is like the natural beliefs: we can be momentarily disturbed by sceptical objections, but not seriously shaken from holding it. But it is *un*like the natural beliefs in that, as far as the *Dialogues* go at least, it is not a belief that is *arrived* at without reasoning.

Penelhum 1, pp. 170f

This is a very persuasive interpretation, but I still feel it is not quite right. It seems to me that Philo's positions in Part XII (and his final attenuated deism is a distinct thing, as Kemp Smith and others have pointed out, from his surprisingly fulsome admission at the start) are the result of combining an argument which he has *not* shown to be a *complete* philosophical failure, with a propensity of the mind to 'see' design in natural order – a propensity which surfaced as Cleanthes 'irregular' argument in *Dialogues* III, and which is better described as a *feeling of design*.

I say Philo's objections to the design argument do not show it to be a *complete* philosophical failure because the form of the argument Philo is attacking prevents this. In the case of the *a priori* argument, the critic (Cleanthes in that instance) can offer a conclusive refutation – 'I propose this [objection] as entirely decisive, and am willing to rest the whole controversy upon it' (*Dialogues*, 189). But with the design argument Philo is attempting to dismantle not a demonstration, but a *probability*. This means that unless he can show up some hidden incoherence in what is asserted (Demea hints at this in his remarks on god's immutability and simplicity, but the point is not pressed, see *Dialogues*, 158f), all the critic can do – and this *is* what Philo does – is to show how weak is the probability which is argued for. Thus in Part II Demea *complains* that the design argument depends upon mere 'experience and probability'. Cleanthes argues that the probability amounts to a certainty, and Philo that it amounts to a probability of the weakest sort (cf. *Dialogues*, 168f and 227), but a probability none the less. As such it attracts 'a plain, philosophical assent', i.e. an assent circumscribed by all the difficulties set out by Philo and by the limitations of our understanding. But this assent is not merely to some absurdly irrelevant principle of order which carries no hint of agency and is nothing but the brute fact *that there is order* by another name. It is assent to the conclusion 'that the cause or causes of order in the universe probably bear some remote analogy *to human intelligence'*, and this assent, although as it stands entirely devoid of religious significance or value, is surely an assent of the reasoning mind to the remote probability that there may be some sort of god.

However the fact remains that Philo's initial admissions in Part XII look more generous than his (or Hume's) final and long-meditated conclusion at the end. So what should we make of this? Penelhum puts it just right when he says 'the theist has merely to refer us once again to the intricacies of nature, and it is as though we had never heard how inadequate a reason they give us to infer [divine intelligence]' (1, p. 171). So the question is: is the collapse of Philo's objections the collapse of excessive scepticism in the face of a natural belief?

It seems indisputable that the arguments proposed by Philo in Parts II to XI (and those of the Epicurean in *Enquiry* XI) are not the arguments of excessive scepticism. They are the normal, hard-hitting, philosophical debate the consequences of which anyone could take on board without losing their footing in reality. One does not have to believe that the universe evinces design, or to have heard of the design argument, in order to act coherently in ordinary life. So before what is Philo, for the time being, collapsing at the start of *Dialogues* XII?

The answer, surely unwelcome to Hume, is that however weak the design argument is shown to be, there remains a propensity to 'see' design in nature. This propensity is articulated by Cleanthes as the 'irregular' argument in *Dialogue* III. It is not that this so-called 'argument' adds any rational weight to the design argument as already presented. It is rather that Cleanthes reaffirms the obviousness of its conclusion: '. . . tell me, from your own feeling, if the idea of a contriver does not immediately flow in upon you with a force like that of sensation' (*Dialogues*, 154f.). As several commentators have observed, Philo can find nothing to say here.

One should perhaps recall the P.S. to Hume's letter of 1751 written to Gilbert Elliot when he was first working on the *Dialogues*:

> If you'll be persuaded to assist me in supporting Cleanthes, I fancy you need not take Matters any higher than Part 3. He allows, indeed, in Part 2, that all our Inference is founded on the Similitude of the Works of Nature to the usual Effects of Mind.

Otherwise they must appear a mere Chaos. The only Difficulty is, why the other Dissimilitudes do not weaken the Argument. And indeed it would seem from Experience & Feeling, that they do not weaken it so much as we might naturally expect. A Theory to solve this would be very acceptable.   *Letters*, I, 157

In the end Hume produced no theory. Instead what he offers us in Part XII of the *Dialogues* is first an acknowledgement of the power of the common *feeling* that natural order is an outcome of design (the enthusiastic concession of Philo's first speech), then a careful statement of the vestigial rational probability established by the design *argument* (the attenuated deism of Philo's last speech). But the feeling for design is not a new argument, irregular or otherwise, nor does it add any new ground of assent to the old design argument. It is something more like the sense of cosmic awe which inspired the Psalmist: 'The heavens declare the glory of God: and the firmament shewith his handywork', or which was to move Wordsworth:

> there is a dark
> Inscrutable workmanship that reconciles
> Discordant elements, makes them cling together
> In one society.

But why should this insistent feeling for the design in things not be treated as a natural belief, as something having epistemic importance? It seems to start as a natural belief (giving us an otherwise inexplicable addiction to the design argument), and to survive philosophical objections. But it is not universal. It need not be and, as the historical processes of secularisation and urbanisation have continued, looks less and less like, an ordinary belief of common life. Finally, and crucially, having the feeling that natural order is design is not a precondition of practical life like belief in an external world. Some of us do not have this feeling: but our life goes on in a state of Epicurean *ataraxia* nevertheless.

So Penelhum's reconciliation of Philo's apparently conflicting positions is to say: his deism is brought about by reasoning (unlike natural beliefs) but (like natural beliefs) is not dislodged when the reasoning that has brought it about is shown to be bad. Philo's deism is thus an anomaly in Hume's system in not being clearly either a reasonable belief or a natural belief or a pathologically caused irrational belief.

My reconciliation is to say: Philo's final attenuated deism is brought about by philosophical reasoning (unlike natural beliefs) and is not in its final vestigial form dislodged because in that form it is a reasonable conclusion: 'it is supported by all the arguments which its nature admits of, even though these arguments be not, in themselves, very numerous or forcible' (*Dialogues*, 216). So Philo's deism is not an anomaly in Hume's system. It is a weakly probable belief. It exists alongside, and is readily and confusingly augmented by, an entirely distinct *feeling for design* which does not have the epistemic status of a natural belief and may or may not be explicable in terms of the pathological causes Hume investigates in the *Natural History of Religion*.

*   *   *

Hume's conclusion that belief in god is not a natural belief has two immediate consequences. One is that to doubt the belief (even if Hume himself did not doubt one very attenuated form of it) would not be excessive scepticism. The other is that the belief is subject to the normal reasonable/unreasonable dichotomy. From Hume's repeated affirmations of a deity, together with Philo's assent to a very restricted sense of the proposition 'there is a god', I have concluded that Hume regards belief in a god as reasonable rather than unreasonable and that he thinks the reasonableness is recognised by most men when they survey the order in nature (*something* of the design argument remains). But this reasonable belief amounts to so very little that the theist and the atheist can agree about it. The belief is without religious significance and leaves Hume free (a) to adopt an attitude of mitigated scepticism to all theological arguments because they are beyond our understanding; (b) to attribute belief in a particular relevation to an irrational faith which he sarcastically refers to as a miracle, and (c) to criticise and condemn religion 'as it has commonly been found in the world'. It is failure to notice the genuineness of Hume's rational assent to the existence of some sort of god which has made it appear as if his assent is insincere, or inconsistent with his critique of religion, or the expression of a natural belief. It is none of these; but neither is it of any advantage to the religious apologist.

But if belief in god is not a natural belief how is it that so very many people at all times and in all places have believed in a god or gods, and have believed in a way which is much more significant and influential than Hume's minimal 'assent of the understanding'? One possible answer, which Hume rejects, is that we have a particular and reliable revelation of God's character and purposes. Another, which he accepts, is that popular religion has a causal origin in human nature. I deal with these, together with the effects Hume considers religion to have on morality, and his own personal beliefs, in the second part of this book.

Part Two
Revealed, Historical and Personal Religion

8

Miracles and Revelation

We know that thou art a teacher come from God: for no man can
do these miracles that thou doest, except God be with him.

> John, III, ii

It often happens, such is our natural love for the marvellous, that
we willingly contribute our own efforts to beguile our better
judgements.   Scott, *Guy Mannering*, chapter IV

The stimulating and confusing thing about Hume's chapter on
miracles in the *Enquiry* is that it brings together, interrelates and
applies to the biblical miracles two items which for the sake of the
clarity should perhaps be kept apart, namely, the credibility of
witnesses and the intrinsic probability or improbability of the event
allegedly witnessed. The result is a piece of argument which has
provoked more comment, criticism and abuse than anything else in
Hume's philosophical writing. To the philosopher 'Of Miracles'
offers, at the very least, an almost irresistible opportunity to try to
distinguish between a miracle, a very unusual event, and an event
which provides a falsifying instance of a natural law; to the historian
or jurist it offers a fascinating discussion of the credibility of
witnesses; to the believing Christian it threatens to demonstrate that
no wise man would give any credit to the New Testament miracles;
and, which is not now so readily perceived, to an eighteenth-
century reader (or to a twentieth-century reader asking questions of
the 'Who moved the stone?' type) it offers a direct confutation of the
crucial argument upon which the rational credibility of the Christian
Revelation had been and is still sometimes made to depend,
namely, the historical truth of the Resurrection.

Hume's chapter is divided into two parts. In the first he is mainly
concerned with what is often described as an *a priori* argument
against justified belief in reported miracles. In the second he is
concerned with four of what are, by contrast, *a posteriori* arguments
against the credibility of miracles, and with applying these
arguments, in as far as was permissible at the time, to the biblical

miracles in general and the Resurrection in particular. I begin with consideration of one of the *a posteriori* arguments from Part II since it has the advantage of highlighting the place of miracles in normal Christian apologetic. I then move to the eighteenth-century context of Hume's arguments to show the radical significance of Hume's conclusion 'that a miracle can never be proved, so as to be the foundation of a system of religion'. In the third and fourth sections of the chapter I proceed to a discussion of Hume's arguments about evidence before adding a few footnotes to the vast and ever-growing literature relating to the philosophical and interpretive problems raised by Hume's outburst in Part II about the 'absolute impossibility' of an event.

THE SIGNIFICANCE OF MIRACLES AND CONTRARY MIRACLES

The fourth of Hume's *a posteriori* arguments to show 'that there never was a miraculous event established on so full an evidence [as to amount to an entire proof]' is what I have called the Contrary Miracles Argument. The argument is as follows:

> . . . let us consider, [p] that, in matters of religion, whatever is different is contrary; and that it is impossible the religions of ancient Rome, of Turkey, of Siam, and of China should, all of them, be established on any solid foundation. [q_1] Every miracle, therefore, pretended to have been wrought in any of these religions (and all of them abound in miracles), as its direct scope is to establish the particular system to which it is attributed; so has it the same force, though more indirectly, to overthrow every other system. [q_2] In destroying a rival system, it likewise destroys the credit of those miracles, on which that system was established; so that all the prodigies of different religions are to be regarded as contrary facts, and the evidences of these prodigies, whether weak or strong, as opposite to each other.   *Enquiry*, 121f: 129f

Using the designations I have interpolated in square brackets, p is the premise or assumption from which *two* conclusions follow, namely the conclusion q_1 that a miracle wrought in one religion serves to overthrow all other religions; and the conclusion q_2 that miracles wrought in different religions are 'contrary facts'.

Bailey, in the 1737 edition of his *Dictionary*, gives (sense 1) 'CONTRARY: opposite things are said to be contrary, the natures or qualities of which are absolutely different, and which destroy one another'. This is evidently closer to the use Hume is making of the term than either the second meaning Bailey gives (sense 2) 'when one thing is opposed to another, as light to darkness', or the meaning from the Square of Opposition which occurs in the 1764 edition of Bailey, and which approaches the modern use (sense 3) in which propositions X and Y are said to be contraries if X and Y are so related that they cannot both be true.

In p Hume is thus asserting that different religions are such that if one is established on a 'solid foundation' the others are destroyed, and that, in the absence of any being so established, whatever evidence tells in favour of any, tells against all the rest. But, as we shall see, this generalisation (in both its parts) holds only for religions (usually monotheistic) which make universal claims of a character which exclude the truth claims of all other religions. It does not hold for religions (usually polytheistic) which eschew such universal and exclusivist claims. The point is in effect made by Hume himself in the *Natural History of Religion*:

> The tolerating spirit of idolaters, both in ancient and modern times, is very obvious to any one, who is the least conversant in the writings of historians or travellers. When the oracle of Delphi was asked, what rites or worship was most acceptable to the gods? Those which are legally established in each city, replied the oracle. Even priests, in those ages, could, it seems, allow salvation to those of the different communion. The Romans commonly adopted the gods of the conquered people; and never disputed the attributes of those local and national deities, in whose territories they resided. . . . The intolerance of almost all religions, which have maintained the unity of God, is as remarkable as the contrary principle of polytheists.   *N.H.R.*, 49f

Hume is of course comparing monotheism and polytheism with respect to tolerance, but their tolerances derive from their claims. Worship of Asclepius at Cos was never supposed to exclude the propriety of worship of Sulis Minerva at Bath. Belief in the real existence of the members of the Roman pantheon did not exclude the possibility that the contemporaneously worshipped primitive gods of south Arabia could have real existence. Worship of Roman gods did not even exclude the reality of Jehovah as the single god of a particular area or nation; but worship of Jehovah, at least by the beginning of the Christian era, had come to exclude the reality of all Roman and other gods.

I say by the beginning of the Christian era, because although 'in the beginning God [by implication the one and only God] created the heavens and the earth', the original commandment in Exodus 20: 4 was not 'There are no other gods save me' but 'You shall have no other gods before (or beside) me'; and the question in Deuteronomy 4: 7 also allows the existence of other, less effective, gods: 'For what great nation is there that has a god so near to it as the Lord our God is to us, whenever we call upon him?' It is only in the sixth century BC that the god of Israel begins to emerge (e.g. in Isaiah ch. 2), not only as somehow the creator spoken of in Genesis and by the psalmists, but also as God *alone and universal*: the notion accepted into early Christianity and made absolutely explicit in the Nicene Creed 'I believe in one God the Father Almighty, Maker of heaven and earth, and of all things visible and invisible'.

The generalisation in Hume's premise, although false in many instances involving polytheistic religions, is thus *true* in the instance which most concerns him: Christianity. It is indeed impossible for Christianity to admit that any polytheistic religion could be established along with it 'on any solid foundation'. But could Christianity admit a related monotheistic religion such as Islam? The modern Christian theologian – pluralistic in outlook, and with enlarged liberal swallow – would almost certainly allow that although, for example, certain descriptions of the deity in the two religions are (sense 3) contraries, nevetheless the intended object of the descriptions is the same. Thus the description 'three persons in one substance' could not be true along with the Muslim's claim that 'Allah is One, the Eternal God. He begot none, nor was he begotten. No one is equal to Him' (*The Koran*, ch. 112). But some generalised principle of theism could be shared by Christianity and Islam, and in that limited sense both could start from a solid foundation. It would, on this showing, be particular doctrines, not the basic theistic assumption of the two religions, which would be contraries in Hume's premise.

So p is reduced to this: it is impossible for Christianity to be well founded along with any polytheistic religion, and it is impossible for the distinctive dogmas of Christianity to be well founded along with contrary (sense 3) dogmas in other monotheistic religions. From this observation Hume draws the conclusion q_1: that a miracle wrought in one religion serves to overthrow all other religions, and the conclusion q_2: that miracles wrought in different religions are 'contrary facts'.

But is it in general the case that the direct scope of every miracle is to establish the particular system to which it is attributed and thus, indirectly, to overthrow other systems? The short answer is – no. It was perfectly possible for miracles to be attributed to the god Asclepius (and indeed the number of plaques found at his temple at Epidauros on the Adriatic recording miraculous cures suggests a veritable pagan Lourdes), without 'overthrowing' whatever divinity Vespasian was, or employed, at Alexandria in AD 69 (Tacitus, *Histories* IV, 81). Why? Because the agents held to be responsible did not exclude each other. But the case was quite different for Christianity. The miracles wrought by Jesus were, from the very beginning, taken to be marvels which transcended what was humanly possible, thereby showing the power of the *one true God* working through him, and confirming that he was the Messiah. This is the traditional Christian 'argument from miracles'. Even Jesus himself, in as far as we can discern his view in the Synoptic gospels, seems to have viewed his ability to cast out devils in this way: 'if it is by the Spirit of God that I cast out demons, then the kingdom of God has come upon you.' The use of miracles as validating signs is even more apparent in John 2: 11; and the final generalisation in John 20: 30f is a short statement of much subsequent orthodoxy:

Now Jesus did many other signs in the presence of the disciples, which are not written in this book; but these are written that you may believe that Jesus is the Christ, the Son of God . . .

The same point is made with great authority by Origen, writing against Celsus, the Pagan critic of Christianity:

Moreover . . . the gospel has a proof which is peculiar to itself, and which is more divine than a Greek proof based on dialectical argument. The more divine demonstration [St. Paul] calls a 'demonstration of the spirit and of power' – of spirit because of the prophecies . . . of power because of the prodigious miracles which may be proved to have happened by this argument among many others, that traces of them still remain among those who live according to the will of the Logos.[1]

In short, the Pagan may admit the miracles of Jesus as real events brought about by some god, and may set them along side the miracles of Asclepius, Apollonius, Vespasian *etc*; but the Christian may not. *His* belief (in *one* God and in Jesus Christ his *only* Son) precludes the possibility that other divinities exist through whom or by whom other miracles could be performed. If other signs appear, they are the works of Satan, not of gods (see 2 Thessalonians 2: 9–12). This means, in effect, that the Christian accepts what C. D. Broad identified as the suppressed premise in Hume's argument – 'that miracles *only* occur in connexion with true religion' – because for the Christian there is only *one* true religion and only *one* divine agent.

In his discussion of this point R. M. Burns writes 'If the miracles associated with any given system were not effected for evidential purposes, then even if they can be proved to have occurred, they cannot possibly help "to overthrow every other system" or "destroy a rival system"'.[2] But he fails to note that in Christianity they *were* taken to have been effected for evidential purposes. This evidential use is not obscurely located in the writings of the first centuries of our era, but is a commonplace oft repeated, particularly by eighteenth-century writers, which is still being affirmed. Thus in the article on miracles in the recent *New Dictionary of Christian Theology* (ed. A. Richardson, London, 1983) we are reminded that 'the early apologists appealed to miracles as confirmation of the truth of the Christian faith'. The evidential use is also in Campbell's 1762 critique of Hume: 'But where are the miracles (*those of holy writ excepted*) of which you can say with propriety, it is their direct scope to establish a particular system?' (my italics).[3] Burns' somewhat uncharacteristic artlessness concerning this subject is emphasised when he continues (pp. 243f):

> Again, in the case of the alleged miracles of Vespasian, granted their occurrence, why should God not have intervened because of the necessity in the design of Providence of having Vespasian confirmed as emperor? Or why should He have refused to heal the blind and the lame, because, as was quite understandable for them in their historical circumstances, they had a devotion to the god Serapis?

Why indeed, when we conceive God in terms of the fairness and social evenhandedness approved by the modern liberal theologian!

But God was *not* so conceived by the first Christians. For them, in effect, *the agency of the one true God was built into the definition of what a miracle was.* Such an agency could not possibly be admitted to be at work in performances within religions which the first Christians 'in their historical circumstance' could only regard as false, and as opposed to their own faith. Hence their eagerness (starting in the gospels) to say that Pagan 'miracles' had not really occurred, or had been misreported, or were cheats, or, in the last resort, were the production of wizards or demons somehow permitted in God's scheme of things.[4]

The outcome of all this is that the challenging polemic of Hume's false generalisation in q_1 reduces to the particular truth that the miracles attributed to Jesus were always regarded as a major part of the evidence which established Christianity and therefore, because of *its* claims to a unique revelation of the one true God, the Christian miracles also served to overthrow other religions, particularly polytheistic religions.

I now turn to the conclusion which Hume offers in q_2: that prodigies of different religions are contrary facts – *things* which destroy one another. In addition Hume wants to say that the *evidence* for the contrary facts are 'opposites'. These are distinct matters. The first is a nonsense; the second is true within certain limits. Let us consider them separately.

It is not immediately evident what 'contrary facts' would be. The apparent example given by Bailey (sense 2) is 'light and darkness'. This suggests existences which cannot co-exist; the intrinsic notion of one is such that it cannot (as with light and darkness) or does not (as with sodium and water) exist with the other in the same area at the same time. But no two miracles wrought in different religions are ever contrary *facts* in this sense. The turning of water into wine by Jesus and the raising from the dead of the daughter of 'a consular family' by Apollonius of Tyana[5] are such that both events could have happened as reported. The mere events as such do not, as it were, cancel each other out.

The judicious Campbell expressed the point very nicely for Hume to see: 'Many facts are related as miraculous, where we may admit the fact, without acknowledging the miracle' (op. cit., p. 173). It is thus nonsense for Hume to suggest that the facts somehow render each other incredible. That this is indeed what he is suggesting is confirmed by the paraphrase of this part of his argument in his letter to Hugh Blair in response to Campbell:

If a miracles proves a doctrine to be revealed from God, and consequently true, a miracle can never be wrought for a contrary doctrine. The facts are therefore as incompatible as the doctrines.

Letters, I, 351

Facts – events in this instance – cannot be incompatible; they just *are*. The contrariety or incompatibility only arises when the *report* of one fact is given in such a way that it excludes the truth of something reported about the other fact.

Now *if* the fact (if it was a fact) that Jesus turned water into wine at Cana is reported (as it was reported) to be a sign that the God *whose existence excluded all other gods* had done this to glorify Jesus, then indeed this report would be contrary to a report that some other god has raised the consul's daughter to glorify Apollonius. The events, in each case, are as they are. But given the Judeo-Christian presuppositions of the writer of St. John's gospel, the accounts given (the attribution to different divine agencies) cannot both be true. We are thus again forced back to the strategic alternatives already met. In summary, there are three:

The Christian apologist can deal with the contrariety by questioning whether the alleged event ever took place, or was a cheat, or was the work of a diabolical spirit. *The Pagan apologist* can in his turn question whether the alleged Christian miracles ever took place etc. or he can resolve the contrariety by accepting that different divine agencies were operating (a resolution explicitly debarred to the Christian by his creed). The *sceptical observer* (which Hume undoubtedly invites us to be) can resolve the matter by concluding from 'the many instances of forged miracles', from the way miracle stories 'abound among ignorant and barbarous nations', and so on, that in all likelihood *none* of the miracles alleged by Christian or Pagan sources really took place in the manner reported.

As set out by Hume, far from being 'over subtle and refined' as he calls it, the Contrary Miracles Argument thus appears on examination to be careless and over-generalised. But when qualified, it still establishes a conclusion which looks deceptively unexciting: that when two religions claim mutually exclusive revelations, it is not possible for both of them to be well evidenced by the way they report their associated miracles. The conclusion has historical interest in as much as it reports the stance of Christian apologists (following the lead of the gospel writers) in the controversy between the early Church and those few Pagan intellectuals who noticed its claims. It has present day relevance in as much as the early apologetic position survives. It has direct relevance to the comprehensive eighteenth-century debate on miracles because the biblical miracles were then still normally taken to be actual happenings indicating, as they had indicated at the beginning of the Christian era, the exclusive revelation of the one true God in Christianity, and warranting the authenticity of that revelation.[6]

THE EIGHTEENTH-CENTURY CONTROVERSY

'Whatever God hath revealed is certainly true; no doubt can be made of it. This is the proper object of faith: but whether it be a divine revelation or no, reason must judge' (Locke, *Essay*, IV, xviii, 10). But how was reason to judge? The eighteenth-century answer was found in two arguments, neither new. One referred to the fulfilment of prophecy. The other was the argument from miracles. Both arguments were set out with great vigour by Samuel Clarke in the Boyle Lecture of 1705: 'The Proof of the Divine Authority of the Christian Revelation, is *confirmed and ascertained*, by the *Exact Completion both of all those Prophecies that went before concerning our Lord*, and *of those that he Himself delivered concerning things that were to happen after*.'[7] And, concerning miracles, 'The Christian Revelation is positively and directly proved, to be actually and immediately sent to us from God, by the many infallible *Signs and Miracles*, which the Author of it worked publickly as the Evidence of his Divine Commission.'[8]

The argument from miracles to the authenticity of the Christian revelation is, as we have seen, exceedingly ancient. In the Restoration period it had been formulated by Stillingfleet[9] among others, and was repeated by Locke in his *Discourse of Miracles*.[10] Indeed it was an argument whose strength was conceded by most writers in the period, the deists included.[11] Together with the argument from prophecy it made up the orthodox early eighteenth-century case for maintaining that the Christian revelation ought to be accepted by every rational man.

The structure and assumptions of the argument from miracles were as follows: Granted both that the power of performing miracles could only be conferred upon a man by God, and that God would not confer such a power upon those misrepresenting him, then any man who performed miracles gave evidence in so doing that he had authority from God to deliver a revelation, and hence that the revelation was true. The argument from prophecy took the same general form, but with the important and distinctive addition that in the New Testament accounts Jesus both delivered prophecies, and more significantly, fulfilled in his own person the prophecies concerning a messiah which had earlier been delivered by others. These arguments were both challenged in the 1720s and, in the course of the extensive controversy which followed, the reasonableness of accepting the Christian revelation came to rely mainly upon one particular version of the argument from miracles – the version which Hume attacks.

The controversy concerning prophecy began in 1724 with a tract from the scholar and mathematician William Whiston which naively and inadvertently provided Antony Collins with an opportunity to attack the argument from prophecy.[12] The argument thus begun continued at a high level of polemic[13] until diverted in 1727 by a new subject even more alarming to orthodox apologists. In that year there appeared the first of six *Discourses on the Miracles of our Saviour* by Thomas Woolston. In the first five discourses Woolston examined fourteen of the miracles with an eye to establishing: 'That the literal History of many of the Miracles of *Jesus*, as recorded by the *Evangelists*, does imply Absurdities, Improbabilities, and Incredibilities; consequently they, either in whole or in part, were never wrought [but must be understood in an allegorical or mystical sense]'.[14] In the final discourse (1729) he dealt with the story of the Resurrection – 'that Sandy Foundation of the Church' – which he set out to show 'to consist of Absurditys, Improbabilitys', and to be a fabrication by the Apostles.

Woolston's argument was vigorous rather than profound, but vigorous upon a most sensitive topic. It was directed at the heart of the argument from miracles, and hence at what was considered to be the essential rational foundation of the Christian revelation. It called forth a storm of refutations[15] of which only those from Sherlock and Pearce (another bishop) need be mentioned. Pearce tacitly admitted that the argument from miracles needed defending. He suggested that if the miracle of the Resurrection could be established as an undoubted historical fact, then this would be sufficient to prove to a rational man that God had invested Jesus with special authority to deliver a revelation. He states the logic of the situation as follows:

Here then a Rational man will take his Stand, and being once convinced that *Jesus* did truly rise from the Dead . . . he will easily admit all the Miracles wrought by *Jesus*, when Alive, to have been True and Real ones: For the Divine Power (we may be sure) would [not have raised up a charlatan]: And if he wrought Undoubted Miracles, will not this Conclusion necessarily follow, That he came from God, teaching the Divine Will, because he made use of his Miracles as so many Proofs of his having a Commission from Heaven?[16]

It was, however, Thomas Sherlock in the *Tryal of the Witnesses of the Resurrection*[17] who argued carefully and persuasively that the testimony of the Apostles established the Resurrection as an historical fact.

The *Tryal* was immensely successful if we may measure success by the number of editions which a book makes in the first twenty years of its life. It was widely acclaimed as a decisive move in the controversy with the deists. Even Annet, one of Sherlock's critics, conceded ten years after its publication that 'The conquest he has gain'd has spread itself far and wide, and reach'd even the remotest corners of infidelity'.[18]

In 1733 Woolston died in prison on a charge of criminal blasphemy, and Chubb and Annet who survived to challenge Sherlock drew abuse and ridicule upon themselves. In these circumstances it is not surprising to find that Hume hesitated to enter a controversy which by this time had acquired a huge literature. In a letter of 1737, addressed to Henry Home (of a branch of the Home or Hume family which had not adopted the reformed spelling of its name), Hume explained why he had decided to omit his remarks on miracles from the *Treatise*: 'Having a frankt Letter I was resolv'd to make Use of it, & accordingly enclose some Reasonings concerning Miracles, which I once thought of publishing with the rest, but which I am afraid will give too much Offence even as the World is dispos'd at present' (*New Letters*, 2). But in 1748 Hume did publish his reasonings – or some later revision of them – in the *Enquiry*. 'I won't justify the prudence of this step', he wrote to the same correspondent, 'any other way than by expressing my indifference about all the consequences that may follow' (*Letters*, I, 111). Hume's new recklessness may have been encouraged by his increasing fame and maturity and by the cooling of tempers and the decline of controversy between 1737 and 1748. Be that as it may, 'Of Miracles' has strong appearances of being intended, not merely as a general summary of the arguments of the sceptical deists, but in part also as a particular response to Sherlock's highly successful *Tryal of the Witnesses*.

We know that as a general policy Hume deliberately avoided personal exchanges which could lead to pamphlet war between himself and others. It is therefore not surprising to find no reference to Sherlock either in the *Enquiry* or in the rather meagre collection of Hume's letters surviving from the years 1737 to 1748. The evidence that Hume is answering the *Tryal* is textual and circumstantial. It consists of five items:

(1) Sherlock's sole concern in the *Tryal* is with weighing and assessing evidence, where the evidence consists exclusively in the reports of witnesses. As Flew observed, this is also Hume's fundamental concern throughout 'Of Miracles'.[19]

(2) This similarity of subject-matter becomes more significant when it is noticed that Hume's final conclusion 'a miracle can never be proved, so as to be the foundation of a system of religion' directly contradicts the conclusion which Sherlock tries to establish, namely, that one particular miracle, the Resurrection, *has* been so conclusively evidenced that it could be used as the rational ground for accepting a system of religion.

(3) Sherlock confines his discussion to the particular question whether the evidence for the Resurrection is good enough to establish that the event in question took place. Hume's argument is sufficiently general to cover the evidence for any miracle but his interest in the particular case of rising from the dead is obviously stressed at several points in his argument. On p. 115: 122 in the middle of his 'proof . . . against the existence of any miracle' he remarks: 'But it is a miracle, that a dead man should come to life; because that has never been observed in any age or country' and on the immediately following page he drives home his reference in another way: 'When anyone tells me, that he saw a dead man restored to life, I immediately consider with myself, whether it be more probable, that this person should either deceive or be deceived, or that the fact, which he relates, should really have happened'. Again, on p. 128: 138, immediately following his conclusion that 'a miracle can never be proved, so as to be the foundation of a system of religion', he discusses what the reaction would be to reports attributing a

resurrection to Queen Elizabeth.[20] He would not have 'the least
inclination to believe so miraculous an event. . . . But should
this miracle be ascribed to any new system of religion; men,
in all ages, have been so much imposed on by ridiculous stories
of that kind, that this very circumstance would be a full
proof of a cheat . . .'. The reference to the Resurrection,
and *via* the conclusion that a miracle can never be proved
so as to be the foundation of a system of religion, to the
Resurrection used to 'ground' the Christian revelation, is thinly
disguised.

(4) Hume could well be alluding to Sherlock on p. 130: 140 of the
Enquiry. At the end of his discussion of miracles he invites his
readers to examine the miracles related in scripture 'according to
the principles of these pretended Christians, not as the word or
testimony of God himself, but as the production of a mere
human writer and historian'. Who are 'these pretended
Christians'? At the beginning of the *Tryal* it is agreed that the
'Argument should be confined merely to the Nature of the
Evidence' and the whole work treats the scriptures expressly
and exclusively as the production of human writers and
historians. Hume might have had other names in mind, but
none would fill the place more easily than Sherlock's, given
the character of the *Tryal* and its fame at the time Hume was
writing.

(5) From a comparison of the arguments deployed by Hume and
Sherlock it would appear that Hume is answering certain vital
points in Sherlock's case.[21] This fifth item requires further
discussion.

In the *Tryal* the *dramatis personae* include Judge, Jury, Counsel for
Woolston (whose business it is to press the charges against the
Apostles) and Counsel for the Apostles. The Judge puts three
charges: *First*, that there is fraud and deceit in the transaction, i.e.
that Jesus himself is a 'trickster' (this is the word being used at the
time); *secondly*, that the evidence is forged by the Apostles; *thirdly*,
that no evidence would be sufficient to support the credit of so
extraordinary an event.

Sherlock dismisses the first charge after a careful cross-
examination of the four narratives. Hume does not re-open this
question although he does insinuate the suggestion that there may
be 'a cheat' in the business (*Enquiry*, 118: 126 and 121: 129) and his

remarks throughout Part II are reminiscent of the violent language in which the controversy had been carried on. The terms 'lies', 'forged miracles', 'imposture', 'holy fraud' and 'cheat' occur in the chapter.

The second charge – that the evidence is forged by the Apostles – is countered by Sherlock with the following superficially powerful argument:

> The Counsel for *Woolston* tells you, that 'tis common for Men to die for false Opinions; and he tells you nothing but the Truth. But even in those Cases their suffering is an Evidence of their Sincerity; and it would be very hard to charge Men who die for the Doctrine they profess, with Insincerity in the Profession. Mistaken they may be; but every mistaken Man is not a Cheat. Now if you will allow the Suffering of the Apostles to prove their Sincerity, which you cannot well disallow; and consider that they died for the Truth of a Matter of Fact which they had seen themselves, you will perceive how strong the Evidence is in this Case.   *Tryal*, p. 77

This argument can be weakened by establishing a non-identity between the witnesses of the events and the narrators of the Gospels, or by establishing a possibility that the witnesses may have genuinely deceived themselves about the nature of the events they describe. Clearly, although Hume may have entertained doubts about the authorship of the Gospels, he did not have the critical equipment required to urge the first alternative very convincingly. He does however adopt the second line of attack. If a report asserts very odd and unlikely events, it must, among other things, be attested 'by a sufficient number of men, of such unquestioned good-sense, education, and learning, as to secure us against all delusion in themselves'. (The passage could be Hume's amplification of Sherlock's concession (p. 46) that miracles 'require more Evidence to give them Credit than ordinary Cases do'). The hint is given, and Hume goes on:

> But if the spirit of religion join itself to the love of wonder, there is an end of common sense; and human testimony, in these circumstances, loses all pretensions to authority. A religionist may be an enthusiast, and imagine he sees what has no reality: He may know his narrative to be false, and yet persevere in it, with

the best intentions in the world, for the sake of promoting so holy a cause. *Enquiry*, 117: 125 (see also 126: 136: 'Even a court of judicature' may have difficulty in settling what is true).

The *possibility* that the Apostles reported an illusion, or persisted in a falsehood for the sake of 'so holy a cause' is sufficient to upset Sherlock's argument that it is altogether beyond belief that the Apostles could have suffered in a false cause. A good example of the sort of way in which the enthusiastic distortion described by Hume could work in an actual example is given by Conyers Middleton. Speaking of Irenaeus he says:

. . . but I have shewn also, that this single witness was of a character, on which we cannot reasonably depend for the truth of a report so extraordinary. I have shewn him to be of so credulous, superstitious and enthusiastical a turn of mind, as would dispose him to embrace and assert any fabulous tale, which tended, as he thought, in any manner, to advance the credit of the Gospel, or to confute an Heretic.[22]

There can be little doubt that Hume would have liked to say this sort of thing about the Apostles had the evidence been available or contemporary opinion permitted.

It is, however, with the third and final charge against the witnesses of the Resurrection – that no evidence would be sufficient to support the credit of so extraordinary an event (see *Tryal*, pp. 43–8 and 73–4) – that Hume is primarily concerned. As Sherlock observes, if this charge can be sustained it 'excludes all evidence out of the case'. In developing the charge the Counsel for Woolston is made to raise two issues[23] which Sherlock in the person of the Counsel for the Apostles then answers.

The first is that the Resurrection is not an event of the kind which is capable of being established by sense-perception (*Tryal*, p. 43). To this Sherlock replies:

A Man rising from the Grave is an Object of Sense, and can give the same Evidence of his being alive, as any other Man in the World can give. So that a Resurrection consider'd only as a Fact to be proved by Evidence, is a plain Case; it requires no greater Ability in the Witnesses, than that they be able to distinguish

between a Man dead, and a Man alive: A Point, in which I believe
every Man living thinks himself a Judge.   *Tryal*, p. 46

Hume does not discuss this matter, although, as already pointed
out, he draws attention to the difficulty which a court of law might
experience in distinguishing a true from a false report – even when
the report concerns the most recent and public events (*Enquiry*, 126:
136).

The second issue is that the Resurrection cannot be proved to the
satisfaction of a rational man (*Tryal*, pp. 43–4). It is a tribute to
Sherlock's intellectual honesty that the case he makes for this
position is a great deal stronger than anything actually to be found in
Woolston's *Discourses*. He argues thus on Woolston's behalf in more
than one place:

> In common Affairs, where nothing is asserted but what is
> probable, and possible, and according to the usual Course of
> Nature, a reasonable Degree of Evidence ought to determine
> every Man. For the very Probability, or Possibility of the thing, is a
> Support to the Evidence. . . . But when the thing testified is
> contrary to the Order of Nature, and, at first sight at least
> impossible, what Evidence can be sufficient to overturn the
> constant Evidence of Nature, which she gives us in the uniform
> and regular Method of her Operations?   *Tryal*, p. 43
> The Testimony of Nature, held forth to us in her constant Method
> of working, [is] a stronger Evidence against the Possibility of a
> Resurrection, than any human Evidence can be for the Reality of
> one.   *Tryal*, p. 73

This is substantially the same *a priori* argument[24] as that
developed at greater length by Hume in the first part of the chapter
on miracles. Sherlock's reply is as follows: 'Our Senses then inform
us rightly what the usual Course of Things is; but when we conclude
that things cannot be otherwise, we outrun the Information of our
Senses' (*Tryal*, p. 47).

Thus although experience indicates that resurrections are
uncommon, it does not entitle us to infer that they can never take
place. This is a good point. But it is only effective against the version
of the *a priori* argument which concludes that a miracle is
impossible. Sherlock does not state this version. The version he has
set himself to answer (the one which Hume officially reiterates

although he later gets carried away by his own argument) concludes that 'the wise man' – the man who learns from the regularities in his experience and proportions his belief to the evidence – will only believe in a miracle if it is supported by overwhelming evidence: evidence stronger than is ever likely to be produced. Against this position Sherlock produces only one reply of consequence. If the sceptic cannot believe reports of a resurrection then: 'A Man who lives in a warm Climate [Hume calls him 'the Indian prince'], and never saw Ice, ought upon no Evidence to believe that Rivers freeze and grow hard in cold Countries; for this is improbable, contrary to the usual Course of Nature; and impossible according to his Notion of Things' (*Tryal*, p. 45).

Let us call this the Indian Prince Argument. The reasoning of the Indian Prince is clearly mistaken. Ice may be impossible according to his experience: but his experience is limited. If the cases are parallel, then the experience of the sceptic is also limited, and his decision to reject resurrection reports is unjustified.

The Indian Prince Argument is given an important place in the *Tryal*. Hume answers it (*Enquiry*, 113: 121) both in the text and in a lengthy footnote.[25] The gist of his answer is that the cases differ; the experience of the Indian Prince is limited in a way in which the sceptic's is not. The Indian Prince has an obvious gap in his experience, namely, cold and its effects. But the sceptic's experience that men die and do not rise from the dead has no obvious gap in it. There is no reply to the sceptic which could take the form 'in *these* conditions, which you have not experienced, resurrections occur'.

It is possible that Sherlock might defend the Indian Prince Argument as follows: Hume is begging the question. If the Gospels are true then a resurrection *has* occurred, and the sceptic's experience is therefore limited in contrast with the experience of the Apostles even if the sceptic's experience has no 'obvious' gap in it. But for the sceptic the fundamental question *is* whether the Gospels are true. Hume does not discuss this question in a direct manner. He does, however, give an account of the way in which a wise man would react to *reports* of a resurrection (and the Gospels considered as historical evidence are merely ancient reports). The wise man would disbelieve the reports unless and until overwhelming evidence was produced that the reports were genuine. The Indian Prince 'reasoned justly' when he required 'very strong testimony' before he would believe reports of events outside the range of his experience. But once very strong testimony was produced, the

Indian Prince, as a rational man, was bound to believe in the freezing of water. Likewise very strong testimony would oblige the sceptic to believe reports of a resurrection. But has sufficiently strong testimony ever in fact been produced? Hume's official answer in 'Of Miracles' is that it *has not*. But at points in what he has to say a second and more problematic answer appears: that sufficiently strong testimony *could not* be produced. I will first consider his official answer. The problematic answer will be considered in the last section of this chapter.

THE RELIABILITY OF WITNESSES

Hume attributes to Archbishop Tillotson the apologetic corrective which he turns against 'all kinds of superstitious delusion'. But the argument which he actually sets out in the first part of the chapter on miracles bears a remarkably close resemblance to the one devised by Sherlock on behalf of Woolston: 'The Testimony of Nature, held forth to us in her constant Method of working, [is] a stronger Evidence against the Possibility of a Resurrection, than any human Evidence can be for the Reality of one' (*Tryal*, p. 73). Hume's official version of this *a priori* argument, rather than the argument as some of his critics have interpreted it and as Hume himself in off-duty moments seems to want us to use it, is as follows:

(1) A weaker evidence can never destroy a stronger.
(2) A wise man proportions his belief to the evidence.
(3) Some things happen invariably in our experience, e.g. that all men die.[26] In matters of fact these invariable experiences constitute certainties and are called laws of nature – 'a firm and unalterable experience has established these laws'.
(4) Other things happen less than always in our experience, e.g. that a day in June is warmer than a day in December. In matters of fact these constitute probabilities which admit of degrees ranging from strong (almost always happens) to weak (very seldom happens).
(5) The veracity of human testimony is, from experience, normally a strong probability and as such amounts to a proof that what is reported took place.
(6) But sometimes the veracity of testimony is a weak probability as when 'the witnesses contradict each other; when they are but

few, or of a doubtful character; when they have an interest in
what they affirm; when they deliver their testimony with
hesitation, or on the contrary, with too violent asseverations'
etc. (*Enquiry*, 112: 120). *Therefore* (from 3 and 4) when testimony
is given which is contrary to our invariable experience, a
probability, whether strong or weak, is opposing a certainty and
(from 1 and 2) the wise man will believe the certainty.

Now by 'miracle' is meant 'a transgression of a law of nature by a
particular volition of the Deity' (*Enquiry*, 115n: 123n) and 'a firm and
unalterable experience has established these laws':

> There must, therefore, be a uniform experience against every
> miraculous event, otherwise the event would not merit that
> appellation. And as an uniform experience amounts to a proof,
> there is here a direct and full *proof*, from the nature of the fact,
> against the existence of any miracle; nor can such a proof be
> destroyed, or a miracle rendered credible, but by an opposite
> proof, which is superior.
>   The plain consequence is, ... 'That no testimony is sufficient to
> establish a miracle, unless the testimony be of such a kind, that its
> falsehood would be more miraculous, than the fact, which it
> endeavours to establish . . .'. [quotation marks in original]
>   *Enquiry*, 116: 123

It is in large measure due to Professor Flew (op. cit., Chapter VIII)
that there can now be no excuse for ignoring Hume's all too easily
ignored official restrictions and reservations on this argument. In
the first place it does not set out to demonstrate that certain
conceivable events, whether called miracles or not, are logically
impossible. Thus Hume is not abandoning, out of prejudice against
miracles or for any other reason, his fundamental thesis that 'The
contrary of every matter of fact is still possible; because it can never
imply a contradiction, and is conceived by the mind with the same
facility and distinctness, as if ever so comfortable to reality' (*Enquiry*,
25: 40). Even if a miracle is at variance with all known facts, if it is
conceivable, like the sun not rising tomorrow, then it is logically
possible. The second restriction upon Hume's argument is that it is
intended as a check upon superstition[27] not as a demonstration that
a miracle could never occur in a religion. Thirdly, the argument is
addressed to the wise, to the man who does in fact proportion his

belief to the evidence, not to him for whom belief is conditioned by real or imagined factors other than evidence (factors such as election by divine grace.) Finally, Hume's argument is concerned with the testimony of witnesses and historians, not with what a man might observe for himself, experimentally reconstruct, or infer from the physical relics of past events.

This last restriction is of great importance and is still being ignored by commentators. Hume's argument tells me that if *I* have seen a miracle I should not expect any reasonable or wise man to believe my report. But my outrage at such scepticism is no objection to Hume (as Newman[28] and Ninian Smart would have it be). Hume is simply warning that incredulity is what I should expect. His argument refers explicitly and totally to the credibility of reports of miracles not to the possibility of actually experiencing one take place. Thus my own experience of seeing water turn into wine is not within the range of his argument. But the report of my experience given to someone else is within its range. From the other person's point of view my experience is simply someone's testimony, and Hume's argument warns me, very realistically I would have thought, that if my experience were very far-fetched I should expect to be pooh-poohed when I tell other people about it. In his otherwise valuable discussion Ninian Smart misconstrues Hume's argument at just this point: 'Hume's general argument, then, fails. We cannot rule out *a priori.*, i.e. without recourse to observing the way the world is, the possibility of miracles; and therefore we cannot frame a rule about believing in them which would rule out the legitimacy of believing what we see, if we were to see a miracle'.[29] But in Hume's official argument there is no attempt to rule out *a priori* the possibility of miracles or anything else taking place and at no point, not even during incautious over-statements of his position, does he ever rule out the legitimacy of believing what we see. His argument is not about what *we* see but about what *others* tell us that they saw. As such, is it a good argument? I shall argue that it is decisive when applied to weak evidence but indecisive when applied to evidence which would be regarded as conclusive apart from the improbability of what is reported.

When Hume lists the factors which put the veracity of an historical report in question, the effect of his argument is to include among them the probability of the event reported. There is nothing particularly odd about this but it has significant consequences when the report concerns events improbable enough to be called miracles. In such reports the improbability of the event, when measured by our normal experience, is so great that it vitally affects the credibility of the evidence. If, on other grounds, the evidence has already been judged weak then the improbability of the event augments this weakness. In Hume's phraseology, a weak probability (the truth of the report) is confronted with a certainty (our experience that events of the kind reported do not happen) and the wise, or even the mildly stupid man, will not believe the report. In just this sort of way the fabulous or miraculous episodes in a legend, which might in other respects contain elements of historical truth, are readily dismissed: no wise man is going to start looking for the skull of a tall one-eyed man from the evidence contained in Book IX of the *Odyssey*. Likewise no wise father is going to look for the old woman on hands and knees his young son says is crawling round the house, although the father may go out and chase the sheep away. Disbelief, when the report is suspect and what is reported is grossly improbable, is both normal and rational, and Hume's argument does little more than codify this response.

But what happens when the evidence is strong when considered in isolation from the probability of what is evidenced? In such a case, as Hume says (*Enquiry*, 116: 123) the evidential proof is diminished by the strength of my certainty that some things just do not happen. Now it is in this situation, when it is 'supposed that the testimony upon which a miracle is founded may possibly amount to an entire proof' that Hume's argument engenders a little unease. There is an uncomfortable sense that by means of it one may well justify disbelieving reports of things which did in fact happen – like your disbelief in my report of seeing water turned into wine if my report had also been vouched by numerous other good and impartial witnesses. While it is certainly true that when something altogether extraordinary is reported, the wise man will require more evidence than usual and will check and re-check the evidence very carefully, nevertheless at some stage in his accumulation of respectable evidence the wise man would be in danger of becoming dogmatic and obscurantist if he did *not* believe the evidence. Such dogmatic obscurantism looks capable of some sort of justification according to Hume's argument, and in a few off-duty moments Hume is himself guilty of it. But, as if sensing that his argument could be unconvincing when brought to bear upon evidence which in itself amounted to a full proof, he begins Part II with what is clearly a premeditated retraction. As far as miracles are concerned his argument has never been confronted with evidence which amounted to a full proof: 'it were easy to shew, that we have been a great deal too liberal in our concession, and that there never was a miraculous event established on so full an evidence'. 'Never was' is stronger and more difficult to establish than is required in order to confute the apologetic position adopted by Sherlock, Pearce, Sykes and the rest, but it has the advantage of comprehending the dangerous particular case – the Resurrection – without naming it.

Hume offers four considerations (or '*a posteriori* arguments') which would justify saying that no miracle has ever been satisfactorily evidenced. He does not quite say in as many words that the biblical narratives in general and the Resurrection story in particular are unsatisfactory and weak as evidence when judged by these, but he does come as close to saying this as a prudent regard to the contemporary state of law and opinion would allow. Thus, as I have already pointed out, at several points in the chapter he adverts to the case of a man rising from the dead and, lest any doubt should remain about the application of his argument, he finally invites his readers to consider the Pentateuch 'according to the measures of probability above established'.

The first consideration which leads Hume to say that a miracle never has been supported by conclusively strong evidence is just a list of tough-minded requirements for such evidence. Hume bluntly says these have never been satisfied. They include guarantees against delusion, deception and falsehood concerning events 'performed in such a public manner, and in so celebrated a part of the world, as to render the detection unavoidable'. In the light of modern scholarship it might seem absurd to expect the biblical narratives to satisfy such requirements and it should come as no surprise to *us* when Hume implies that the biblical narratives do not satisfy the requirements. But Hume's background was a theology which took the Gospels as straightforward factual reports. Against *that* background it would be quite in order (as Sherlock shows) to expect the Gospels to satisfy tough evidence criteria and to be shocked if it is said or implied that they do not.

The second develops an old observation about human credulity. Although belief in a wise man is fixed by evidence, there is in human nature an irrational interest in and love of the marvellous. As Scott was to observe a little later – 'such is our natural love for the marvellous, that we willingly contribute our own efforts to beguile our better judgements'. In just such a way could we account for the spread of stories about the odd, strange, interesting or marvellous.

> But if the spirit of religion join itself to the love of wonder, there is an end of common sense. . . . A religionist may be an enthusiast, and imagine he sees what has no reality: He may know his narrative to be false, and yet persevere in it, with the best intentions in the world, for the sake of promoting so holy a cause.
>
> *Enquiry*, 117: 125

The remark about enthusiastic self-deception is of particular importance in relation to what C. D. Broad calls the indirect evidence for the Resurrection:

> The direct testimony for this event appears to me to be very feeble. . . . But the indirect evidence is much stronger. We have testimony to the effect that the disciples were exceedingly depressed at the time of the Crucifixion; that they had extremely little faith in the future; and that, after a certain time, this depression disappeared, and they believed that they had evidence that their Master had risen from the dead.[30]

As already indicated, a good part of Sherlock's case rests on indirect evidence of this sort and the possibility of enthusiastic self-deception is one of Hume's few available counters to it apart from questioning the *entire* record of events (which, it seems to me, he does in fact wish to do).

The third consideration which leads Hume to say there never was a miracle established on full evidence is the way in which miraculous narratives are devalued by abounding among primitive and barbarous peoples and in 'the first histories of all nations'. So common are miracles in such histories (and so easily dismissed by the wise) that in the essay 'Of the Authenticity of Ossian's Poems' Hume is able to make the *lack* of miracles in the narrations an objection to their authenticity: 'Why is this characteristic wanting, so essential to rude and ignorant ages? . . . the incidents, if you will pardon the antithesis, are the most unnatural, merely because they are natural'.

The fourth consideration is the Contrary Miracles Argument. It has already been discussed in the first section of this Chapter.

Now if the New Testament – and not just the Pentateuch as Hume tactfully suggests – is examined, not as the testimony 'of God himself, who conducted the pen of the inspired writers', but 'as the production of a mere human writer and historian', what happens? Manifestly the narratives cannot satisfy the tough-minded criteria for evidence which Hume first produces. The early spread of Christianity in Roman society *could* be accounted for by enthusiastic self-deception together with the interest always excited by the marvellous or odd. Christianity *did* start among uncultured and uncritical people in a remote part of the Roman world, and, because of the exclusivist 'one true God' claims of the early Church, Christianity *is* subject to the Contrary Miracles Argument. But of course none of this would be very new or shocking, at least to modern New Testament scholars. With the exception of contrary miracles it is exactly the sort of thing which they have been saying in vast detail throughout the present century. As C. S. Peirce remarks 'The whole of modern "higher criticism" of ancient history in general, and of Biblical history in particular, is based upon the same logic that is used by Hume'.[31]

Thus Hume's contention at the beginning of Part II, that the evidence for a miracle has never amounted to a full proof, if not capable of justification for *all* cases, is at least justified when applied to the miracles which really matter: the biblical miracles in general and the Resurrection miracle in particular. This being so, the full force of Hume's '*a priori*' argument, as it applied to weak evidence, can be turned upon the Resurrection narrative, that is, upon the keystone of eighteenth-century attempts to show that the Christian Revelation was so well-authenticated that it could not be rejected by any rational and unbiased man:

It is experience only, which gives authority to human testimony; and it is the same experience, which assures us of the laws of nature. When, therefore, these two kinds of experience are contrary, we have nothing to do but subtract the one from the other, and embrace an opinion, either on one side or the other with that . assurance which arises from the remainder. But according to the principle here explained, this subtraction, with regard to all popular religions,[32] amounts to an entire annihilation; and therefore we may establish it as a maxim, that no human testimony can have such force as to prove a miracle, and make if a just foundation for any such system of religion.

Enquiry, 127: 137

What Hume does not do in this argument, what he does not need to do, and what it may not be possible to do, is to show that miracles could never happen and that the evidence for a miracle could never be credible to a rational man. But giving his argument the limited application which it requires in order to upset the position of eighteenth-century rational apologists (and modern funda-mentalists) it does all that Hume could have required of it. This success is however achieved by playing down the occasional extravagances in Hume's statements, by giving more weight than he himself always gives to the restrictions on his argument, and by ignoring the contentious points which have always proved an irresistible fly-paper to the passing philosopher.

LAWS OF NATURE

Among the incautious, possibily incorrect, and certainly debatable items which appear in 'Of Miracles' the following stand out: Hume's inference that if an event happened more than once it would not be a miracle: the conflict between his own account of laws of nature and the definition of a miracle which he quotes; his apparent gaffe in talking about the 'absolute impossibility' of an event and his over-hasty dismissal of the evidence for unusual events which may indeed have happened whether or not they warrant the title 'miracle'.

The most detailed definition of a miracle which Hume offers is in the footnote on p. 115: 123: *'a transgression of a law of nature by a particular volition of the Deity, or by the interposition of some invisible agent'*. In the main text, just preceding this note, he remarks: 'Nothing is esteemed a miracle, if it ever happen in the common course of nature' and 'There must, therefore, be a uniform experience against every miraculous event, otherwise the event would not merit that appellation'. These observations contain both a mistake and an insight. The mistake is in thinking that an event would not be a miracle if it happened more than once. But if due weight is given to a miracle being a particular volition of the Deity it is manifestly possible that the Deity, like all lesser agents, is able to will the same thing more than once, and, if resurrections are miracles and took place as reported, he *has* willed the same thing more than once (Jesus, Lazarus and Jairus' daughter). The insight, on the other hand, is in noticing that no happening 'in the common course of nature' could be called a miracle even if, in some way, it could be known to be a regular volition of the Deity. To be recognised, a miracle has to be a *particular* volition. To mortal man a *regular* volition would be indistinguishable from a law of nature, and an unrecognised miracle would be, for evidential and religious purposes, as good as no miracle at all.

But for anyone already believing in a god who works miracles, the possible repetition of a miracle and our inability to recognise a miracle occurring in the common course of nature, are not in any real, practical, conflict. Providing the Deity does not will resurrections for a significant proportion of men within three days of their deaths it seems perfectly possible to preserve the universal generalisation that death is for ever except for the three or four occasions when the Deity has particularly willed it otherwise. These particular occasions, the believer may say, no more invalidate the universal generalisation than a man picking up a stone invalidates the law of gravity. But the case is different for a man who does not already believe in a god who works miracles. A unique event which his devout friend calls a miracle may ultimately have to be just accepted by the sceptic as an unpalatable aberration in the nature of things. But an odd event repeated several times would almost certainly be taken as a challenge to explanations of the way the world works: revise your old explanations or devise new ones to account for the repeating oddity. Thus faith healings appear to constitute a sufficiently numerous and well-attested class of events for the sceptic to look seriously for the conditions which produce them quite apart from reference to repeated volitions of the deity. The difficulty for the believer occurs when the sceptic comes up with a sufficient explanation for the odd events he is investigating. The believer then has to face the alternatives of retracting his judgement that the odd events were miracles or revising his definition of what constitutes a miracle so that an event whose causes are known can still 'be seen to have religious significance' or something of that sort. The believer in miracles is always vulnerable to this sort of attack but he is much less liable to be attacked if his miracle constitutes a unique event rather than one of a class of oddities.

The second debatable topic in 'Of Miracles' is the tension between Hume's own account of what constitutes a law of nature and the definition of a miracle. For Hume, a law of nature is, very roughly,, the way in which we describe what always happens in our experience together with an expectation that our experience will be the same in the future as it has been in the past. In 'Of Miracles' this appears simply as 'a firm and unalterable experience has established these laws'. (Even here there is an incipient mistake. The word 'unalterable', although possibly justifiable on some account of the laws of nature, is not justifiable on Hume's. What he should have written is something like 'unvaried'.) Now if a miracle is 'a transgression of a law of nature' this simply means it is at variance with all our past experience and consequently with our expectations. But an event of this sort could equally well be either a transgression of a law of nature or an indication that our experience has not been sufficiently extensive for us to be able to formulate the laws of nature correctly; what we have could be either a miracle or a very uncommon natural event. Flew puts his finger right on the crucial point when he writes: 'Hume can provide no conception of a law of nature sufficiently strong to allow for any real distinction between the miraculous and extremely unusual' (op. cit., p. 204). But of course (a point Flew does not miss) the converse of what is a weakness in Hume's account of laws of nature is a weakness in the religious man's definition of a miracle as 'a transgression of a law of nature' etc. It is incumbent upon *him* to be able to identify a transgression of a law of nature which results from a particular volition of the deity and to differentiate it from the odd event which can safely be left to the scientist to absorb into an amended statement of the laws. Hume on the other hand does not really *need* to make this highly complex and problematic distinction (albeit that he could not). But to the believer in miracles it is of the utmost importance. Nevertheless Hume does pitch headlong into a somewhat similar distinction which he is just as unentitled to make. It is the distinction between what could happen and what is 'absolutely impossible'.

It is as clear as anything could be that in his own person Hume strenuously and totally disbelieved in miracles. This disbelief breaks through his official argument both in an over-hasty rejection of his own examples and in two appeals to the impossibility of something happening. The first of these occurs when he is considering the miracles performed at the tomb of the Abbé Paris. He concludes 'And what have we to oppose such a cloud of witnesses, but the absolute impossibility or miraculous nature of the events, which they relate? And this surely, in the eyes of all reasonable people, will alone be regarded as a sufficient refutation'. The second occurs in his invented resurrection of Elizabeth I – 'I should only assert [her death] to have been pretended, and that it neither was, nor possibly could be real.' How should these outbursts be interpreted?

The interpretation which has provoked most discussion is that Hume is appealing to a distinction between the very unusual and the totally impossible which, like the distinction between the marvellous and the miraculous, he is simply not in a position to make. The distinction is doubly unfortunate from Hume's point of view. On the one hand he almost seems to say, as R. C. Wallace puts it, 'that occurrences are to be ruled out as impossible, solely on the grounds that they would conflict with the scientists' nomologicals',[33] and Hume can give no sufficient account of such nomologicals[34] (It is an open question whether anyone has or could, but that it is not to the point.) On the other hand if he is in fact using 'law of nature' as 'firm and *unalterable* experience' (that is, with a different meaning to that employed in the rest of his philosophy), then, again in Wallace's words, he is 'using a line of argument which would exclude not only miracles, but also events which at present appear to be anomalous and inexplicable, but which may in time be incorporated into our pattern of explanation' (op. cit., p. 236). In short, Hume's account of the laws of nature is either too weak to facilitate the distinction which he seems to use between the impossible and the unusual or too strong to admit the unusual when the unusual is a genuine indication that the laws of nature should be re-formulated.

In an exceedingly interesting attempt to find a way out of this difficulty, Flew (op. cit., p. 186f) suggests that when Hume talks about the impossibility of an event he is talking about physical impossibility and 'the criterion of physical as opposed to logical impossibility simply is logical incompatibility with a law of nature, in the broadest sense'.

> The qualification *in the broadest sense* is necessary. The expression *law of nature* is sometimes taken as a prerogative of science. Whereas the notion of physical or empirical impossibility is quite untechnical, and surely antedates the emergence of science proper. . . . It is only and precisely our knowledge, or presumed knowledge, of such nomological propositions which enables us to make the ordinary lay distinction between the immensely improbable and the sheerly impossible.

Now in speaking of 'absolute impossibility' it is unreasonable to presume that Hume is suddenly and inconsistently abandoning his distinction between matters of fact whose negation is conceivable and relations of ideas whose negation is not, in other words, he is not attempting to say that certain events are *logically* impossible. The impossibility he is talking about almost certainly is something like what Flew calls physical impossibility. But the questions are, is Hume entitled to talk about such impossibility and in what sense does such impossibility entail that certain conceivable events could not happen?

In answer to the first question it would seem that Hume is just as entitled as anyone else to use the lay distinction between the highly improbable and the absolutely impossible. It is just impossible for me to be beheaded and then for the headless body to get up an hour later and walk away. It is just impossible for the sun to stand still in the sky in response to the fiat of a man. These things are equally impossible in my understanding of the world and in Hume's. They simply do not happen in the nature of things and there is nothing in Hume's account of the laws of nature (as invariable experience plus strong expectation) which prevents him from saying they are impossible in the sense of *do not happen*. But does impossibility of this sort mean that these things *could not happen*? Since logical impossibility is ruled out, the force of 'could not' can only be either an emphatic and deceptive repetition of 'do not' or shorthand for a statement of the sort 'is logically incompatible with a universal statement to which we attribute a law-like character'. The second of these alternatives does not however get us very close to the notion of 'could not happen'. The difficulty is in the word 'attribute' and it is one which has already shown up in Flew's phrase 'knowledge, or presumed knowledge'. Our attribution could be incorrect, and if our knowledge could be presumed knowledge, it could also be false belief. The point is that, once formulated, laws of nature certainly imply the physical impossibility of events incompatible with them, but their real authority to say certain events could not happen is no better than the evidence which has been used to establish them in the first place. But there is no means of knowing that such evidence is of the sort (whatever that sort would be) which could give the laws of nature the psuedo-logical strength which would be required in order to rule out certain events as physically impossible in the sense of *could not happen*. Consider an example.

Hume could have said (with complete justification) that it was physically impossible, according to the best laws of nature at his disposal, for a man in England to be able to talk to and see a man who is at the same time in America. Now if he had taken this to mean 'it could not happen that . . .' then we would simply retort it *has* happened. In short, if we are to employ the notion of physical impossibility, the most this can mean is that: within 'our' experience of the world the event has not happened, nor are we able to conceive how it could happen, nor could it possibly happen *if* the laws of nature have in fact the form and content which we attribute to them.

What force then has such impossibility got as used by a 'just reasoner' against a report of a miracle? No more force than Hume's original argument that the event is against all our past and what we presume to be our invariable experience. That is, there is a strong and rational presumption against the event but not a demonstration of its 'absolute impossibility' in any sense of that phrase in which it can be taken to imply *'could not happen'*. When Hume is on his guard he shows himself perfectly well aware of this:

> I beg the limitations here made may be remarked, when I say, that a miracle can never be proved, so as to be the foundation of a system of religion. For I own, that otherwise, there may possibly be miracles, or violations of the usual course of nature, of such a kind as to admit of proof from human testimony; though, perhaps, it will be impossible to find any such in all the records of history.   *Enquiry*, 127: 137

Hume's 'absolute impossibility' is thus merely a robust appeal to the familiar and useful notion of 'physical impossibility' where that is construed in such a way that it does *not* entail that the impossible event *could not* happen – however confident we may be that in fact it *will not* happen.

If all this seems over-subtle and refined a much simpler interpretation is available: In Hume's observation about laws of nature the word 'unalterable' should have been 'unvaried'. The 'impossibility' gaffes are nothing but overstatements of his official argument brought on by his enthusiastic disbelief in miracles. They are at variance with his official argument and its appendage that *in fact* 'There never was' a miracle founded on good evidence. They are at variance with what he needs to establish in confronting the apologetic position of Sherlock and the rest. They are, in their simplest and most obvious meaning, at variance with his own philosophical position about matters of fact and they are minute points in a much longer argument.

However the most objectionable aspect of the chapter consists not in Hume's proper or improper appeals to physical impossibility, but in his precipitate readiness to play the Indian Prince and dismiss events which could very well have happened (and not even be miracles) solely on the grounds that they do not conform to his rather imperfect grasp of what constitute laws of nature. It is not that *we* have a perfect grasp of such laws but that, in general, a certain humility about our knowledge seems appropriate. Thus Hume's impatient dismissal of the Abbe Paris cures and of the Vespasian cure of the blind man seems both obscurantist and unnecessary, and quite a lot else in the tone of the chapter conveys a sense of undue and slightly arrogant confidence about what is or is not physically possible.

*   *   *

'Of Miracles' has received more critical attention than anything else Hume wrote on religion. Its particular merits may not justify this but its importance in his whole critique of religion within the limits of reason alone can scarcely be over-estimated. It is the only piece in which he systematically attacks the reasonableness of belief in revealed religion. He does so by means of an argued rejection of the thesis that miracles in general and the Resurrection in particular authenticate the Christian revelation in a manner which should satisfy any reasonable man. But despite this, and his highly critical survey of the arguments of natural religion, he does not say that no reasonable man can believe in any religion. A reasonable man can have a non-natural belief which goes beyond the evidence and may not be due to general pathological causes of the sort Hume examines in the *Natural History of Religion*. But the belief will exist alongside, rather than as part of, the rational man. It will subvert 'all the principles of his understanding' and be brought home to him 'by the immediate operation of the Holy Spirit': an operation which Hume ironically describes as 'a continued miracle'. Another such irrational oddity confirmed by a suspect revelation is belief in personal immortality.

9

The Revelation of Immortality

The soul, secur'd in her existence, smiles
At the drawn dagger, and defies its point.
The stars shall fade away, the sun himself
Grow dim with age, and nature sink in years;
But thou shalt flourish in immortal youth,
Unhurt amidst the war of elements,
The wrecks of matter, and the crush of worlds.

Addison, *Cato*, V i

At no time in his adult life did Hume ever believe in any form of personal immortality. This biographical fact, so challengingly at variance with the professed beliefs of most of his contemporaries, is given little expression in his philosophical writings. There is the brief, aphoristic essay 'Of the Immortality of the Soul' which Hume perforce never published during his lifetime, and there are sections in the *Treatise*, in particular 'Of the Immateriality of the Soul' which were construed as attacks upon the immortality doctrine. There are a few wayward remarks elsewhere in his private papers and published works – mostly of biographical interest – and that is all. The excuse for devoting a chapter to the present topic is thus not its prominence in Hume's writing but its importance in the philosophy of religion together with the controversial significance of those relatively brief things which Hume has to say. These add up to a case against immortality which at least one writer has found 'almost irresistible'.[1]

SPECIES OF IMMORTALITY

'Whether we are to live in a future state, as it is the most important question which can possibly be asked, so it is the most intelligible

166

question which can be expressed in language.' The confident opening sentence of Bishop Butler's dissertation 'Of Personal Identity' asserts one thing and asks another. It asserts, what subsequent philosophical discussion has taken to be highly debatable, that the immortality of a person is a coherent doctrine. It asks whether the doctrine is true. Now Hume's contribution to the subject is to argue that one very important version of the immortality doctrine is incoherent and that even if it were coherent it would, along with other versions of the doctrine, be false or pernicious or both. But first, what versions of the doctrine are there and what problems do they raise?

There are unproblematic palliatives such as speaking of a man's children or his works or his moral acts as 'his immortality'. There are modernistic re-thinks of Christianity which would rob 'eternal life' of any reference to life after death. There is a doctrine that a 'shadow' or 'astral' body breaks away from the physical body at death and in certain abnormal pre-mortem experiences. This has had a certain vogue among modern devotees of psychical exotica. None of these doctrines are the concern of eighteenth-century thinking nor, for that matter, are they the concern of any of the great religions of the western world. For *their* purposes the immortality doctrine exists in only two historically important forms: as the bodily resurrection of the whole person, or as the survival of the soul.

Bodily Resurrection

This is the orthodox Christian (and Muslim) doctrine. It is that at 'the general resurrection in the last day' the corruptible body which each person has in earthly life will be restored incorruptible: 'It is sown a natural body; it is raised a Spiritual body';[2] 'For this corruptible must put on incorruption, and this mortal must put on immortality.'[3] in case anyone should construe 'spiritual body' as a sort of ghost rather than flesh and blood there is St Augustine's authoritative and forthright gloss:

> Bodies which have a living soul, but not yet a life-giving spirit, are called *animal* (that is, bodies with *anima* – 'life' or 'soul'; and yet they are not souls but bodies). In the same way, those other bodies are called *spiritual*. Yet we must not allow ourselves to believe that they will be spirits: we must think of them as bodies

having the substance of flesh, though never having to experience corruption or lethargy, being preserved from such a fate by the life-giving spirit. Then man will no longer be earthly, but heavenly, not because his body, made of earth, will not be the same, but because the heavenly gift will fit it for living in heaven itself, not by a loss of its natural substance, but by a change in its quality.[4]

About this doctrine as such Hume makes no *direct* critical comment although some of his remarks on personal identity could be developed into an objection to it, as they could to almost any doctrine of personal immortality. But even in Christianity the doctrine of immortality by bodily resurrection in the last day or at death (which will be the same thing for those who are dead if there is to be no existence between death and the general resurrection) exists along with a second doctrine, one version of which is the main butt of Hume's attack.

Immortal Soul

In this account of immortality man is thought of as the combination of a mortal and perishable body with an immortal and imperishable soul. The soul is identified with the essential person, with 'mind' or 'self' or the 'Hidden Thing within': that which is supposed to make me what I am, a thinking, conscious being apart from the accidents of the bodily encumbrance which I happen to carry in mortal life.[5] The body is subject to death. But the essential person survives death.

This account of immortality comes in at least two versions. In one the distinction is made between the material substance of the body and the immaterial or spiritual substance of the soul. The material body corrupts at death but the immaterial soul is released and remains incorruptible. In the other the distinction is again made between body and soul but the vehicle of the soul's immortality is not specified as a substance – immaterial or otherwise. It is mainly the former of these which Hume attacks: very sharply under the heading 'metaphysical topics' in 'Of the Immortality of the Soul'; less sharply, but with more sophistication, in the *Treatise* chapter 'Of the Immateriality of the Soul'.

The doctrine of an immortal soul has a venerable lineage from Plato's *Phaedo* and earlier to the present day. It still provides the commonest background assumption to popular talk about immortality. In Christianity, despite the more canonical bodily resurrection doctrine, talk about an immortal soul, whether or not the soul is identified with an immaterial or spiritual substance, is and always has been very common.[6] Because of this, Hume's attack upon the notion of an immaterial soul was commonly understood as an attack upon any belief in immortality. *A Letter* (1745) defends him from this interpretation. But given his own disbelief in immortality the defence may well be disingenuous and adapted, like the *Letter* itself, for particular local purposes.

In some variations of the immortal soul doctrine (but not in the Christian assimilation of it) the soul is thought of as existing both before and after its sojourn in the mortal body. This is the version of the doctrine which Hume briskly rejects when he remarks 'The soul, therefore, if immortal, existed before our birth: And if the former state of existence no wise concerned us, neither will the latter.'

Both the doctrine of bodily resurrection (or whole man reconstitution as it is sometimes called) and that of an immortal soul pose questions of the highest complexity. How is the resurrected body or the immortal soul to be identified as the *same person* as some once living man? What is meant by 'soul' or 'self'? (A problem spotted by Berkeley – 'the grand mistake is that we know not what we mean by we, selves, mind etc'.[7]) What is it to be the same person at different times? Is the phrase 'immaterial soul' intelligible? If these and other questions about the coherence of either doctrine can be given a satisfactory answer, then the matter-of-fact question can be asked: Is there any evidence that men have an immortality of the sort spoken of? In what follows, and in accordance with the design of this book, I confine discussion of these and the like questions to points raised by Hume or arising *directly* in connection with what he says. Accordingly I omit, in this edition, any discussion of his *Treatise* chapter 'Of Personal Identity'. The discussion of personal identity in general is highly relevant to questions about the coherence of the idea of personal immortality, but the direct relevance of what Hume says is slight.

HUME'S ARGUMENTS

In the short essay 'Of the Immortality of the Soul' (which I shall generally refer to in this chapter simply as 'the essay') Hume divides the discussion into metaphysical topics and physical and moral arguments. *Metaphysical topics* are the difficulties with the immortal soul doctrine which result from considerations of coherence or intelligibility. *Physical arguments* are those which would seek to show that the doctrine of the immortality of the soul is false, even if we allow it to be coherent. The most important of those touched upon in this essay are what I shall call the Concomitant Variation Argument and the Secret Dread Argument. *Moral arguments* are those objections which, according to Hume, would be made on moral grounds to the Christian doctrine of immortality whatever its ontological status.

Metaphysical Topics

At the beginning of the essay 'Of the Immortality of the Soul' Hume remarks that 'metaphysical topics are founded on the supposition that the soul is immaterial, and that it is impossible for thought to belong to a material substance'. His reply is:

> But just metaphysics teach us, that the notion of substance is wholly confused and imperfect, and that we have no other idea of any substance than as an aggregate of particular qualities, inhering in an unknown something. Matter, therefore, and spirit are at bottom equally unknown; and we cannot determine what qualities may inhere in the one or the other.

This reads very like a summary of part of Hume's argument in the chapter 'Of the Immateriality of the Soul' in the *Treatise*. His conclusion there is that 'the question concerning the substance of the soul is absolutely unintelligible' (*Treatise*, 250). This conclusion rests upon four arguments.

The first and most general of these arguments in the *Treatise* is that since we have no idea of *any* substance ('matter and spirit are at bottom equally unknown') we cannot dispute meaningfully whether something is or is not a material or an immaterial substance. (This is the road which Locke might have taken when he remarks 'Self is that conscious thinking thing, whatever substance made up of (whether spiritual or material, simple or compounded, it matters not) . . .'.[8] Locke's later preference for the soul being an immaterial substance is the one which Hume attacks.) Hume's reasons for concluding that the notion of a substance is meaningless form a significant part of the critical epistemology of the *Treatise*. For example, he says that we have no idea of any substance derived from our impressions (our sensible and reflective experiences) therefore we can attach no meaning to the term. And again, if we define a substance as 'something which may exist by itself' then this is vacuous because it 'agrees to every thing, that can possibly be conceiv'd; and never will serve to distinguish substance from accident, or the soul from its perceptions' (*Treatise*, 233). Hume's objections to the doctrine of substance – whether supposed to be material or spiritual – are part of the history of philosophy known to every undergraduate and discussed by every critic. I do not propose to rake over the ashes again here. Suffice it to say that with certain additions and qualifications they are widely held to be important objections to the notion of material substance as Locke was supposed to have used it,[9] and may also be significant objections to Berkeley's account of minds if his account can be shown to depend upon us having a notion of a spiritual substance.

Hume's second argument in the *Treatise* to show that 'the question concerning the substance of the soul is absolutely unintelligible' consists in an attack upon one of the arguments which had been used to show that the soul must be an immaterial substance. There is, he says, an argument for the soul's immateriality which runs as follows. Thought or consciousness (the supposed primary function of the soul) does not have extension or location. Everything which is of material substance does have extension and location. Therefore thought cannot inhere in a material substance. Therefore it inheres in an immaterial substance (which is the indestructible stuff of the soul). In order to discuss this argument Hume suspends his contention that all talk of substances is meaningless. His reply is then a prolonged advocacy of the thesis that 'an object may exist, and yet be nowhere'. For example, 'A moral reflection cannot be plac'd on the right or on the left hand of a passion, nor can a smell or sound be either of a circular or a square figure' (*Treatise*, 236). The fact that it makes no sense to ask for the location of a thought or the extension of a consciousness does not, according to Hume, imply that these objects are non-existent or that they must exist in an immaterial substance which is incapable of location or extension. Instead it implies that thought and consciousness are not members of that category of objects to which the concepts 'location' and 'extension' can be meaningfully applied. The argument (that thought cannot inhere in a material substance therefore it inheres in an immaterial substance) is thus, according to Hume, a confusion derived from a category mistake. It leads to questions as absurd as 'Is the . . . immaterial substance . . . on the left or the right hand of the perception? (*Treatise*, 240) and is, for example, as foolish as asking if the sportsmanship of the village cricket team is at deep mid-wicket or silly mid-on, failing to get an answer, and therefore concluding that the sportsmanship inheres in a locationless spiritual ether. Hume does not use the modern expression 'category mistake'. But he does in effect characterise the mistake and use it to ridicule the contention that thought must inhere in an immaterial substance.

His third argument is an attack upon yet another argument for the soul's immateriality. Motion and matter, it is sometime said, however subdivided or compounded, are still motion and matter and never become pleasures or moral reflections or thoughts. 'Now as these different shocks, and variations, and mixtures are the only changes, of which matter is susceptible, and as these never afford us any idea of thought or perception, 'tis concluded to be impossible, that thought can ever be caus'd by matter' (*Treatise*, 247). This argument is the fusion of two arguments. One concludes that the movements and combinations of physical things are in a different category from thoughts, hopes, pleasures and intentions. The other concludes that the movements of matter can never produce (cause) thoughts etc. The former conclusion is true but, as Hume has already indicated, does not imply that thoughts must exist in a non-material substance. The latter conclusion asserts a matter of fact which on the best information available seems to be just false. As Philo remarks 'we every day see [reason] arise from [generation] and never [generation] from [reason]' (*Dialogues*, 197). The line Hume takes in the *Treatise* is a more general rejection of the matter of fact argument: 'as the constant conjunction of objects constitutes the very essence of cause and effect, matter and motion may often be regarded as the causes of thought, as far as we have any notion of that relation' (*Treatise*, 250).

It may well be true that thought is commonly observed to be an effect of some modification of matter and hence that it is not *necessary* for thought to inhere in some immaterial substance. But it is a pity Hume's own preconceptions prevent him using the most obvious argument against thought belonging to an immaterial substance. If he had been able to accept that he was acquainted with material things and that these, not their qualities (the Cheshire cat but not its grin), are substances, that is, can significantly be said to exist separately or in their own right, then he could have attributed thought to the corporeal person and left the immaterial soul-substance as a pseudo-notion.[10] As it is, he will have nothing to do with any talk of substances: an unwillingness which both deprives him of a good argument against immaterial substances and puts some of his own metaphysic in question. In particular, for Hume, the essential person or soul is left as *neither* material *nor* immaterial substance and this means that he is officially unable to say that the person is corporeal: an official prohibition which he comes close to waiving on at least one occasion (see below p. 177).

There is a fourth and somewhat curious reason given by Hume for reaching the conclusion that 'the question concerning the substance of the soul is absolutely unintelligible'. It is this. If Spinoza's doctrine of the unity of the substance of the universe (each individual object being merely a modification of it) is held to be absurd and atheistical then 'this hideous hypothesis is almost the same with that of the immateriality of the soul, which has become so popular' (*Treatise*, 241). It is almost the same because the whole of our experience can be considered in two ways. 'I observe first the universe of objects or of body', the sun, moon, mountains etc. and these, for Spinoza, are all modifications of one substance. 'I then observe a universe of thought, or my impressions and ideas' and there I discover another sun, moon, mountains etc. These, for 'certain theologians' (Berkeley?), are all modifications of one single immaterial substance which is my soul. Both hypotheses are equally absurd according to Hume. I say this in a 'somewhat curious' argument because its force depends on the one hand upon a carelessly developed paraphrase of a profoundly complicated philosophical position while on the other hand it depends upon Hume's readers being prejudiced against Spinoza on the grounds of his supposed atheism. Neither of these characteristics is likely to commend Hume's arguments in the present matter to the modern reader and his thesis that 'immaterial substance' is meaningless is sufficiently argued without the Spinoza outburst. (Whenever Hume mentions Spinoza he does so in order to condemn him (see, for example, *A Letter*, 13). I have never been able to decide if this is because Hume genuinely disliked Spinoza's 'absurd' metaphysics or because he thought it prudent to identify himself or occasions with those who condemn Spinoza's 'atheism'.)

Hume has thus argued 'concerning *the Immateriality of the Soul* (from which the Argument is taken for its natural Immortality, or that it cannot perish by Dissolution as the Body)' (*A Letter*, 13) that the notion of an immaterial substance is unintelligible and that nothing shows that thought must 'inhere' in such a substance. Hence if immortality depends upon the soul being an immaterial substance no coherent account of immortality is possible.

Hume's parting shot on the subject is in 'Of the Immortality of the Soul'. If we suppose 'spiritual substance' (Hume uses 'immaterial' and 'spiritual' interchangeably, as I have done) to be a coherent concept and to be instantiated, then nature appears to employ such a substance much as she does ordinary matter:

> [Nature] modifies it into a variety of forms and existences; dissolves after a time each modification; and from its substance erects a new form. As the same material substance may succesively compose the bodies of all animals, the same spiritual substance may compose their minds: Their consciousness, or that system of thought, which they formed during life, may be continually dissolved by death; and nothing interests them in the new modification. . . . And that an immaterial substance, as well as a material, may lose its memory or consciousness, appears, in part, from experience, if the soul be immaterial.

The suggestion is strikingly destructive. What Hume is saying is that even if we allow that the soul is immaterial the immortality of its stuff may be of no more significance to our immortality as persons than is the immortality of the stuff of our bodies. In this sense the doctrine of metempsychosis could be true but totally banal. The soul may transmigrate but the transmigration would be of no more interest to the person whose soul it was, and no more identical with him as a person, than the maggots which devoured the dead body of the king would be of interest to or identical with the king. Hume's piquant conclusion to the passage quoted – if experience shows anything it shows that immaterial substance can lose its memory – refers, presumably, to both geriatric and post-mortem amnesia!

It will be observed that in all this Hume has said and implied nothing about the doctrine of immortality through bodily resurrection. The final shot apart, all he has said is that the soul cannot be immortal if the vehicle of its immortality is the incoherent doctrine of immaterial substance. As he remarks in his own defence: 'The Author has not anywhere that I remember denied the

Immateriality of the Soul in the common Sense of the Word. He only says, That the Question did not admit of any distinct Meaning; because we had no distinct Idea of Substance. This Opinion may be found everywhere in Mr *Lock*, as well as Bishop *Berkley'* (*A Letter*, 30). But this is slightly disingenuous. What is 'the common sense of the word' (presumably the word 'soul') which differs from the sense Hume gives it? If the soul is the essential person, and the soul cannot be said to be an immaterial substance and thus both immune from the body's corruption and able to provide some sort of vehicle for continuing personal identity, how is anyone going to be able to characterise immortality except through the *intrinsically* improbable credo of bodily resurrection, or through some unexplained non-substantial person for which the word 'soul' is supposed to stand? The suspicion that Hume means more destruction than he finds it prudent to admit is, I think, confirmed by the remainder of his discussion which is capable of application to doctrines of immortality which do not depend upon speaking of an immaterial soul-substance.

Physical Arguments

These are Hume's several (brief) arguments in the essay which maintain that even if it were coherent, the doctrine of the immortality of the soul would very probably be false. There are four.

(1) The first is what I shall call the Concomitant Variation Argument. It is an application of what J. S. Mill was to call the 'Method of Concomitant Variations' in his list of sound experimental procedures. Hume's statement of the method in the essay is this:

> Where any two subjects are so closely connected, that all alterations, which we have ever seen in the one, are attended with proportionable alterations in the other; we ought to conclude, by all the rules of analogy, that, when there are still greater alterations produced in the former, and it is totally dissolved, there follows a total dissolution of the latter.

Now, argues Hume, there is a very striking concomitant variation in the state of our body and the state of our soul (where 'soul' or 'mind' is understood to mean the sequence of perceptions which is the essential person). For example:

> Sleep, a very small effect on the body, is attended with a temporary extinction; at least, a great confusion in the soul. The weakness of the body and that of the mind in infancy are exactly proportioned; their vigour in manhood; their sympathetic disorder in sickness; their common gradual decay in old age. The step further seems unavoidable; their common dissolution in death.

These reflections are by no means original. They have a history going at least as far back as the Epicureans, and Bertrand Russell is unlikely to be the last distinguished thinker who will appeal to them.[11] But what *is* unusual in Hume's use of them is that he makes the argument an application of a respectable general procedure for securing true results in empirical investigations. If we are to think of a living man as a conjunction of two parts, a soul (or essential person) and a body, then to all appearances the two parts have a common rise and fall. The argument to their mutual dissolution is of exactly the same character as the observation that the health of the red corpuscles in the blood varies with the health of the marrow, to the extent that in the end, if the latter is destroyed by disease, so is the former. Hume is in effect arguing that we cannot accept the concomitant variation between two physical processes and reject it between a physical process (bodily health and maturity) and something else which we have no decisive reason to suppose is *not* a physical process: the conscious soul. It will be observed that this argument is primarily applicable to forms of the immortality doctrine in which the soul, substantial or otherwise, operates as the bearer of the person's immortality.

(2) The second argument to show that the soul is mortal looks like an extension of the first but on closer inspection it proves to be something more: 'Every thing is in common betwixt soul and body. The organs of the one are all of them the organs of the other. The existence therefore of the one must be dependent on that of the other.' Now this certainly could be read as a reassertion of the Concomitant Variation Argument. But it could also be read as Hume's nearest approach to saying that soul and body are not separable, independent objects, but interrelated

features of one unified thing – the whole corporeal man. In 'Of Personal Identity' Hume set out with a preconception which he shared with Locke: that he should look for and that it would be possible to find a single non-corporeal criterion of personal identity which would be decisive in all cases however peculiar. Having failed to find anything which would do the job he admitted failure in his quest and never returned to it. What he should have done, we may say, was to pay more attention to this hint in the essay and say that the quest was futile. It is futile for the reason quoted: the quest depends upon being able to isolate parts of the whole man and treat one of the parts as the essential person. But there are no separable parts in the sense supposed. There are only different aspects of the whole man: body and soul make one, not two. As Bernard Williams has remarked, 'when we are asked to distinguish a man's personality from his body, we do not really know what to distinguish from what'.[12] Now if 'every thing is common betwixt soul [essential person] and body' and the identity of the whole man consists in body and soul, then if the body is destroyed the soul is destroyed. Once again it will be noted that there is much less difficulty here for immortality by bodily resurrection complete with soul.

(3) The third 'matter of fact' argument which Hume produces is an appeal to the universality of Heraclitean flux.

> Nothing in this world is perpetual. Every being, however seemingly firm, is in continual flux and change: The world itself gives symptoms of frailty and dissolution: How contrary to analogy, therefore, to imagine, that one single form, seemingly the frailest of any, and, from the slightest causes subject to the greatest disorders, is immortal and indissoluble? What a daring theory is that!

The reference of the word 'form' (it appears from a few sentences earlier) is 'the soul'. Why, asks Hume, and with good reason, should this one part or aspect of the whole man be excepted from the universal rule of change, decay, corruption.

(4) The final 'physical argument' is a reversal of the old argument that since men look for immortality there must be something there to look for. The old argument can be found, for example, in several of Berkeley's sermons and elsewhere in his work.[13] It is

also given splendid rhetorical statement by Addison in the lines
which precede the motto to this chapter:

It must be so – Plato, thou reason'st well! –
Else whence this pleasing hope, this fond desire
This longing after immortality?
Or whence this secret dread, and inward horror,
Of falling into nought? why shrinks the soul
Back on herself, and startles at destruction?

If we call this the Pleasing Hope Argument then Hume's counter
to it (apart from his point that it is highly suspect because it is
interested pleading) could be called the Secret Dread Argument:
if the pleasing hope requires an object so does the secret dread.
If, according to Hume in the essay, the horror of annihilation
were an 'original passion' it would prove the mortality of the
soul since nature, which does nothing superfluously 'would
never gives us a horror against an impossible event' – 'She may
give us a horror against an unavoidable event, provided our
endeavours, as in the present case, may often remove it to some
distance. Death is in the end unavoidable; yet the human species
could not be preserved, had not nature inspired us with an
aversion towards it'. It is not entirely clear that Hume intends to
say the Pleasing Hope and the Secret Dread Arguments are both
nonsense because if one is valid, the other is valid and they
cannot both be valid because they establish contradictory
conclusions. He could be saying this, or he could be saying that
the Pleasing Hope Argument is unsound because the Secret
Dread Argument shows not that annihilation is objectively real,
but that aversion to death is useful as a means of preserving the
species in a way in which the hope for immortality is not. Either
way the Pleasing Hope shrivels (like Lamia) under the cold
touch of Hume's philosophy.

I have listed these four 'matter-of-fact' objections to the
immortality of the soul more or less as Hume gives them. The last two
are also objections to a rational belief in bodily resurrection though
not to the coherence of such a doctrine if it could be otherwise
established, say by divine revelation. Hume does not develop these
arguments elsewhere either in private or published writings
although he does affirm his disbelief in any form of immortality –

a disbelief which we can only assume to be influenced by arguments of this sort.

There is one other matter-of-fact (or perhaps it should be called matter-of-taste) argument against immortality which Hume produces in the essay and which he returned to in his deathbed interview with Boswell. In the essay he puts it thus: 'How to dispose of the infinite number of posthumous existences ought also to embarrass the religious theory. . . . For these, then, a new universe must, every generation, be created, beyond the bounds of the present universe.' In Boswell's report the same objection – 'That immortality if it were at all, must be general' – reduces to Hume saying that if he is immortal, then Wilkes must be immortal: a consideration which perhaps makes the thought of personal immortality unseemly without diminishing its probability. But as Hume says in the essay (concerning a universe crowded with the dead) 'The want of arguments, without revelation, sufficiently establishes the negative.' No need then to fear Wilkes in the future state, or the tedious company of 'every stupid clown that ever existed'!

Moral Arguments

It will be noticed that nothing which Hume has so far said is specifically directed at immortality by bodily resurrection. But he does confront the Christian doctrine with about the most damaging objection which could be devised. He says, not that it is incoherent or false, but that it is immoral. It is immoral in three ways according to Hume in the essay.

First, given the fine balance between our needs and our ability to satisfy our needs, all our energy and attention have to be directed to this world (the point is in the essay but is repeated in *Dialogues*, 208) and in practical life we cannot regulate our conduct by reference to an hereafter. Secondly, the benefits of the after-life are reserved for one species of virtue but:

> According to human sentiments, sense, courage, good manners, industry, prudence, genius, are essential parts of personal merit [a point argued at length in the *Enquiry concerning the Principles of Morals* – J. G.]. Shall we therefore erect an elysium for poets and heroes, like that of the ancient mythology? Why confine all rewards to one species of virtue?

Finally, the use of heaven and hell as an ultimate, everlasting
reward and punishment is a moral scandal. This is because (a)
'Punishment, without any proper end or purpose, is inconsistent
with *our* ideas of goodness and justice; and no end can be served by
it after the whole scene is closed'. (b) 'Punishment, according to *our*
conceptions, should bear some proportion to the offence. Why then
eternal punishment for the temporary offences of so frail a creature
as man?' (c) 'Heaven and hell suppose two distinct species of men,
the good and the bad. But the greatest part of mankind float betwixt
vice and virtue'. (d) The very concepts of reward and punishment
are inappropriate to non-rational creatures and very many men
come into this category, for example 'Nature has rendered human
infancy peculiarly frail and mortal; as it were on purpose to refute
the notion of a probationary state. The half of mankind die before
they are rational creatures.'

Hume's emphasis on the word '*our*' ideas of goodness and justice
should be noted. It is a point which has already been considered (see
p. 105 above). Hume's return to it under the topic of immortality
emphasises its importance: 'To suppose measures of approbation
and blame, different from the human, confounds every thing.'

The contention that the Christian view of immortality is immoral
is in striking contrast to the often heard view that the 'weights' of
heaven and hell are at least a significant motive to do good and may
even be the ultimate pivot upon which the justice or injustice of
things is balanced. As D. Z. Phillips remarks 'In this world, there
may be moments when one wonders whether justice and goodness
are worth pursuing. One's immediate reading of the scale of
probabilities makes the matter look doubtful. At such times, Geach
would say, what we need to do is to extend the scale so that it
includes an assessment of life after death.'[14] I would not care to
conjecture from the source given [15] whether Geach would or would
not say exactly this, but there is no doubt that very many people
would say it. To such people Hume's reasoned contention, that
immortality of the type popularly and traditionally supposed in
Christianity is flagrantly contrary to all human moral decencies,
may even now come as a startling affront to their religion. But I
suspect Hume's intention is not to say that the Christian scheme of
immortality is in fact morally offensive, but that because it would be
morally offensive there can be no such scheme.

*   *   *

Hume did not believe in any form of personal immortality. His reasons for this negative belief are as complete as the nature of the case will permit. The belief in its vulgar (and not so vulgar)[16] form as the immortality of an immaterial soul (thought of as the essential person and characterised by consciousness or perceptions or thoughts) is incoherent. The question concerning the materiality or immateriality of the soul is wholly unintelligible. There is nothing to show that thought does inhere in an immaterial substance nor even that it would be meaningful to say that it did so inhere. Even if it did there is nothing to show that the immaterial stuff preserves its form any more than the material stuff does. Such observations as we can make show that whenever thought occurs it occurs in conjunction with a body. The concomitant variation of bodily vitality and the vitality of the soul or supposed essential person, the inextricable fusion of body and soul which makes the identity of the living man, the precariousness of human life and our consequent *interest* in securing immortality – all this argues against that aspect of the living man which we call 'soul' being immortal. But, finally, even if the immortality promised in the Christian religion were coherent and true it would be morally offensive.

In the light of what he had written about the credentials of revelation in the *Enquiry*, Hume's final flourish in the essay can only be read as sarcastic irony. He says that only divine revelation can give us information about immortality:

> Nothing could set in a fuller light the infinite obligations which mankind have to Divine revelation; since we find, that no other medium could ascertain this great and important truth.

Since not even divine revelation could substantiate an incoherence, Hume is presumably not referring here to immortality via an immaterial soul but to some other characterisation of immortality such as the survival of disembodied experiences or the resurrection of the body complete with soul. That the Christian belief should be whole-person immortality – preserving body and soul into everlasting life – and therefore least *metaphysically* objectionable is not a consideration which gives the belief any significant probability. Hume's prudential device of foisting improbable beliefs onto divine revelation is like saying that the beliefs are probably false and certainly independent of evidence, though they are of much too much public importance to be freely dismissed.

I said at the start of this Section of the present chapter that a sentence in the essay 'Of the Immortality of the Soul' reads very like a summary of part of the chapter in the *Treatise* called 'Of the Immateriality of the Soul'. But there is more to it than that. At the end of the chapter 'Of the Immateriality of the Soul' Hume remarks: 'In both cases the metaphysical arguments for the immortality of the soul are equally inconclusive; and in both cases the moral arguments and those deriv'd from the analogy of nature are equally strong and convincing' (*Treatise*, 250). In the light of what I have been saying, to describe the metaphysical arguments as 'inconclusive' is erring on the side of modesty; but to describe the moral and physical arguments as 'strong and convincing' is downright deception *unless one had already read* 'Of the Immortality of the Soul'. If one had read that essay it would not require much intellectual detective work to notice the *irony* (no longer the deception), and one would easily appreciate what is now completely hidden: that Hume means 'strongly and convincingly *against* the immortality of the soul'. This cross-reference between the essay and 'Of the Immateriality of the Soul', together with the appearance which the metaphysical topics in the essay have of being a *summary* of the *Treatise* section, leads me to the following conjecture.

We know that Hume produced 'Of the Immortality of the Soul' and 'Of Suicide' in 1755 in a hurry to fill up a gap in a volume at the printers (*Letters*, II, 253). I would suggest that the immortality essay came so easily to hand because it was one of the parts of the *Treatise* which twenty years earlier he had decided not to publish for fear of public outcry (see *New Letters*, pp. 2–3). It could have been a separate section coming immediately after the section 'Of the Immateriality of the Soul' or, much more likely, it could have formed the concluding pages to that section itself. When the two were pulled apart the essay required a summary (which it has) of the metaphysical topics which had originally preceded it in detail, while the *Treatise* section required a new and truncated ending – possibly the paragraph on the middle of p. 250 beginning ''Tis certainly a kind of indignity . . .'. This would then leave the irony of the 'strong and convincing' physical and moral arguments high and dry (as it now is) and without any reference to what precedes it in the *Treatise* as actually published.

10
The Causes and Corruptions of Religion

> The theologian may indulge the pleasing task of describing Religion as she descended from Heaven, arrayed in her native purity. A more melancholy duty is imposed on the historian. He must discover the inevitable mixture of error and corruption, which she contracted in a long residence upon earth, among a weak and degenerate race of beings.   Gibbon, *Roman Empire*, ch. XV

Hume's critique of religion includes not only the traditional arguments for rational theism and the supposed authenticating marks of revelation but also the causes of religion in human nature and its effects in society. The *effects* of religion upon society are the concern of Hume the historian and moralist rather than Hume the philosopher. But an adequate account of the *causes* of religious belief, though not itself philosophy, is an essential complement to his philosophical thinking about religion. If, as Hume seems to conclude, the arguments of natural religion are bad or establish only a hesitant and highly attenuated conclusion, and if the authenticity of revelation is suspect, then an appeal will almost inevitably be made by the believer to the argument from general consent: why is it that religious belief is and always has been so very prevalent? The argument, as J. S. Mill observes, 'admonishes us to look out for and weigh the reasons on which this conviction of mankind or of wise men was founded'. The short and conciliatory answer – that belief in god is a natural belief – is, as I have shown, not adopted by Hume and not adopted for the very good reason that belief in god does not satisfy the conditions for a natural belief. Thus, the only answer which remains for Hume, in the absence of new and valid reasons, is that there must be causes for religious belief which operate sufficiently widely for them to influence most men. 'What those principles are, which give rise to the original belief, and what those accidents and causes are, which direct its operation, is the subject of our present enquiry' (*N.H.R.*, 21; 'Introduction').

In this chapter I shall give some account of what Hume has to say in the *Natural History of Religion*[1] and some account of his insufficiently noticed distinction between 'true' and 'corrupt' religion.

AN ORIGIN IN HUMAN NATURE

The main points which Hume makes in the *Natural History of Religion* are these:

(1) 'It is a matter of fact incontestable that about 1,700 years ago all mankind were polytheists' (*N.H.R.*, 23). This assertion would now be subject to many qualifications and footnotes. There is, for example, a dim possibility that some primeval religion might be more aptly described as monotheistic. Nevertheless, what Hume says here (as in the rest of the *N.H.R.*) could be re-dressed in modern terms as acceptable generalisations. Something very like it is affirmed, for example, by Ninian Smart: 'whether or not primeval religion was monotheistic, early religion was polytheistic but shows a tendency to evolve towards monotheism or monism'.[2]

(2) Polytheism does not owe its origin to contemplation of the order in nature by rational men:

> But farther, if men were at first led into the belief of one Supreme Being, by reasoning from the frame of nature, they could never possibly leave that belief, in order to embrace polytheism; but the same principles of reason, which at first produced and diffused over mankind, so magnificent an opinion, must be able, with greater facility, to preserve it.   *N.H.R.*, 25, see also 26

(3) The origin of polytheism is fear of the unknown causes of the apparently capricious events which govern human life:

> On the other hand, if, leaving the works of nature, we trace the footsteps of invisible power in the various and contrary events of human life, we are necessarily led into polytheism and to the acknowledgement of several limited and imperfect deities . . . the first ideas of religion arose not from a

contemplation of the works of nature, but from a concern with regard to the events of life, and from the incessant hopes and fears ['especially the latter' – p. 28] which actuate the human mind.   *N.H.R.*, 27

Thus in (1) to (3) Hume is saying that because polytheism is the primary religion of mankind; because 'the primary religion of mankind arises chiefly from an anxious fear of future events' (*N.H.R.*, 65); *therefore* the origin of religion as a whole lies in fear of the unknown, not in a rational contemplation of the order of nature. To the twentieth-century reader this may seem so obvious as to be scarcely worth insisting upon. But in the eighteenth century it was strikingly at variance with the sort of thinking (not all of it heterodox) which gave rise to deism and an excessive reliance on the arguments of natural religion. An assumption of deism, quite often shared by orthodox divines, was that monotheism was both the rational and natural religion of mankind. 'Natural' in the sense that, quite apart from the influence of priests and revelations, all men could and should arrive at it. 'Natural Religion is the Belief we have of an eternal intellectual Being, and of the Duty which we owe him, manifested to us by our Reason, without Revelation or positive law'.[3] In such a context 'reason' is thought of as a timeless and classless capacity by which man will always be able to reach the conclusions of rational theism. No, says Hume; fear, not reason, is the source of religion. Polytheism, not theism, is the original religion of mankind.

(4) 'The only point of theology, in which we shall find a consent of mankind almost universal, is, that there is invisible, intelligent power in the world;' (*N.H.R.*, 32). But whether this power be one or many, supreme or subordinate is in perpetual dispute. In other words there is no significant common notion of god which influences all belief or which looks in the direction of theism. The contrast between this and the tone of an earlier enquiry into the most general features of religions – Herbert of Cherbury's *De Veritate* (1624) – could hardly be more striking:

No general agreement exists concerning the gods, but there is universal recognition of God. Every religion in the past, every religion in the future, did and will acknowledge some sovereign deity among the gods. . . . Accordingly that which is everywhere accepted as the supreme manifestation of deity, by whatever name it may be called, I term God.[4]

Lord Herbert's quest for monotheism in the diversity of actual world religions leads him to call by the name 'God' what Hume finds to be merely the tendency of polytheism to promote one deity above the rest: 'They may either suppose, that, in the distribution of power and territory among the gods, their nation was subjected to the jurisdiction of that particular deity; or reducing heavenly objects to the model of things below, they may represent one god as the prince or supreme magistrate of the rest . . .' (*N.H.R.*, 43).

(5) From fear of this dominant god, his praises are ever extended and magnified, 'till at last they arrive at infinity itself' and thus theism is reached not by reason, 'but by the adulation and fears of the most vulgar superstition' (*N.H.R.*, 43).

(6) Although attributes are ascribed to the single, theistic deity which are quite inappropriate to a man or anything like a man, nevertheless the common people still try to propitiate him in a way appropriate to the old, local, anthropomorphic deity.

(7) So remote and incomprehensible are the attributes of the theistic god – infinity, perfection, etc. – that 'they require to be supported by the notion of inferior mediators or subordinate agents' (*N.H.R.*, 47), which in turn become objects of devotion (such as the Virgin Mary), until a reaction towards pure theism intervenes. Thus there is a flux and reflux of polytheism and theism.

(8) The effects of polytheism are in many ways preferable to those of monotheism. Polytheism is more tolerant (by its very nature). It does not appeal to reason and therefore avoids the entanglement of philosophy with religion which is characteristic of monotheism. This entanglement starts with the recognition by philosophy of the reasonableness of the basic tenet of monotheism. It finishes with philosophy 'perverted to serve the purposes of superstition' (*N.H.R.*, 54; see also *Enquiry*, 15: 25). But worst of all, monotheism as it occurs in the popular religions of the world, has a pernicious and distorting effect upon morality. The main reason for this mentioned in the *N.H.R.* is that 'as men farther exalt their idea of their divinity; it is the notion of his power and knowledge, not of his goodness, which is improved' (*N.H.R.*, 67).

Although the authorities and evidence which Hume produces for his conclusions in the *N.H.R.* are almost all drawn from the observations of ancient authors, the problem which he discusses – the psychological and anthropological causes and origins of religious belief and its effects – is, as Mossner observes, essentially modern, 'and to Hume should go the credit for being the first great modern to treat of it systematically. From it arises much modern thinking on the subject'.[5] But quite apart from the *N.H.R.*, being the first move in what might now be called the sociology of religion, some of what Hume has to say has a bearing upon the philosophical acceptability of religion to a reasonable man. For one thing Hume does not distinguish between the historical conditions in which religious belief originated and the conditions which continue to operate to produce religious belief in subsequent periods. For example, if the origins of religion are fear and ignorance, he takes it for granted that fear and ignorance will at other times be the factors which foster religion, and with which religion will tend to be associated. If this is so, then a reasonable man, not a prey to the conditions Hume describes, may well conclude that he should have nothing to do with religion, its miserable effects or its degrading causes. But Hume appears to have a way out for the reasonable man. He is always careful to speak of 'vulgar religion', 'popular superstition', 'the opinion of the vulgar', 'barbarous and ignorant nations' etc. and to contrast this with a not very conspicuous alternative – 'the notion of a perfect being, the creator of the world' – which is conformable to 'the principles of reason and true philosophy' (*N.H.R.*, 43). Thus it is implied that the religion of the reasonable man, if he has any religion, will be something very different from the causally conditioned religion of the vulgar. His religion will be philosophical, rarified, 'true' by contrast with religion as it has commonly been found in the world. By opening up this distinction we shall see both what Hume thinks religion should be and why he condemns what it is.

TRUE AND CORRUPT RELIGION

Hume's account of the 'true religion', hinted at in the *N.H.R.*, is given in the *Dialogues* and in an unpublished preface to Volume II of the *History*. The preface has been printed in full in Mossner's *Life*, pp. 306–7. A truncated and amended version of it also appears as a footnote on p. 449 of Volume II of the first edition of the *History* (London, 1757). It disappears altogether in later editions. In a sentence which appears identically in the preface and in the footnote true religion is described in terms which have a mildly masonic flavour: 'The proper office of religion is to reform men's lives, to purify their hearts, to enforce all moral duties, and to secure obedience to the laws and civil magistrate'.

In the *Dialogues* similar words are given to Cleanthes, and Philo does not demur at the description: 'The proper office of religion is to regulate the heart of men, humanise their conduct, infuse the spirit of temperance, order and obedience' (*Dialogues*, 220). Now this characterisation of religion by means of its non-distinctive features, morality etc., without reference to any of its distinctive features, devotion, prayer etc., is entirely consistent with what one would expect from a man who could admit, on numerous occasions (see below p. 219) to a formal belief in god, but who also kept to his earlier 'Objection both to Devotion & Prayer & indeed to every thing we commonly call Religion, except the Practice of Morality, and the Assent of the Understanding to the Proposition *that God exists*' (*New Letters*, 12). On this ground alone, apart from the evidence of the repetition of the account in both the *Dialogues* and in the footnote to the *History*, there can be little doubt that Hume speaks sincerely. He does think true religion would have the functions he suggests. But later in the footnote, and also in Cleanthes' next sentence, it is made abundantly clear that Hume does not think this sort of religion would be at all conspicuous in the world, or active as an influence in history: 'and as its operation is silent and only enforces the motives of morality and justice, it is in danger of being overlooked, and confused with these other motives' (*Dialogues*, 220). But Philo takes the matter further. Although true religion thus described has no pernicious consequences, 'we must treat of religion, as it has commonly been found in the world' (*Dialogues*, 223).

It has commonly been found, according to Hume, in the corrupt forms of superstition and enthusiasm. He characterises and condemns these (in the essay 'Of Superstition and Enthusiasm') in a conventional eighteenth-century manner: enthusiasm is a species of emotional fanaticism or religious mania; superstition is a state in which 'unknown evils are dreaded from unknown agents'. Its source is 'weakness, fear, melancholy . . . and ignorance' and it manifests itself in 'ceremonies, observances, mortifications, sacrifices, presents' directed towards the unknown agent.

However, what is not conventional eighteenth-century thinking is Hume's analysis of the prevalence of these corruptions, particularly of superstition. Again in the unpublished preface to the *History* (but this time not surviving in the footnote) he writes:

> The Idea of an infinite Mind, the Author of the Universe seems at first Sight a Worship absolutely pure, simple, unadorned; without Rites, Institutions, Ceremonies; even without Temples, Priests or Verbal Prayer & Supplication; Yet has this Species of Devotion been often found to degenerate into the most dangerous Fanaticism. When we have recourse to the aid of the Senses & Imagination, in order to adapt our Religion, in some degree to human Infirmity; it is very difficult & almost impossible, to prevent altogether the Intrusion of Superstition, or keep Men from laying too great Stress on the ceremonial & ornamental Parts of their Worship.

As we have seen, in the *N.H.R.*, a reason for the prevalence of superstition is suggested: namely, that religion in general and superstition in particular have the same causes, to wit, fear and ignorance.

> Each element is subjected to its invisible power or agent. . . . Nor are the operations of the same god always certain and invariable. Today he protects: Tomorrow he abandons us. Prayers and sacrifices, rites and ceremonies, well or ill performed, are the sources of his favour or enmity, and produce all the good or ill fortune, which are to be found amongst mankind.   *N.H.R.*, 27

The similarity between this account of the origin of religion in general and the account of the origin of superstition in which 'unknown evils are dreaded from unknown agents' is too obvious to need further elaboration.

The point is that, for Hume, religion as it has commonly been found in the world, the vulgar religion whose causes and effects are considered in the *N.H.R.* and whose working in human history and society is so baleful, *is* superstition. Thus in the *N.H.R.* 'popular religion' and 'superstition' are treated as interchangeable terms. It is recognition of Hume's identification of popular religion with superstition which provoked much of the uproar over the *N.H.R.* and the *History*. An early critic of the *History* complained that Hume represented all religion as tending towards superstition or enthusiasm. The ever vigilant Warburton likewise remarked 'This [the *N.H.R.*] fully justifies the censure which has been passed upon his *History of Great Britain*; namely that he owned no Religion but what might be resolved into Superstition or Fanaticism'. Even after Hume's death the row continued: 'We all know, Sir, what the word SUPERSTITION denoted, in Mr Hume's vocabulary, and against what Religion his shafts are levelled, under that name.'[6] But what is it that is so alarming for the religious man, the Christian in particular, in Hume's identification of vulgar religion with superstition, *provided* he leaves room for 'true religion'? The quotation marks round 'true religion' indicate the answer. Such religion, as characterised by Hume, whatever it *ought* to have been in history and society, most certainly is not religion as it has commonly been found in the world. *That* religion, 'vulgar religion', contains virtually all the religion there actually is, a few saintly stoics like Marcus Aurelius only excepted. Vulgar religion, described in Hume's depressingly monochromatic terms, must, for example, comprehend practically the whole history of Christianity. Hume's self-defence in a letter may be disingenuous or it may be that he just does not grasp the implications of what he has done:

> There is no passage in the History which strikes in the least at revelation. But as I run over all the sects successively, and speak of each of them with some mark of disregard, the reader, putting the whole together, concludes that I am of no sect; which to him will appear the same thing as the being of no religion. *Letters*, I, 237

This remark sounds and probably is sincere. It also sounds like a reasonable and enlightened defence until it is noticed that 'all the sects' constitute pretty well all the religion there actually is. They *are* the 'vulgar religion' of the *N.H.R.* What Hume is doing is to define for himself something called 'true religion' which has none of the distinctive features of actual religions. He himself points out that it will be hard to distinguish such religion from secular morality. He then contrasts true religion with vulgar religion in order both to commend the former and to be able to claim that he has himself some religion. Now I do not wish to suggest that Hume was in the least insincere in this. All I wish to argue is that he cannot conceal his critical analysis of actual religion behind a commendation of something as unreligiously abstract as the 'true religion' which he describes and which he admits (*Dialogues*, 223), will be 'always confined to a very few persons'. Whether Hume's analysis of the causes and origins of religion is true, or near enough true, may be argued one way or the other. That it is intended to apply to religion as it has actually appeared in the world cannot be doubted. This means that his contemporary critics were right. He *is* saying that religion, including Christianity, is subject to the analysis given in the *N.H.R.* and exemplified in the *History*. It *is* caused by fear and fostered by ignorance. It *does* corrupt morality and condone misery.

This last charge is so massive and so serious, and Hume spends so much time on it, and on trying to show that the morality that matters to us all is entirely independent of religion, that I deal with the subject in a separate chapter.

11

The Corruptions Caused by Religion

What have we sons of God to do
with morality!

Nietzsche

Tantum religio potuit suadere malorum.

Lucretius

Towards the end of the *Natural History of Religion* Hume's passionate hostility to the mischief brought about by popular religion explodes into oratory:

> What a noble privilege it is of human reason to attain the knowledge of the supreme Being; and, from the visible works of nature, be enabled to infer so sublime a principle as its supreme Creator? But turn the reverse of the medal. Survey most nations and most ages. Examine the religious principles, which have, in fact, prevailed in the world. You will scarcely be persuaded, that they are any thing but sick men's dreams. . . . What so pure as some of the morals, included in some theological systems? What so corrupt as some of the practices, to which these systems give rise?
> *N.H.R.*, 75f

His charges are that religion is inimical to happiness and detrimental to morality. I shall examine these charges separately, and then see how they are focused by Hume upon the particular issue whether suicide be criminal.

SICK MEN'S DREAMS

To the question 'How is it that religion brings about misery?' Hume has two answers. In the first place, the conditions which cause religion are also, according to Hume, the conditions which religion fosters, and in which it thrives. Men turn to religion when they are in some way miserable or afraid:

> It is true; both fear and hope enter into religion; because both these passions, at different times, agitate the human mind, and each of them forms a species of divinity, suitable to itself. But when a man is in a cheerful disposition, he is fit for business or company or entertainment of any kind; and he naturally applies himself to these, and thinks not of religion. When melancholy, and dejected, he has nothing to do but brood upon the terrors of the invisible world, and to plunge himself still deeper in affliction. . . . But still it must be acknowledged, that, as terror is the primary principle of religion, it is the passion which always predominates in it, and admits but of short intervals of pleasure.
>
> *Dialogues*, 225

This is the explicit statement of a view which lies behind a great deal of Hume's understanding (and some of his misunderstanding) of religion. As early as the *Treatise* he remarks 'that in matters of religion men take a pleasure in being terrify'd, and that no preachers are so popular, as those who excite the most dismal and gloomy passions' (*Treatise*, 115). As late as his deathbed interview with Boswell he can still talk about religion seeing immortality 'through a gloomy medium'. The pity about this assessment of religion is not that it is wrong, but that it is so excessively one-sided. It is certainly true that a happy and busy people do not readily turn to religion. It is also true that when men are worried, apprehensive or terrified, the churches are filled. But this does not mean that religion must foster or increase the terror and gloom. It *may* do so. But then again it may alleviate the terror: religion *might* have delivered Ivan Ilyitch from his fear of death.

It cannot be known for certain why Hume had such a distorted and one-sided picture of the psychology of religious practice, but a very obvious possibility is his study of seventeenth-century history, and the dour and narrow presbyterianism of the Scotland into which he was born. Be that as it may, his picture, though distorted, may be salutary. There is and always has been an aspect of religion which is as Hume describes: morbid, preciously self-pitying, almost pathologically preoccupied with sin and sometimes hypocritical as well – the type is finely portrayed in Scott's *Old Mortality*. Furthermore Hume's observation of the psychology of this sort of religion can sometimes be a great deal more subtle than his general condemnation would lead us to expect: 'The steady attention alone to so important an interest as that of external salvation is apt to extinguish the benevolent affections, and beget a narrow, contracted selfishness. And when such a temper is encouraged, it easily eludes all the general precepts of charity and benevolence' (*Dialogues*, 222).[1]

Secondly, religion, particularly monotheism, is detrimental to happiness, according to Hume, because of the bigotry, cruelty and persecuting zeal with which it has been so often accompanied. The charge is put in a circumspect and generalised way in the *N.H.R.*, 48–51. It is exemplified in detail in the *History*. The 'barbarous zeal and theological fervour' of the Scots, 'the dismal fanaticism' of the English parliamentarians, 'the vicious cruelty' of the inquisitions of Madrid and Rome receive frequent mention. And worse – 'The greatest and truest zeal gives us no security against hypocrisy': a generalisation (in *N.H.R.*, 73) which Hume gives particular illustration from the activity of the independent committees which controlled parts of England in 1647:

> The sanctified hypocrites, who called their oppressions the spoiling of the Egyptians, and their rigid severity the dominion of the Elect, interlarded all their iniquities with long and fervent prayers, saved themselves from blushing by their pious grimaces, and exercised, in the name of the Lord, all their cruelty on men.
>
> *History*, VII, 94

As Gibbon observes, the historian must 'discover the inevitable mixture of error and corruption' which disfigures religion. Whether the disfigurement is as extensive as Hume suggests other historians will judge. That it exists no honest man can deny.

FRIVOLOUS SPECIES OF MERIT

It is, however, Hume's charge that religion corrupts morality, rather than his historical analysis of the misery it has produced, which is the more serious. Although the two matters are related, the misery might be argued off as an accidental though frequent aberration. But the immorality, on Hume's understanding, is almost inseparable from popular religion as such. Hume has two charges to put.

In the first place, religion begins in worship (through fear) of capricious amoral power 'But as men farther exalt their idea of their divinity; it is the notion of his power and knowledge only, not of his goodness, which is improved' (*N.H.R.*, 67). As an historical generalisation about world religions this judgement is questionable. As a charge against the sort of God which Christians have traditionally worshipped it has more substance than appears at first sight. The God of St Peter and St Paul embodies curiously discordant elements. He is certainly powerful: the creator and sustainer of all things visible and invisible. He is the God of mercy and love. But he is *also* the God who countenances the everlasting torments of Hell. This last element – now weakened by the liberal draughts with which twentieth-century Christians wash away the taste of traditional teachings – may well be the occasion for the remarks with which Hume follows the generalisation just quoted: 'And while their gloomy apprehensions make them ascribe to him [the god] measures of conduct, which, in human creatures, would be highly blamed, they must still affect to praise and admire that conduct in the object of their devotional addresses.' Two interpretations are, I think, possible. The first is the one already indicated: that Hume is taking seriously the Christian doctrine of Hell, a monstrosity condemned outright in his essay 'Of the Immortality of the Soul' (see above pp. 179f). The second (which does not exclude the first) is that he is underlining the moral double-dealing and psychological tensions involved in worship of a God who is capable of inflicting everlasting torments but whom we still feel obliged to think of as good: 'The heart secretly detests such measures of cruel and implacable vengeance; but the judgement dares not but pronounce them perfect and adorable' (*N.H.R.*, 67). But this danger of moral double-talk in the interests of theology is scarcely as serious as Hume's second and fundamental charge: that religion involves the creation of amoral species of merit.

The *Enquiry Concerning the Principles of Morals* contains Hume's systematic analysis of 'that complication of mental qualities which form what, in common life, we call PERSONAL MERIT'. The analysis is Aristotelian in tone but with a very strong utilitarian bias. Each of the qualities Hume finds to be admired is *useful* to society.

They have a 'tendency to promote the interests of our species, and bestow happiness on human society' and 'the moral obligation holds proportion with the *usefulness*'. But this moral obligation is not difficult or disagreeable or in any way contrary to our nature as normal people. It is an 'interested obligation' and we are inclined to observe it by a combination of many factors: our participation in the feelings of others through sympathy or fellow feeling, our concern to be well thought of in society and live at peace with ourselves and others, our aversion to criminal punishment and disgrace, our calculation of our own greatest happiness etc. In brief, happiness for people and usefulness for society, are the criteria for the morality of an action, and action in accordance with these criteria is both in a man's best interest and in harmony with his normal personality. Morality is social, utilitarian and secular. The will of god and the rewards and punishments of an afterlife play no part in Hume's scheme of morals.[2]

But when Hume examines the observances which are principally associated with religion, he finds not the 'virtue and good morals' which theism appears to enjoin and which would be in accord with a social, utilitarian morality, but always some non-utilitarian, non-moral species of merit:

> It is certain, that, in every religion, however sublime the verbal definition which it gives of its divinity, many of the votaries, perhaps the greatest number, will still seek the divine favour, not by virtue and good morals, which alone can be acceptable to a perfect being, but either by frivolous observances, by intemperate zeal, by rapturous extasies, or by the belief of mysterious and absurd opinions. *N.H.R.*, 70

The observances of popular religion or 'superstition' are 'frivolous'[3] by contrast with the observances of morality because the former is 'useless, and burdensome; the latter is absolutely requisite to the well-being of mankind and the existence of society' (*Moral Enquiry*, 199: 29). What is more, if men were to judge of things 'by their natural, unprejudiced reason, without the delusive glosses of superstition and false religion' (and, Hume might have added, of political creeds treated like religion) they would never adopt non-utilitarian substitutes for morality:

Celibacy, fasting, penance, mortification, self-denial, humility, silence, solitude, and the whole train of monkish virtues; for what reason are they every where rejected by men of sense, but because they serve no manner of purpose; neither advance a man's fortune in the world, not render him a more valuable member of society; neither qualify him for the entertainment of company, nor increase his power of self-enjoyment? We observe, on the contrary, that they cross all these desirable ends; stupify the understanding and harden the heart, obscure the fancy and sour the temper. *Moral Enquiry*, 270: 91

A similar point is made, more sharply, by Philo towards the end of the *Dialogues*. The common people cannot conceive a deity 'pleased with nothing but virtue in human behaviour.[4] The recommendations to the Divinity are generally supposed to be either frivolous observances, or rapturous ecstacies, or a bigoted credulity'. He continues:

But even though superstition or enthusiasm should not put itself in direct opposition to morality; the very diverting of the attention, the raising up of a new and frivolous species of merit, the preposterous distribution which it makes of praise and blame, must have the most pernicious consequences, and weaken extremely men's attachment to the natural motives of justice and humanity. *Dialogues*, 222

In the *N.H.R.* a reason is suggested for the raising up of 'new and frivolous species of merit' in religion:

In restoring a loan, or paying a debt, his divinity is nowise beholden to him; because these acts of justice are what he was bound to perform, and what many would have performed, were there no god in the universe. But if he fast a day . . . this has a direct reference . . . to the service of God [because it could have no other possible use]. *N.H.R.*, 72

In all this two questions stand out. Do specifically religious observances have the rationale Hume suggests? Do such observances compete with morality?

The peculiarity about the first question is that for practical purposes there is no way of knowing what the answer really is. If a devotee of some religion is asked whether he is fasting rather than doing good works because fasting is a way in which he can specially commend himself to his god, he may not be able to answer either yes or no. He could be fasting because that is the accepted way within his religion of commending himself to god, *or* of atoning for his sins, *or* of reminding himself of his dependence upon god, *or* of separating himself from the cares of the world and the dictates of the flesh. Any one of these, among other possible answers, could be true, and only the first invites the repetition of Hume's question: why is fasting supposed to commend you to god? The answer, 'I don't know. That's just the way we believe the relationship of god and man to be', is not flagrantly absurd even if it permits someone like Hume, already persuaded that only virtue and good morals 'can be acceptable to a perfect being', to reply that the devotee has misunderstood the relationship. But misunderstanding the relationship is a somewhat less perversely silly thing than doing something because it is so useless from every human point of view that it could only be of service to the deity. After all, the devotee may well retort '*you* have misunderstood the relationship. Good works are not *alone* acceptable to the supreme being. We have other information on the subject'. Put in this way the dispute becomes one between different sects disagreeing about what is pleasing to god. But this misses the point of what Hume has to say. The strength of his rationale of religious observances and of the 'monkish virtues' followed for the sake of the deity alone, is not that his rationale holds for every devotee, but that to the outsider, the non-participant in religious life, it can be known to hold in some cases on the admission of the devotee himself, while in other cases it seems to have a psychological plausibility. How could a thing so utterly useless as fasting be undertaken for any other than something like the reason Hume suggests? This is the sort of question which commends Hume's analysis to the secular outsider, the man of the world, but leaves the believer unmoved.

The second question – do such observances compete with morality? – admits of a somewhat more determinate answer. Yes they do. But whether the competition is or is not an adverse reflection upon religion depends upon the point of view. From the point of view of the devotee, the 'frivolous species of merit' introduced into life by his religion, while admittedly not sanctioned by and possibly even contrary to secular utilitarian morality, is far from frivolous. It may be amongst the most significant concerns of his life. But Hume's charge that religion corrupts morality does not pretend to judge religion from its own point of view. The point of view is that of the world at large: the world of people who do not share the particular religious beliefs of the devotee. From *this* point of view the religious observance or 'species of merit'[5] could be positively evil, as with the inquisitorial hunting out and burning of heretics; non-moral, as with the habitual Roman Catholic attendance at mass each Sunday; or positively virtuous, as with any religious observance which inculcates the precept 'love thy neighbour as thyself'. Concerning the man-of-the-world condemnation of such religious virtues as heretic burning Hume has nothing to add. But he has something extra to say about non-moral religious virtues, namely, that it is very easy for these to become alternatives to morality, diverting the attention of the devotee. The virtue of attending ceremonies can easily become a substitute for loving one's neighbour. Even when religious virtue is identical with secular utilitarian virtue Hume still prefers the latter. Religion too easily gives morality a dismal face and is too easily diverted into observances. If a popular religion were founded

in which it was expressly declared, that nothing but morality could gain the divine favour; if an order of priests were instituted to inculcate this opinion, in daily sermons, and with all the arts of persuasion; yet so inveterate are the people's prejudices, that, for want of some other superstition, they would make the very attendance on these sermons the essentials of religion, rather than place them in virtue and good morals.   *N.H.R.*, 70

In a letter, Hume once wrote 'I am a Citizen of the World', meaning 'I have not the particular interests and prejudices of a Whig, a Tory, a Christian, a Scotsman, an Englishman or whatever.' This stance, or something like it, is also characteristic of his moral judgement of religion. From the point of view, not simply of an 'outsider' to religion, but of a 'citizen' of the world', a point of view concerned with happiness and the good of society, some religious species of merit are frivolous, some are vicious, some are agreeable to the good of mankind. Only the last, consistently and cheerfully pursued, would be 'true religion' in Hume's understanding of that term. It may of course be, as we are continually told in sociology and in trifles culled from Wittgenstein, that there can be no such thing as the view of an impartial citizen of the world. Every view is partial. Every sect has its own species of 'truth' and plays its own verbal 'game'. But this depressing possibility need not keep a man from the admirable and important enterprise of *trying* to see what the moral standards of mankind would be like apart from the 'virtues' preached by particular religious or political sects – 'virtues' which may on occasions seem to the world at large little better than 'sick men's dreams'.

But in all this discussion of the moral effects of religion one cardinal point is missing. The moral precepts of the Christian religion (never mind its practices for the moment) overlap very considerably with the precepts of secular utilitarianism of the type Hume sets out in the *Moral Enquiry*, and the moral precepts of Christianity are guarded by the threat of everlasting punishment and sweetened with the promise of eternal life. As Paley says in his influential *Moral and Political Philosophy*, 'Virtue is, *"the doing good to mankind, in obedience to the will of God, and for the sake of everlasting happiness"* . . . and "everlasting happiness" is the motive of human virtue.'[6] This motive receives not so much as a mention in the *Moral Enquiry*. Why has Hume so ignored it? His own reasons for rejecting doctrines of personal immortality are beside the point here since, *de facto*, very many men accept, or say they accept, a doctrine of immortality which involves moral retribution. On the one hand, the hopes and fears of immortality may constitute (as Paley's definition of virtue would suggest) the *only* motive to observe morality. On the other hand such hopes and fears surely, it may be argued, constitute *one* important motive among others. Either way there is a great advantage on the side of morality and even Hume ought to be able to recognise a profitable error even if he himself cannot admit the religious belief in immortality.

Hume's reply to the assertion that the hopes and fears of immortality constitute the *only* motive of morality is in the *Moral Enquiry*. If retributive immortality is indeed a motive to do good, it is, as a matter of common observation, not the only motive. Our 'interested obligation' to do good has many facets (see above p. 196) and a normal man is influenced by many of them. There is no one necessary motive, such as the hope of everlasting happiness, in the absence of which any normal man will at once rush off into a life of vicious debauchery. Anyone doing such a thing is a fool or a lunatic, not an unfortunate victim of an omission in Hume's appraisal of the moral worth of religion. But surely retributive immortality constitutes one of the important motives of morality among others, and deserves a mention which it does not get in the *Moral Enquiry*?

And in particular, does not this apply to secret viciousness which is neither accessible to public opinion nor punishable at law? The point was well made in 1779 in the first review of the *Dialogues*:

> But suppose that Mr Hume's principles are let loose among mankind, and generally adopted, what will then be the consequence? Will those who think they are to die like brutes, ever act like men? Their language will be, *let us eat and drink, for tomorrow we die*. When men are once led to believe that death puts a final period to their existence, and are set free from the idea of their being accountable creatures, what is left to restrain them from the gratification of their passions but the authority of the laws? But the best system of laws that can be formed by human wisdom is far from being sufficient to prevent many of those evils which break in upon the peace, order and welfare of society. A man may be a cruel husband, a cruel father, a domestic tyrant; he may seduce his neighbour's wife or his daughter, without having any thing to fear from the law; and if he takes pleasure in the gratification of his irregular appetites, is it to be supposed that he will not gratify them? What, indeed, is to restrain him?[7]

A very similar argument had in fact already been expressed by Hume himself in the first *Enquiry* where, addressing his 'sceptical friend' he says:

> Men reason not in the same manner you do, but draw many consequences from the belief of a divine Existence, and suppose that the Deity will inflict punishments on vice, and bestow rewards on virtue, beyond what appear in the ordinary course of nature. Whether this reasoning of theirs be just or not, is no matter. Its influence on their life and conduct must still be the same. And, those, who attempt to disabuse them of such prejudices . . . free men from one restraint upon their passions, and make the infringement of the laws of society, in one respect, more easy and secure.   *Enquiry*, 147: 155

The status of this passage is somewhat ambiguous. In the chapter from which it is taken Hume is at exceptional pains to obscure his own position. The remarks quoted are in his own first person but I take it that they do *not* represent his own committed opinion because if they did there would be some mention of them in the

Moral Enquiry where men's interests in morality are discussed at full length. Accordingly I take it that Philo voices Hume's reply towards the end of the *Dialogues*. His reply is that while the hopes and fears of immortality could be expected to influence moral conduct *in fact* they do not. Cleanthes remarks 'For if finite and temporary rewards and punishments have so great an effect, as we daily find: How much greater must be expected from such as are infinite and eternal?' To which Philo replies, two paragraphs later:

> Your reasonings are more easily eluded than my facts. The inference is not just: because finite and temporary rewards and punishments have so great influence, that therefore such as are infinite and eternal must have so much greater. Consider – I beseech you, the attachment which we have [if indeed we consider the matter merely in an abstract light: If we compare only the importance of the motives, and then reflect on the natural self-love of mankind: we shall not only look for a great effect from religious considerations; but we must really esteem them absolutely irresistible and infallible in their operation. For what other motive can reasonably counter-balance them even for a moment? But this is not found to hold in reality; and therefore, we may be certain that there is some other principle of human nature, which we have here overlooked, and which diminishes, at least, the force of these motives. This principle is the attachment, which we have] to present things, and the little concern which we discover for objects so remote and uncertain (*Dialogues*, 220: the passage enclosed in square brackets, though a clear development of Hume's point, is deleted in the MS and not usually printed).

A criticism sometimes made of the *Moral Enquiry* is that Hume ignores the hope of everlasting happiness as a motive for morality because he himself rejects such a possibility.[8] He takes it that it does not influence men because it ought not to influence men. But (See *Enquiry*, 147: 166) the reverse is his actual position. In the *Dialogues* he admits it ought to influence men but points out that in practice it does not. A parallel observation is afforded by the modern anti-smoking campaign. The smoker is threatened with the probability of heart disease and cancer at some remote but indeterminate time in his future. The threat is exceedingly unpleasant but because of its 'remote and uncertain' character it in fact influences the smoker less than a few pence *now* on a packet of twenty. Likewise the threat of possible eternal punishment *at some time* is less of an influence than the certainty *now* of being expelled from the club for bad behaviour. The point is driven home by Hume in sentences immediately following upon those just quoted from the *Dialogues*:

> When divines are declaiming against the common behaviour and conduct of the world, they always represent [the attachment which we have to present things] as the strongest imaginable (which indeed it is) and describe almost all human kind as lying under the influence of it, and sunk in the deepest lethargy and unconcern about their religious interests. Yet these same divines, when they refute their speculative antagonists, suppose the motives of religion to be so powerful, that, without them, it were impossible for civil society to exist.   *Dialogues*, 221

In short, the hope of everlasting happiness and the fear of eternal punishment is not regarded by Hume as a significant contribution by popular religion to social morality. It is thus not mentioned by him in his analysis in the *Moral Enquiry*. These religious motives, Hume maintains, do not in fact influence men as actively as we might suppose during their lives: Faustian repentances as the gates of Hell open being too late to serve the interests of human society.

IF SUICIDE BE CRIMINAL

In 1755 Hume wrote to his publisher offering him material for a volume 'a fourth less than my Enquiry; as nearly as I can calculate' (*Letters*, I, 223), the volume to consist of 'four short Dissertations'. A succinct account of the vicissitudes suffered by these dissertations is given by Hume in a letter of 1772:

> I intended to print four Dissertations, the natural History of Religion, on the Passions, on Tragedy, and on the metaphysical Principles of Geometry. I sent them up to Mr Millar; but before the last was printed, I happened to meet with Lord Stanhope, who was in this Country, and he convinced me, that either there was some Defect in the Argument or in its perspicuity; I forget which; and I wrote to Mr Millar, that I would not print that Essay; but upon his remonstrating that the other Essays would not make a

Volume, I sent him up these two which I had never intended to have published. They were printed; but it was no sooner done than I repented; and Mr Millar and I agreed to suppress them at common Charges, and I wrote a new Essay on the Standard of Taste, to supply their place. *Letters*, II, 253

Fortunately the two suppressed dissertations survive both in pirated copies and in a copy which Hume authorised 'to be considered as a Manuscript'.[9] One is the relatively simple 'Of the Immortality of the Soul' (see Chapter 9 above). The other is the profound and complex 'Of Suicide'. This work is important[10] as a rare and bold statement in English of a view of suicide more readily associated with Voltaire and Montesquieu. It is flatly contrary to the well-established Christian habit of setting suicide apart as a thing accursed. The dissertation also shows Hume actually applying to conduct of a peculiarly high moral voltage his general thesis in the *Moral Enquiry* that the morality of an act has nothing to do with religious permissions, and that such permissions (or prohibitions) can, and in the case of suicide actually do, foster and extend misery and suffering.

Only philosophy (Hume begins in typical vein in the two pages of introductory material) can afford an antidote to 'superstition and false religion'.[11] One misery of the superstitious man is that he may not terminate his misery, however great and incurable, because of a 'vain fear lest he offend his maker, by using the power, with which that beneficent being has endowed him'. The argument then follows in three sections of very unequal length: 'If suicide be criminal, it must be a transgression of our duty either to God [five pages], or our neighbour [one page], or ourselves' [half a page]. Hume is thus primarily concerned with the religious prohibition of suicide. If that can be countered, then the remaining social and personal considerations can be discussed in a calm and rational way free from the prejudices engendered by 'false' religion.

Hume takes for granted two assumptions for the purposes of 'Of Suicide'. One is that there is a God who exercises some sort of providential interest in mankind. If there is not, then no duty to God can exist, and there can be no coherent religious position to answer. But it is evident that the vast majority of people reading the dissertation would not take that view, or be impressed with a vindication of suicide which depended upon it. Better then to tackle your opponents on their own terms! Hume's second assumption is that suicide is not something that happens to its victims, but a voluntary act subject to reasoned decision and therefore susceptible to moral judgement. He is thus *not* concerned with self-destruction by the insane and, like the Stoics, he would *not* accept that all suicides must fall into that category. I believe that he is right in the second part of this assumption. If he is not, then the religious sanctions against suicide also become an absurdity: akin to punishing someone for manifesting the seizures of epilepsy. In Hume's writing, and in what follows, 'suicide' thus means *rational* suicide, not pathological self-destruction.

Hume is precisely correct in reminding us in the footnote which concludes 'Of Suicide' that 'There is not a single text of Scripture which prohibits it.' Indeed the few suicides recorded in the O.T. are reported with complete moral neutrality, while that of Judas in the N.T. seems to be regarded as the natural outcome of his remorse. It is only with Augustine[12] – after a long period during which many Christians had deliberately sought martyrdom with an enthusiasm close to a quest for suicide – that Christianity embarked upon the reasoning which led first to a sanctified prohibition, and then to the unreserved damnation of suicide as a mortal, even *the* mortal sin. So great and so persistent was this damnation that to this day, even outside countries like the Republic or Ireland where it is still a version of criminal killing, there persists an anxiety to treat suicide, if not as a sin, then as an illness; and if not an illness, at the very least as a vaguely embarrassing subject not quite fit for ordinary discussion. I emphasise this point because in appraising the significance of what Hume had to say, it is essential to be aware of the fixed intensity of Christian feeling on the subject. Indeed he could scarcely have chosen a more sensitive or more deeply entrenched taboo over which to confront the special dictates of Christian morality.

The arguments with which Christianity established and sustained its revulsion to suicide include: (a) special re-readings of the commandment 'Thou shalt not commit murder'[13] or of the Lord's assertion in Deuteromony 'I kill and make alive'; (b) variations on the themes that life is God's gift, and as such ought not to be destroyed, or is not really our own to do with as we please; (c) the argument that suicide is in some way a violation of Natural Law: that is to say of the laws of the created universe which move all things according to God's purposes in so far as these purposes apply to man in ways in which he, as a rational being, can chose to conform or not to conform to them.[14] Hume is particularly concerned with (c), not in its Thomistic form[15] which would have been obscure to most of his contemporaries, but as one of 'the common arguments against Suicide' concerned with man's interference with those eighteenth-century familiars: the laws of nature.

Hume's arguments in 'Of Suicide' are dense and varied, and a full discussion of them is neither possible nor warranted here. But his main thesis is as follows. General and immutable laws (L) govern the natural world. Various bodily and mental powers (P) govern the animal world. Both P and L are established by the deity as his governance of all things. P and L are in a free interplay with each other so that P sometimes disturbs the outcome of L (as when a man catches a falling stone and puts it where it would not naturally have fallen); while L sometimes overrides P (as when a man is crushed to death contrary to his endeavours by a falling boulder). There is 'No one event, however important to us, which he has exempted from the general laws that govern the universe, or which he has peculiarly reserved for his own immediate action and operation.' And this includes the event of suicide.

A possible objection is that God has reserved the lives of men for his own special decision. But, Hume continues, this is plainly false. Human life stands or falls exactly on a par with the life of any other living thing, and may fall from the most trivial of natural causes. So perhaps it would be against the will of God to disturb natural causes? But this is absurd. It would mean that we ought to take no action to avoid death or injury from natural causes, or to interfere in any way with the course of nature as dictated by L.

> Putting together, therefore, these conclusions, we find *that* human life depends upon the general laws of matter and motion, and *that* it is no encroachment on the office of providence to disturb or alter these laws.

And such disturbance includes the discontinuation of our own lives. Hume concludes this section of his argument with the pious injunction to *thank* God for the power of self-destruction rather than *repine* at supposedly immovable and unendurable misery.

Before leaving the subject of our duty to God, Hume turns briefly to versions of the (b) Christian arguments above. The ones he produces are that we are placed 'like a centinel' and may not desert our station; and that we are placed in a room by Providence. The first

analogy is Ciceronian, the second Platonic.[16] Both had been adapted
to Christian purposes. In both instances Hume's reply is in effect to
deny the analogy. It does not *matter* in the grand design whether I
stand or fall, am in my room or out of it. 'The one change is more
important to me than the other; but not more so to the universe.'

In all this (and there is much more detail to Hume's arguments
than I can give) it should be noted that Hume's central argument
does not seek to *justify* suicide on the ground that it comes within the
power of a man operating within the physically possible. Such an
argument would also justify murder and every imaginable moral
outrage. His tactic is to point out *that* no inspired (i.e. biblical)
sources state or imply any prohibition of suicide; *that* nothing which
can be identified in the overlap between our powers and the laws of
nature shows that the deity has somehow made the death of a man a
special case among natural events reserved uniquely for his
decision: *therefore* its moral status must be decided by reference to
the extent to which suicide disturbs society. That is to say by
reference to its tendency to promote happiness or diminish misery
('the *moral obligation* holds proportion with the usefulness' – *Moral
Enquiry*, 206: 35; see above p. 196). The means whereby this decision
is arrived at ('our duty to . . . our neighbour or ourselves') need not
concern us here. His conclusions are that circumstances of old age,
infirmity or public duty could make the act of suicide morally neutral
and, on occasions, even positively laudable. The overall effect of
Hume's argument is thus to show that there is no valid secular
reason to condemn suicide in all instances, and that only
superstition and false religion leads to such a misery-producing
condemnation.

* * *

At the beginning of the previous chapter I asked how Hume would
answer the argument from general consent. His reply should now
be apparent. The explanation why so many men believe in a god,
despite the tenuous reasons for doing so, is not that it is a natural
belief, but that there are general causes for the belief in human
nature. These general causes produce the popular religions of the
world. These popular religions or 'superstitions' are distinct from
the 'true' religion of the rational and civilised man, but they, not true
religion, are the religions whose influence is seen in history and in
society. This influence is almost always deplorable from the
standpoint of those who seek the general welfare and happiness of

mankind. Even the eternal penalties which religion attaches to immoral behaviour do not in reality have the beneficial influence which in theory they should have. At best popular religion is non-moral; at worst it is capable of intruding great misery into the world: 'the dreadful tribunal of the inquisition, that utmost instance of human depravity, is a durable monument to instruct us what a pitch iniquity and cruelty may rise to, when covered with the sacred mantle of religion'. (*History*, 1st edn only, Edinburgh 1754, p. 27).

A crucial instance of this is suicide. Here it can be seen that religion distorts morality not only with frivolous species of merit but with false species of crime. The prohibition of suicide can result in great suffering for those who would otherwise escape without social condemnation. It also results in spiritual anguish for those who imagine that what they may do, or their friends or relatives have done, is a mortal sin in the sight of God and the Church. It is perhaps unnecessary to point out that the process of the secularisation of ethics which Hume helped to begin, and the identification of false species of crime with which 'Of Suicide' is concerned, still continue.[17]

12

The Dispassionate Sceptic

Those who seek to learn my personal opinions on the various questions show an unreasonable degree of curiosity. In discussion it is not so much weight of authority as force of argument that should be demanded. *De Natura Deorum*, I

From accusing me of believing nothing, they now charge me with believing every thing. I hope you will be perswaded, that the Truth lyes in the middle betwixt these Accusations.

New Letters, 231

In any substantial discussion of Hume's critique of religion two questions cannot be entirely ignored. These are: What were Hume's personal beliefs about religion and what are the shortcomings of his critique? The first question, which has attracted a great deal of attention at various times, can, despite Cicero's warning, be answered much more completely than most of Hume's commentators seem willing to allow. It is, however, caught up with two tangled and interdependent subsidiary questions both of which have inflamed such protracted controversy as to be in danger of becoming tedious. The first of these subsidiary questions is: who speaks for Hume in the *Dialogues*. The second asks whether the *Dialogues* are concerned with what can be known about god (his nature) or with the existence of god (his being).

HUME'S BELIEFS AND PHILO'S ARGUMENTS

It has so far been my policy (see p. 16) to treat the two works in which Hume is at pains to conceal his personal position – the *Dialogues* and *Enquiry* Section XI – simply as philosophical arguments in which any point made can be attributed to Hume himself. The only instance in which this policy presented a difficulty was in Chapter 11 (p. 202) where a well-argued point in the *Enquiry* XI contradicted a well-argued point in the *Dialogues*. On that occasion it was necessary to appeal to the *Moral Enquiry* in order to settle *pro tem.*, which was Hume's own position. I mention this in order to emphasise, what is very well illustrated by the Swinbourne/Olding controversy cited in Chapter 2 (and apparently forgotten in some discussion), that it is perfectly possible to carry on a detailed discussion of the philosophical arguments in Hume's works without bothering about who said what and to whom and whether Hume himself would have agreed. But once the interpretation of the *Dialogues* (and to a much lesser extent *Enquiry* XI) is under discussion, it becomes essential to decide which characters speak for Hume himself.

The *Dialogues* are introduced, reported and concluded by one Pamphilus. They take place between Philo, the *careless sceptic*; Cleanthes, the *accurate philosopher*; and the *rigidly orthodox* Demea. (The italics indicate descriptions given by Pamphilus.) Philo criticises the design argument, plays upon the problem of evil and maintains the incomprehensible nature of the divine attributes. Cleanthes defends the design argument, offers solutions to the problem of evil, stresses the need for a comprehensible divine nature and attacks the ontological argument. Demea advocates the ontological argument and maintains that god's nature is a mystery. Lest there should be any premature identification of Hume with Philo, in the final part of the *Dialogues* Philo appears to back out of his opposition to the design argument and Pamphilus sums up: 'I cannot but think that Philo's principles are more probable than Demea's; but that those of Cleanthes approach still nearer the truth.'

Of these four characters Pamphilus (which is as good as to say Cleanthes because of the summing up) has been identified as Hume by Dugald Stewart, Hill Burton (Hume's second biographer), Pringle-Pattison, A. E. Taylor, C. W. Hendel and Andre Leroy among others. Those who have selected Philo include the first reviewer of the *Dialogues* in the *Monthly Review* for 1779,[1] Sir Leslie Stephen, T. H. Huxley, N. Kemp Smith in his introduction to the *Dialogues* in 1935,[2] and, much more recently, G. Carabelli in *Hume e la Retorica dell'ideologia*.[3] For a short time it appeared as if the scope and thoroughness of Kemp Smith's case, which is argued in minute detail, might have closed the subject. But, in the Joint Session meeting for 1939 (*Hume and Present Day Problems*), Professor Laird shed doubt upon the whole enterprise of identifying Hume in the *Dialogues*: 'the Ciceronian type of dialogue that Hume chose does not permit such canons of interpretation. Each collocutor develops his point of view in successive short speeches and the author has failed if the voice of any one of them is definitely his own'. More recently there have been other rumbles of dissent. For example, James Noxon, in an article since enshrined in V. C. Chappell's useful collection of essays,[4] has objected to Kemp Smith's identification and his objections have been taken up by others: 'Smith has been conclusively refuted by James Noxon', remarks a recent essayist.[5] I shall dispute this later.

Kemp Smith's thesis is 'that Philo, from start to finish, represents Hume; and that Cleanthes can be regarded as Hume's mouthpiece only in those passages in which he is explicitly agreeing with Philo, or in those other passages in which, while refuting Demea, he is also being used to prepare the way for one or other of Philo's independent conclusions' (p. 59). But Smith is careful not to let this general identification tie him down to the absurd rigidity of saying that every word, phrase and sentence in the work is apportioned in this way: *something* of Hume's beliefs can be found in all three speakers. Smith provides a great profusion of evidence. He points out, for example, the dominant position given to Philo both in the extent of what he has to say and in its philosophical importance. He notes that crucial points made by Philo are repeatedly left uncontroverted; that towards the end the dialogue becomes little more than a monologue for Philo with a few bursts of protest from Cleanthes (Demea having departed in disgust); that Philo's final acceptance of the design argument is so hedged and qualified that it seems, much more than is, an agreement with Cleanthes, and so on.

There are a number of additional points which tend to confirm Kemp Smith's thesis. First there is the untutored response of the new reader of the *Dialogues*. Without the prompting of an editorial apparatus I have never yet known any new reader, already familiar with Hume through the *Enquiry*, who did not at once pick out Philo as the hero of the piece. The choice of Philo would have little significance but for the fact that it is exactly what should be expected from the letter in which Hume remarks that he *makes* Cleanthes the hero but could very easily take upon himself the character of Philo (*Letters*, I, 153f). Cleanthes is the contrived hero but Philo, as the naive reader senses, has Hume's favour. Secondly, if Hume does not for the most part identify with Philo's mitigated scepticism, whatever was the point in the first place of all Hume's efforts to cover his tracks? If Hume should really be identified with Cleanthes, he had everything to gain from making this absolutely clear in the text, rather than leaving it to an apparently disingenuous comment from a spectator in the last two lines of the work. The *only* character Hume could not publicly avow in the *Dialogues* is Philo; the only friend he could not admit to being himself is the 'sceptical friend' in *Enquiry* XI. In terms of the politics and prejudices of his day all the cover-up loses its point if Hume is *not*, for the most part, Philo. Thirdly, the scepticism of Philo with regard to theological argument and debate about god's attributes, together with his highly qualified assent to the propositions that god exists and that his existence is recognisable from the order in nature, and much else in Philo's utterances, are exactly what one finds in the Hume revealed by his private letters and papers: one who doubted, one who believed little, one who disliked religious practices and observances, one who rejected popular religion and all dogmatism and yet retained some belief in a god. It is these similarities which justify speaking of Hume 'covering his tracks' in the *Dialogues* rather than not knowing where he was going or being so uncertain about his position that he communicates his uncertainty to his readers. Much of Philo and much of Hume is so nearly of a piece that it requires a positive effort not to identify Hume and Philo. Finally, Kemp Smith's thesis has been usefully complemented by at least two articles. One is E. C. Mossner's 'The Enigma of Hume'[6] in which the identification of Demea with Samuel Clarke and his less august followers, and of Cleanthes with Butler, is argued in detail. Without going the whole way with Mossner, it is clear that Demea could easily represent the same type of theologian as Clarke and Cleanthes the same type as Butler. This once again leaves Philo as Hume if only on the negative ground that there is no one else he could be: Philo has no matrix outside his creator's mind. The other article is J. V. Price's 'Scepticism in Cicero and Hume'.[7] In this, Price, following up some clues given by Kemp Smith (*Dialogues*, 60f), traces parallels between Philo in the *Dialogues* and Cotta in Cicero's *De Natura Deorum*. He concludes (p. 106) 'Philo is a skilful blend of Ciceronian structure and Humean philosophy.'

Since Kemp Smith's thesis was set out in 1935 no writer known to me has systematically disputed his evidence. What has been done is for a critic to present some general view or hunch which is at variance with Smith's position. An example of this was Laird's contention that the *Dialogues* are Ciceronian in style and as such no speaker is identifiable with the author. This contention seems to be, not so much at variance with Smith, as inviting his conclusions with slightly different emphasis. Thus even in a Ciceronian dialogue one may ask which of the opinions expressed command the author's sympathy and in the case of the *Dialogues* Smith's answer comes again with very little modification: Philo's almost entirely; Cleanthes' in part; Demea's scarcely at all. Another way of attacking Smith's position is that attempted by Noxon in the influential article already cited. There is, as usual, no attempt at reinterpretation or refutation of Smith's actual evidence. What Noxon does is to raise a number of individual points calculated to shed general doubt on Smith's thesis. The points are not numbered by Noxon but I distinguish at least six.[8] They are of enough importance to comment upon in detail in each case.

(1) Cleanthes, Noxon says (p. 366) adopts 'one of Hume's most important principles' when he contends (*Dialogues*, 154) that some beliefs (natural beliefs) are 'neither acquired by rational means nor vulnerable to rational criticism'. The words which Noxon quotes Cleanthes as using when Cleanthes is said to adopt Hume's principle are as follows: 'the arguments for Natural Religion . . . immediately flow in upon you with a force like that of sensation'. But this misrepresents the sense of the original. The subject of Cleanthes' comment is not 'the arguments for natural religion', but, very differently, 'the idea of a contriver'. However the main objection to Noxon's evidence here is that Cleanthes' belief in a designer is *not* parallel, as Noxon seems to imply it is, to a natural belief like belief in an external world. The beliefs are not parallel for a reason already pointed out by Philo and followed up in detail by my argument in Chapter 7. If the philosophical sceptic discovers no rational justification for believing, say in an external world, he still 'must act and live, and converse like other men' (*Dialogues*, 34). The excessive sceptic is under an 'absolute necessity' to do so, and his philosophical scepticism must give way whenever he attends to the ordinary world of his experience. But the religious sceptic is not in this situation. His mitigated scepticism is not rendered academic and unrealistic when he attends to the ordinary world of his experience. Quite the reverse. Such is the remoteness of theological speculation by contrast with our normal experience that 'We must be far removed from the smallest tendency to scepticism not to be apprehensive, that we have here got quite beyond the reach of our faculties' (*Dialogues*,

135; Philo speaking). Thus I would contend that *if* Cleanthes is adopting 'one of Hume's most important principles' then he is mistaking the application – not a very good ground for identifying Cleanthes with Hume.

(2) Noxon draws attention (pp. 368–70) to two passages in Section XI of the *Enquiry* in which Hume appears to voice in his own person opinions which are echoed by Cleanthes in the *Dialogues*. But Noxon also admits the obvious truth that Section XI is so contrived that it is not always possible to isolate Hume's own opinions in it in order to contrast them with opinions which he expresses elsewhere. Moreover one of the passages Noxon cites from the *Enquiry* – to the effect that 'Religion, however corrupted, is still better than no religion at all' (*Dialogues*, 219; cf. *Enquiry*, 147: 155) – is *not* one of Hume's own opinions: not only because it does not appear in the *Moral Enquiry*, but also because he rejects this view in letters, in his continual depreciation in the *History* of the effects of vulgar religion, and in essays (e.g. the opening remarks in 'Of Superstition and Enthusiasm').

(3) In 1776 Hume wrote to Strahan, his publisher, concerning the *Dialogues*: 'I there introduce a Sceptic, who is indeed refuted, and at last gives up the Argument, nay confesses that he was only amusing himself by all his Cavils; yet before he is silenced, he advances several Topics, which will give Umbrage . . .' (*Letters*, II, 323). Is it likely, asks Noxon, that Hume would refer to his own arguments as 'indeed refuted'? Yes, I would reply, it is likely in the dramatic context of a dialogue of which Hume himself judged 'nothing can be more cautiously and more artfully written' (*Letters*, II, 334). Philo is 'indeed refuted' for the sake of the drama and public opinion; he is not *in fact* refuted in his arguments. If he were *in fact* refuted why do eminent philosophers continue to take his arguments so seriously? The same contrast between Hume's comments on the dramatic setting and his feeling for the actual arguments can be found in an earlier letter already quoted in which on the one hand he remarks that 'I *make* Cleanthes the Hero of the Dialogue', and that 'the Confusion in which I represent the Sceptic *seems* natural' (*Letters*, I, 153; italics mine), while on the other hand he confesses that he needs help with Cleanthes' arguments and says: 'Had it been my good Fortune to live near you, I shou'd have taken on me the Character of Philo, in the *Dialogue*, which you'll own I could have supported naturally enough'. The

inference is clear, Hume's sympathies are with Philo, but he contrives to make Cleanthes the hero (a contrivance which, as already pointed out, even the naive reader is quite likely to see through).

(4) Kemp Smith's judgement is that Philo's final appeal to revealed truth (*Dialogues*, 227, i.e. after his highly qualified acceptance of something in the design argument) is a 'conventionally required proviso'. Noxon asks (presumably to imply the proviso is genuine) 'why Hume would pay such deference to social convention in a work planned for posthumous publication when he has shown so little in books published during his lifetime'. But the implication in this question is just not true. Hume *had* displayed a great deal of concern with social convention in his publications: he withdrew 'Of Miracles' and possibly other items (see p. 182) from the *Treatise*, he modified Section XI of the *Enquiry* into a dialogue in which his own opinions are hard to isolate, he withdrew two of the *Five Dissertations* from publication, he modified passages in the *History* and he postponed publication of the *Dialogues* for twenty-six years out of deference to the offence they might cause, despite their being 'artfully written'.

(5) The *Dialogues*, says Noxon, furnish one 'vital piece of evidence' namely a single paragraph, 'in which Hume quite clearly speaks for himself' in the dispute between Cleanthes and Philo. The paragraph is a footnote on p. 219.

> It seems evident, that the dispute between the sceptics and dogmatists is entirely verbal, or at least regards only the degrees of doubt and assurance, which we ought to indulge with regard to all reasoning: And such disputes are commonly at the bottom, verbal, and admit not of any precise determination. No philosophical dogmatist denies, that there are difficulties both with regard to the senses and to all science: and that these difficulties are in a regular, logical method, absolutely insolveable. No sceptic denies, that we lie under an absolute necessity, notwithstanding these difficulties, of thinking, and believing, and reasoning with regard to all kind of subjects, and even of frequently assenting with confidence and security . . .

Unfortunately it is by no means 'quite clear' from the MS (*cf.* edition by J. V. Price, Oxford, 1976, p. 250) whether this footnote should stand as a comment by Hume speaking for himself, or whether it is intended as a footnote which extends Philo's long paragraph on scepticism which just precedes it. But for the sake of Noxon's argument let us presume what is probable: that it is Hume speaking for himself. Noxon interprets the footnote as an affirmation of Hume's mitigated scepticism in contrast to what, in Noxon's estimate, is Philo's excessive scepticism. I cannot accept this interpretation. In Part I of the *Dialogues* Cleanthes has already *mistaken* Philo's position as one of excessive scepticism and has had his mistake corrected:

> *Cleanthes*: Whether your scepticism be as absolute and sincere as you pretend, we shall learn bye and bye, when the company breaks up: We shall then see, whether you go out at the door or the window . . . (p. 132).

> *Philo*: To whatever length any one may push his speculative principles of scepticism, he must act, I own, and live, and converse like other men; . . . But when we look beyond human affairs and the properties of the surrounding bodies: When we carry our speculations into the two eternities, before and after the present state of things; into the creation and formation of the universe; the existence and properties of spirits; the powers and operations of one universal spirit, . . . We must be far removed from the smallest tendency to scepticism not to be apprehensive, that we have here got quite beyond the reach of our faculties.   pp. 134–5

The type of scepticism which Philo here professes is identical in character to the mitigated scepticism which Hume, unequivocally in his own person, defends at the end of the *Enquiry*:

> Another species of *mitigated* skepticism which may be of advantage to mankind, and which may be the natural result of the Pyrrhonian doubts and scruples, is the limitation of our enquiries to such subjects as are best adapted to the narrow capacity of human understanding . . . [A correct judgement] . . . confines itself to common life . . . leaving the more sublime topics to the embellishment of poets and orators, or to the arts of priests and politicians.   *Enquiry*, 162: 170

Thus whatever construction should be put upon the footnote, the construction which Noxon puts upon it will not do.[9]

(6) 'Another of the difficulties involved in identifying Hume with Philo is raised by the complete reversal of standpoint made by Philo in the twelfth and final dialogue', writes Noxon. 'Some attempts must be made to interpret this admittedly unexpected finale.' Kemp Smith's explanation (which Noxon does not examine) consists in showing in detail that Philo's concessions, when they are carefully examined, fall very far short of a 'completed reversal of stand-point'. They amount to saying, as I have already argued in Chapters 2 and 7, that objections to the design argument do not add up to a total, knockdown, disproof. A weak probability that the cause of order in the universe is an intelligent agent survives, and is dramatically overstated by Philo in his apparent reversal of standpoint: 'Here then the existence of a Deity is plainly ascertained by reason' (*Dialogues*, 215). I say 'overstated' because the deity thus ascertained is something exceedingly far short of the god of conventional theism: so far short that, as Philo points out (and he is not controverted by Cleanthes), the atheist and the theist can agree that 'the principle which first arranged, and still maintains, order in this universe, bears . . . some remote inconceivable analogy to the other operations of nature, and among the rest to the economy of human mind and thought'. Again, in the final paragraph given to Philo (written in 1776, the year of Hume's death), the limitations of the possibility left open by Philo's criticisms of the design argument are stressed:

If the whole of natural theology, as some people seem to maintain, resolves itself into one simple, though somewhat ambiguous, at least undefined proposition, *that the cause or causes of order in the universe probably bear some remote analogy to human intelligence*: If this proposition be not capable of extension, variation, or more particular explication: If it afford no inference that affects human life, or can be the source of any action or forebearance: And if the analogy, imperfect as it is, can be carried no farther than to human intelligence . . . what can [a man] do more than give a plain, philosophical assent to the proposition, as often as it occurs.

Dialogues, 227

But it is apparent that in this conclusion the atheist can stress the improbability and the theist the probability of the analogy, and this is what Hume allows for in his comments that the dispute is 'merely verbal' and 'incurably ambiguous'.

From these six considerations Noxon arrives at his assessment: 'In one way, Hume was all or two of his characters; in another he was none or neither.'[10] It seems scarcely fair to Noxon to report this conclusion as a 'total' refutation of Kemp Smith. I myself find it difficult to see that Kemp Smith's position has been disturbed in any serious way. Hume is still Philo except when Cleanthes refutes Demea. Not every single sentence fits this formula, but most of the *Dialogues* do, and that is sufficient identification for the sympathies of their author in a Ciceronian dialogue.

The second question of interpretation is whether Hume in the *Dialogues* is concerned with questioning the existence of god, his being, or with questioning what can be said or known about him, his attributes. Now at the commonsense level it seems clear that if we believe in the existence of something, we believe in the existence of a thing with at least one attribute ('existence' itself not counting). If there are no attributes at all – or none which can be known – then nothing exists to believe in. Having said that, the puzzle in the *Dialogues* is supposed to take shape because Pamphilus prefaces the whole discussion with the comment 'What truth so obvious, so certain, as the *being* of a God. . . . what obscure questions occur, concerning the *nature* of that divine Being . . .' and this is agreed to be Cleanthes, Demea *and* by Philo: 'the question can never be concerning the *being*, but only the *nature* of the Deity' (p. 142). But Philo (and Demea, somewhat gullibly, but quite in keeping with this theology) also seems to say, what he does not in fact quite say, that the deity is unknowable, that nothing can be said about him, that, in effect, he has *no* attributes. This appearance has led one group of interpreters to conclude, with various shades of emphasis, that Hume does not believe in a god at all, whereas another group says he does; the debate in the *Dialogues* is entirely about god's nature. My own position on this matter is a central thesis in this book and has already been developed in earlier chapters but I shall reiterate it here.

THE ATTENUATED DEIST

In one of the mottos to this chapter Hume says in effect that the truth about his belief 'lyes in the middle' between the extremes of believing everything and believing nothing. But what does Hume call the middle? Again and again in private and published work Hume gives explicit or implicit assent to the proposition *that there is a god*. Examples, in chronological order, are:

1740: A footnote to the Appendix to the *Treatise*, unequivocally in Hume's own person:

> The order of the universe proves an omnipotent mind; that is, a mind whose will is *constantly attended* with the obedience of every creature and being. Nothing more is requisite to give a foundation to all the articles of religion . . . *Treatise, 633*

1742: In the essay 'The Stoic', which in isolation could be construed as representing the Stoics' view rather than Hume's own but *in company* seems merely to repeat what Hume says elsewhere, he remarks:

> There surely is a being who presides over the universe; and who with infinite power and wisdom, has reduced the jarring elements into just order and proportion (see also 'The Platonist' – another essay of 1742).

1743: In this year there is a letter in which Hume hopes that Mr Leechman would answer an objection to:

> every thing we commonly call Religion, except the Practice of Morality & the Assent of the Understanding to the Proposition *that God exists* (*New Letters*, 13).

1757: The 'Introduction' to the *Natural History of Religion* remarks:

> The whole frame of nature bespeaks an intelligent author; and no rational enquirer can, after serious reflection, suspend his belief a moment with regard to the primary principles of genuine Theism and Religion.

And the same type of thought appears at least five times in the *N.H.R.* (pp. 24, 26, 38, 42, 75).

1776: In the *Dialogues*, as I have already pointed out, each of the speakers assents to the being of *some* god, and even at the end Philo is left agreeing (however qualified his agreement eventually becomes) that 'the existence of a Deity is plainly ascertained by reason'.

Now all this is not avowal of belief in a god outlandishly defined, but one associated with order and intelligence in a way familiar to deist or theist. We should beware of so relying upon Hume's irony that we read an often repeated declaration as an often repeated denial, especially when such anecdotes as there are seem to give some backing to a non-ironical reading of the declarations I have just quoted.

Let me quote again the famous anecdote known earlier but published in its fullest version in 1938 in a volume of Diderot's letters:

> The first time that M. Hume found himself at the table of the Baron, he was seated beside him. I don't know for what purpose the English philosopher took it into his head to remark to the Baron that he did not believe in atheists, that he had never seen any. The Baron said to him: 'Count how many we are here.' We were eighteen. The Baron added: 'It isn't too bad a showing to be able to point out to you fifteen at once: the three others haven't made up their minds.'   Quoted in *Life*, p. 483

Clearly this anecdote could indicate merely Hume's facility in feeding a good conversational line to his neighbour at dinner: he already knew the atheistical reputation of the *philosophes* and was needling them. Alternatively it could indicate Hume trying the ground before declaring his own atheistical position. But set the story alongside the following remark from Sir James Macdonald in Paris to an English correspondent:

> (So that) poor Hume, who on your side of the water was thought to have too little religion, is here thought to have too much.
>
> *Life*, p. 485

In the light of this, surely the interpretation which best fits the Diderot anecdote is that Hume was combining an ironical conversational gambit with a quiet hint that he himself, as we would expect from his philosophy, did not see things in the dogmatic or confident way in which atheists see them. A similar pointer is given by one of Boswell's most delightful reminiscences. The note which he added after the close of the account of his last interview with Hume reads:

> Speaking of his singular notion that men of religion were generally bad, he said, 'One of the men' (or 'The man' – I am not sure which) 'of the greatest honour that I ever knew is my Lord Marischal, who is a downright atheist. I remember I once hinted something as if I believed in the being of a God, and he would not speak to me for a week.' (Hume) said this with his usual grunting pleasantry, with that thick breath which fatness had rendered habitual to him, and that smile of simplicity which his good humour constantly produced.[11]

So my contention is that Hume gives some sort of genuine assent to the proposition *that there is a god*. This assent that 'lyes in the middle' is between deism and atheism. It is fostered by the feeling of design and given a weak rational basis by recognition that the order to be found in nature *could* (not must) be explained as the work of an ordering agent. But this ordering agent – and this is the aspect of the *Dialogues* which easily deceives those in search of Hume's theism or his atheism – cannot be known to have any attributes other than those just sufficient to produce the given result; that is to say, the power of an agent together with 'some remote analogy to human intelligence'.

In particular this god cannot be known to have any *moral* attributes: 'The true conclusion is, that the original source of all things . . . has no more regard to good above ill than to heat above cold . . .' (*Dialogues*, 212; see also 211). The alliance between Philo and Demea over the incomprehensible nature of the deity is thus a way of showing (as Demea eventually grasps) that the nature of the deity as allowed by Philo is not a fit subject for adoration as a sacred mystery. The adorable mystery of god which evokes a religious response is quite different from an original source of the order to be found in nature which *might* bear some remote analogy 'to the other operations of nature and among the rest to the œconomy of human mind and thought'. Such an original source of order could scarcely function even as the start for belief in a personal God exercising a moral jurisdiction, accessible to prayer, performing acts of intervention in his creation, and worthy of adoration. In such a God as this Hume seems to have had no belief at any period in his adult life. But at the ultimate point of decision in looking for the source of order in nature – when it could be regarded as an inherent principle in things ('brute fact' is the more fashionable phrase) *or* as something which also warrants very circumspect use of the word 'intelligent' – at this point of ultimate ambiguity Hume inclines to the latter of the two possibilities.

This is Hume's 'some belief'. This is the modest persuasion which caused him to be shocked at the dogmatic atheism of the *philosophes* and perturbed at the inconoclastic sneers of Frederick the Great (*Letters*, I, 327). It is not in itself atheism nor is it defended positively. But it *is* atheism as far as the Christian God is concerned just as belief in the Christian God was atheism as far as the classical Roman religion was concerned.[12] This sort of atheism is about as damaging to Christianity as any atheism could possibly be. For it avoids the dogmatism, which many people find distasteful, of denying the existence of all gods whatsoever and yet its diffident affirmation is completely without religious implications. As Hume points out, by a suitable emphasis and choice of words both the atheist and theist can agree about it (*Dialogues*, 218) and the dispute between them becomes 'merely verbal'. But assent to the existence of god in the sense allowed by Hume is valueless for any theistic religion. It carries no duties, invites no action, allows no inferences and involves no devotion. In the light of this the *Dialogues* can be understood as a discussion of the nature of god, what can be known about him, not a discusion of the question whether a god exists. But in the course of the *Dialogues* it becomes apparent that Hume (Philo) is arguing that we can say very little about god's nature and what little we can say cannot be said dogmatically. But the little we can say is neither so little as to invoke the logical objection that Hume is assenting to the existence of a being with no attributes at all, nor so much as to arrive at anything like the Christian God. This position is confusing to the reader who consciously or unconsciously looks at the *Dialogues* with Christian preconceptions: Hume's critical discussion of god's nature *does* turn out to be a discussion of the existence of the Christian God because he argues that the god for whose existence there is some very weak and ambiguous evidence could not be known to have any of the distinguishing features which the Christian God is supposed to have. Thus from the point of view of assenting to the existence of *some* god the discussion in the *Dialogues* is 'concerning the nature of that divine Being'. But from the point of view of assenting to the existence of the *Christian* God (or anything like him) the question concerns the being of God.

I shall call the 'plain, philosophical assent' to the existence of a god as indicated by the vestiges of the design argument, a god whose sole attribute is an intelligence which may bear some remote analogy to the intelligence of man, 'attenuated deism'.[13] Hume would not have welcomed the appellation,[14] but it fits. From this attenuated deism certain other of his opinions follow, but in each case there is independent evidence that he holds the opinion. The opinions are these four:

(1) That religious observances as such are at best worthless[15] and at worst mischievous with the solitary exception of 'virtue and good morals', which 'alone could be acceptable to a perfect being'. But virtue and good morals are not distinctively religious; prayer and love of god which are, excite Hume's explicit censure. His specific objection to 'loving' god is that in real terms this is not possible:

> A remote Ancestor, who has left us Estates & Honours, acquir'd with Virtue, is a great Benefactor, & yet 'tis impossible to bear him any Affection, because unknown to us; tho in general we know him to be a man or a Human Creature, which brings him vastly nearer our Comprehension than an invisible infinite Spirit. A man, therefore . . . from this Circumstance of the Invisibility & Incomprehensibility of the Deity may feel no Affection towards him. And indeed I am afraid, that all Enthusiasts mightily deceive themselves. Hope & Fear perhaps agitate their Breast when they think of the Deity: Or they degrade him into a Resemblance with themselves, & by that means render him into a Resemblance with themselves, & by that means render him more comprehensible. . . . Please to observe, that I not only exclude the turbulent Passions, but the calm Affections. Neither of them can operate without the Assistance of the Senses, & Imagination, or at least a more compleat Knowledge of the Object than we have of the Deity.
>
> *New Letters*, 13

Hence there can be no duty to love god. The remarkable consistency of view between this early letter (1743) and the views expressed in the *N.H.R.* and *Dialogues* can hardly escape notice. In the same letter Hume also provides the only extant explanation of his rejection of prayer. Its rejection is of course a corollary of his attenuated deism but more specifically: our prayers can have no influence on the deity but

> we can make use of no Expression or even Thought, in Prayers & Entreaties, which does not imply that these Prayers have an Influence. . . . This Figure is very dangerous & leads directly & even unavoidably to Impiety & Blasphemy. Tis a natural Infirmity of Men to imagine, that their Prayers have a direct Influence, & this Infirmity must be extremely foster'd & encourag'd by the constant Use of Prayer (ibid).

The objection holds for both Hume's concept of god – how could we suppose the source of order in the universe to be interested in our little wishes – and for the Christian concept of God – if He knows our future as we know our own past how could petitionary prayer move Him to change what is to be? Whether this is or is not a good objection to the Christian use of petitionary prayer has been discussed at length elsewhere and I shall not pursue the matter here. But what cannot be ignored is the exception which Hume makes of virtue and good morals. Why should he suppose that these 'alone could be acceptable to a perfect being'? (*N.H.R.*, 70). There are at least two possiblities. The untidy one is that here we have an odd end of Hume's thought (or lack of it) which refuses to be tied in with the rest. It is an ill-considered vestige of Christianity retained as the absent-minded assumption that if anything is acceptable to the deity, good morals must be. The tidier possibility is that in these contexts (*N.H.R.*, 70; *New Letters*, 12) Hume is not talking about himself. He is saying *if* there were a perfect being as implied in Christianity *then* only good living could be pleasing to him. Hume has an objection to all religion *except* in as far as it is associated with good morality. But this does not entail that he himself practises good morality *because* it would be acceptable to god as he understands that term. Far from it. His social utilitarianism is independent of religion. It is his secular morality which makes him approve of religion if and when it inculcates morality – as 'true religion' would and as 'vulgar superstition' seldom does.

(2) That conventionally required religious observances are of too little real importance to justify making an issue out of disregarding them: 'It is putting too great a respect on the Vulgar, and on their Superstitions, to pique one' self on Sincerity with regard to them . . .' (*New Letters*, 83; see also *Letters*, I, 151f). Hume was not of the scrupulous and dogmatic stuff of which humanist martyrs are made!

(3) That morally contentious issues, for example suicide, and moral distinctions in general, should not be referred to the decision of religious teaching but should be settled by reference to the needs and happiness of people. The most aggressively challenging application of this to a particular case is in the essay 'Of Suicide' but the whole movement of argument in the *Moral Enquiry* is in favour of the independence of utilitarian morality from religion.

(4) That theological argument and dispute is 'sophistry and illusion'. The celebrated final paragraph of the *Enquiry* is the best-known statement of this position but much of the *Dialogues* and considerable areas of the *Enquiry* itself consist in showing, in particular instances, the futility of attempting to reach reasoned conclusions in theology. The futility is amplified in a letter: 'In Politics & natural Philosophy, whatever Conclusion is contrary to certain Matter of Fact must certainly be wrong, and there must some Error lie somewhere in the Arguments, whether we be able to show it or not. But in Metaphysics or Theology, I cannot see how either of these plain & obvious Standards of Truth can have place' (*Letters*, I, 152). There are no basic data in theology – as would be expected if Hume's attenuated deism is the only rational religion.

Other opinions concerning 'the great questions of religion' which Hume certainly held but which do not follow from his attenuated deism are these five:

(1) That the origin of religion is fear of the unknown causes of natural events and that its commonest manifestations are the corrupt forms of superstition and enthusiasm. These *are* religion as it has commonly been found in the world and whose social and moral effects are bad.

(2) That true religion, if any such could be found, would be an inconspicuous personal thing which would enforce morality.

(3) That the priesthood, particularly in institutionalised religion,

have an interest in promoting superstition, ignorance, persecution, and, in themselves, hypocrisy. This theme occurs throughout Hume's writings. His earliest and most moderate expression is in the *Treatise*: '. . . in matters of religion men take a pleasure in being terrify'd, and . . . no preachers are so popular, as those who excite the most dismal and gloomy passions' (p. 115). By 1742 he is more explicit:

> And the same principles of priestly government continuing, after Christianity became the established religion, they have engendered a spirit of persecution, which has ever since been the poison of human society, and the source of the most inveterate factions in every government.
>
> essay 'Of Parties in General'

In the *Three Essays Moral and Political* of 1748 occurs the celebrated note to the essay 'Of National Characters':

> [the clergy] must set a guard over their looks and works and actions: And in order to support the veneration paid them by the multitude, they must not only keep a remarkable reserve, but must promote the spirit of superstition, by a continued grimace and hypocrisy. . . . The ambition of the clergy can often be satisfied only by promoting ignorance and superstition and implicit faith and pious frauds. And having got what Archimedes only wanted, (namely, another world, on which he could fix his engines) no wonder they move this world at their pleasure.

Hume's letters are also liberally sprinkled with comments in a similar vein and even in the *History* he remarks '. . . in every religion, except the true, [the diligence of the clergy] is highly pernicious, and it has even a natural tendency to pervert the true, by infusing into it a strong mixture of superstition, folly, and delusion' (*History*, IV, 31). In the late twentieth century these sentiments may appear illiberal and harsh. In eighteenth-century Scotland and to a man born within living memory of the covenanters they might seem little more than indiscreet.

(4) That there has been no particular revelation of the divine nature and purposes which could establish its authenticity to the satisfaction of an impartial, rational man. The evidence for this is 'Of Miracles' together with the total absence of anything to the

contrary in any private letter or document. But at certain points in his published discussion of items in the philosophy of religion Hume is in fact apt to refer his readers to revelation. Thus, at the end of the *Dialogues*, Philo advises a person 'seasoned with a just sense of the imperfections of natural reason' to 'fly to revealed truth'. Likewise at the end of the essay 'Of the Immortality of the Soul' he remarks on 'the infinite obligations which mankind have to Divine revelation' for ascertaining 'this great and important truth' and in somewhat similar manner at the beginning and end of the chapter on miracles he talks about being moved by faith or by the Holy Spirit. What should we make of these references? There are a number of possiblities. They could be sincere directions to a source of information about god which is reliable despite its defiance of reason and evidence. But given Hume's other opinions, and his attack upon the authenticity of revelation, the sincerity of such directions is quite excessively improbable. Alternatively they could be ironic sarcasms which, in moments of political pressure, allow themselves to be feigned as real. While this could well be the case in 'Of the Immortality of the Soul' the suggestion will not fit the *Dialogues* since the paragraph from which the quotation is taken was written when Hume knew he would not live to see their publication. A third possibility, and one most in keeping with the Calvinism with which Hume was so familiar, is that at these points in his work he is saying that faith in a revelation, possibly arrived at through 'the immediate operation of the Holy Spirit', is the only attitude which is possible for a thinking man who retains a religion more extensive than the possiblity of attenuated deism which Philo allows for. But this attitude of faith is not a ground of assent. It is an arbitrary, anti-rational thing which a reasonable man can neither explain nor defend:

So that, upon the whole, we may conclude, that the *Christian Religion* not only was at first attended with miracles, but even at this day cannot be believed by any reasonable person without one. Mere reason is insufficient to convince us of its veracity; And whoever is moved by *Faith* to assent to it, is conscious of a continued miracle in his own person, which subverts all the principles of his understanding, and gives him a determination to believe what is most contrary to custom and experience.   *Enquiry*, 131:141

Whoever is moved by faith may well be moved in this way but Hume himself was not of that company: He neither believed in miracles nor was himself the subject of one.

(5) That there is no life after death. I would have thought this so clearly and obviously was Hume's belief that no discussion would be necessary, but in a preliminary attempt to establish his contention that 'Hume has left his readers to wonder about his personal convictions on the great question of religion' Noxon questions it. He dismisses the evidence of Boswell's deathbed interview with Hume: 'Boswell was not persuaded of the philosopher's sincerity nor was Samuel Johnson' (when he heard about the interview). Part of this statement is however contrary to Boswell's explicit report in the passage to which Noxon refers us: 'I had a strong curiosity to be satisfied if he persisted in disbelieving a future state even when he had death before his eyes. I was persuaded from what he now said, and from his manner of saying it, that he did persist'.[16] What is more, Johnson scarcely knew Hume, and *his* refusal to believe that Hume died persuaded of his imminent annihilation is no evidence at all about Hume's belief although it may possibly be evidence about Johnson's.[17] But if there were any genuine doubt whether Boswell's deathbed interview revealed Hume's true belief about immortality then there is plenty of evidence elsewhere. His earliest extant note[18] on the subject reveals the scepticism which appeared in full-blown form in 'Of the Immortality of the Soul' and which sufficiently infected the *Treatise* for his disbelief in a future state to be one of the complaints against him in 1745. Indeed his disbelief in this matter formed one of the recurring themes in the complaints of his contemporaries. There is Boswell's report in 1769 (see note 17). There is the calm, Epicurean acceptance of death displayed by Hume in his last letters and recorded in the 'Letter from Adam Smith' (reprinted in *Dialogues*, 243–8) and in Dr Cullen's letter to Dr Hunter (17 September 1776).[19] As late as 1827 Sir Walter Scott remarks in his journal on the dying philosopher's untroubled end[20] – a cause for surprise among the many who knew of his disbelief in immortality. We cannot of course ask him what he believed at the very last moment of consciousness although he was asked that question in a letter which probably never reached him. William Strahan, in a letter headed London, 19 August 1776 (Hume died on 25 August), writes: 'Our soul, or

immaterial part of us, some say, is able, when on the brink of dissolution, to take a glimpse of futurity; and for that reason I earnestly wish to have your *last thoughts* on this important subject'.[21] It is almost as if those who knew him waited in apprehensive hope for some dying affirmation of belief from the great sceptic. But none came. That he was TRUE TO THE END, according to his family motto, we may be certain from the lack of any contrary evidence – evidence so eagerly sought by those about him that had any existed it could never have been concealed.

THE CITIZEN OF THE WORLD

It is always tempting for a biographer or critic to attribute to the object of his study more positive opinions than he had or more consistent beliefs than he at any time possessed. Nevertheless, in Hume's case, as more than one writer has noted, there is a certain unity in his views from start to finish. He was not a man given to different 'periods' of thought. Having had the one colossal re-think which preceded and produced the *Treatise*, much of the rest of his work on philosophy and religion seems to be a consistent working out and application of the one re-think. This, together with the large number of clues and the evidence which Hume has left us, is the justification for attempting to itemise his beliefs and opinions about religion in the way I have done: a basic assent of the understanding to the proposition that a god exists, together with nine other items ranging from immortality to the character of the clergy. But what overall picture do they give us of Hume?

The conventional ascriptions 'atheist', 'agnostic', 'materialist' and even 'sceptic' catch neither the complexity nor the range of his conclusions about religion.[22] His beliefs, as I have already suggested, are perhaps better described as a highly attenuated deism which is not positively advocated. It is the religion of a 'citizen of the world' who has, after due consideration, rejected the beliefs of all particular sects in favour of a true religion whose sole credo is a diffidently held belief in an intelligent origin of natural order and whose sole observance is the morality which would anyway have been followed for other reasons 'were there no god in the universe'.

When one tries to assess Hume's critique of religion as a whole one is immediately struck by its critical aloofness and by Hume's unusual degree of externality to religion. A. E. Taylor made this a cause of /complaint and nothing more: 'Criticism is always superficial unless it is inspired by sympathetic insight and an adequate sense of the significance of the issues at stake.'[23] But this is a perverse judgement. That Hume did not have an insider's sympathy with religion and that he was not worried or emotionally involved in the issues which he discusses means, at least in part, that he is the more able to go wherever the argument leads. This treatment of religion as an objective system subject to disinterested discussion was typical of his century. But in Hume's writing one gets very strongly the sense of religion as a public, inspectable phenomenon. Its belief can be examined and its practices observed. There is no hint that he ever views religion from within as a way of life, a metaphysic of existence, a worthwhile thing to which total commitment is possible.

Indeed to Hume religion as it has commonly been found is not a worthwhile thing. At best it is an amiable, possibly polytheistic, superstition with undemanding rites; at worst it is the poison (Hume's word) of human society, persecuting and torturing people for imaginary crimes, and creating a false morality which fosters anxiety and conserves suffering.

But the limited, external, view of religion is perhaps better in the founder[24] of the philosophy of religion than the reverse: a profound awareness of the possibilities of the religious life without any ability to step back from one's commitment and ask: Is what I believe true? Is my religion a commitment to anything real? Is the social and personal result of what I believe better or worse than the result of not having the belief? In the two centuries which have passed since Hume's death 'total commitment' has proved the easy way out for every anti-rational theology and it is sometimes said that by displaying the barrenness of natural theology Hume opened the way for such developments. He did not. He showed instead what a modest thing a rational man's religion would be and how diffidently it should be held.

*   *   *

There is in the Old Calton Burying Ground in Edinburgh an austere monument over the tomb of the Great Sceptic. At his own request it records only his name and the dates of his birth and death, posterity being left to add the rest. Posterity has added a great deal – perhaps at times too much. No one survives being over estimated.

Nevertheless, within the limitations of human existence, posterity
has already fulfilled the promise of Colonel Edmondstoune in his
last letter to the dying philosopher: 'You can't die, you must live in
the memory of all your friends and acquaintances, and your works
will render you immortal'.

L'envoy 1978

So for the present, gentle reader! and
　Still gentler purchaser! the bard – that's I –
Must, with permission, shake you by the hand,
　And so your humble servant, and good-b'ye!
We meet again, if we should understand
　Each other; and if not, I shall not try
Your patience further than by this short sample –
'Twere well if others follow'd my example.

Don Juan

P.S. 1987

You approved,
　But I've amended:
I trust your friendship
　Is not ended.

J. G.

Notes

CHAPTER 1: INTRODUCTION: HUME ON RELIGION

1. See List of Abbreviations.
2. E. C. Mossner, 'Hume's Early Memoranda, 1729–1740: The Complete Text', *Journal of the History of Ideas* (1948).
3. See list of abbreviations. The details of this story were finely researched by M. A. Stewart for a paper delivered at the Hume Society meeting in Trinity College Dublin in 1981.
4. A discussion of the evidence is contained in E. C. Mossner's 'Hume's Four Dissertations', *Modern Philology* (1950).
5. It contains corrections in Hume's hand which have never been incorporated in any printed edition of the essays. The corrections are noted in my article 'Hume's Suppressed Dissertations – an Authentic Text', *Hermathena* (1968). I adopt these in quotations from the essays in the present work.
6. *English Philosophy since 1900* (Oxford, 1958) p. 164.
7. Lincoln, Nebraska, 1965.
8. Stockholm, 1966.
9. The large-scale pre-war study by A. Leroy, *La Critique et la Religion chez David Hume* (Paris, 1930) has always been somewhat inaccessible to English readers and is now almost unobtainable. A more recent European work is Giancarlo Carabelli's *Hume e la Retorica dell'ideologia* (Florence, 1972). This is a detailed study of the *Dialogues* in relation to the background in the Scottish and European enlightment.

CHAPTER 2: ORDER AND DESIGN

1. Plato: *Timaeus* 47; Xenophon: *Memorabilia*, 1 iv 4–8; Cicero; *De Natura Deorum*, II xxxiv–xxxv; Aquinas: *Summa Theologiae*, 1 Quest, 11 Art. 3; Newton: *Principia Mathematica*, General Scholium; Berkeley: *Alciphron* IV.
2. *The World as I See It* (London, 1935) p. 28.
3. See List of Abbreviations.
4. *Analogy of Religion*, ch. 3.
5. Richard Swinburne, *The Existence of God* (Oxford, 1979) p. 136.
6. Although Hume does not have the theory of natural selection at hand he does make a suggestion (*Dialogues*, 185) which comes remarkably close to anticipating the theory as an objection to the teleological argument. See below p. 44.
7. Colin Maclaurin, *An Account of Sir Isaac Newton's Discoveries*, 3rd edition (London, 1775) p. 400.
8. Richard Swinburne, 'The Argument from Design', *Philosophy* (1968)

pp. 199–212. I shall subsequently refer to this article as 'Swinburne' followed by the page.
9. *Three Essays on Religion* (London, 1875) p. 38.
10. *Alciphron,* fourth dialogue, para. 5.
11. See Rule I of the 'Rules of Reasoning in Philosophy', *Principia Mathematica,* Bk III.
12. A. Olding, 'The Argument from Design – a Reply to R. G. Swinburne', *Religious Studies* (1971) p. 370.
13. McPherson, *The Argument from Design* (London, 1972) p. 73.
14. Antony Flew, *Hume's Philosophy of Belief* (London, 1961) p. 231.
15. Nelson Pike, *Dialogues concerning Natural Religion with commentary* (New York, 1970) pp. 150–5.
16. It is only fair to point out that in a later article Swinburne retracts this judgement 'The Argument from Design – a Defence' *Religious Studies* (1972) p. 203.
17. *Three Essays on Religion,* p. 170. See also W. C. Salmon, *Philosophical Studies* (1978) p. 145.
18. Paris, 1970; London, 1972.
19. L. Pearl, 'Hume's Criticism of the Design Argument', *Monist* (1970) p. 282.
20. Swinburne, 'The Argument from Design – a Defence', *Religious Studies* (1972) p. 199.
21. See Chapter 3 below.
22. I say 'appears' because the dialogue context of the discussion makes it particularly difficult in this instance to identify exactly Hume's personal conclusions.
23. The answer Hume eventually gives is that sceptics and mystics do not *really* differ: see *Dialogues,* Part XII.
24. Whether any worthwhile and possible simplification is achieved in ultimately reducing explanation in terms of laws of nature to explanation in terms of agents is one of the matters explored at some length in the Swinburne–Olding controversy (Swinburne, *Philosophy* (1968) 199–212; Olding, *Religious Studies* (1971) 361–73; Swinburne, *Religious Studies* (1972) 193–205; Olding, *Religious Studies* (1973) 229–32). I shall not follow the argument here since most of the issues lie well beyond those raised by Hume.
25. By 'chaos' Hume probably means something like the 'formless void' of Milton. In the terms I use below, p. 49, this could mean either total mechanical *and* statistical disorder or it could mean matter subject to processes but lacking structures (forms).
26. 'Hume's Immanent God' in *Hume,* ed. V. C. Chappell (New York, 1966).
27. In his book *David Hume: The Newtonian Philosopher* (Boston, 1975), Nicholas Capaldi remarks 'there is no context in which Hume ever challenges the argument from design' (p. 190). While I agree with much of what Capaldi says this particular judgement seems to be at variance with any straightforward reading of the evidence.
28. P. S. Wadia, 'Professor Pike on Part III of Hume's *Dialogues*', *Religious Studies* (1978) pp. 329f.

CHAPTER 3: EVIL, FREEDOM AND THE RELIGIOUS HYPOTHESIS

1. M. B. Ahern, *The Problem of Evil* (London, 1971) p. 61.
2. *Evil and the God of Love* (London, 1966) p. 341.
3. Nelson Pike, 'Hume on Evil', *Philosophical Review* (1963); reprinted in *God and Evil*, ed. Pike (New Jersey, 1964) p. 96.
4. For a discussion of this point see R. Puccetti, 'Is Pain Necessary', *Philosophy* (1975).
5. Antony Flew, 'Divine Omnipotence and Human Freedom', in *New Essays in Philosophical Theology*, eds Flew and MacIntyre (London, 1955); J. L. Mackie, 'Evil and Omnipotence', *Mind* (1955).
6. Flew has reformulated this position in 'Compatibilism, Free Will and God', *Philosophy* (1973).
7. Antony Flew, *Hume's Philosophy of Belief* (London, 1961) p. 162.

CHAPTER 4: BEING AND NECESSITY

1. See letter written to Michael Ramsey, 31 Aug. 1737, published in *Archievum Historii Filozofie i Mysli Spolecznej* (1963) (the journal of the Philosophical and Sociological Institute of the Polish Academy of Science).
2. Clarke gave the Boyle Lectures in 1704 and 1705. These were published as *A Discourse concerning the Being and Attributes of God, the obligations of Natural Religion, and the Truth and Certainty of the Christian Revelation.* Page references are to the 9th edn (London, 1738).
3. 'Hume and the "Metaphysical Argument a Priori" ' in *Philosophy, Its History and Historiography* (The Hague, 1985).
4. 'Part IX of Hume's *Dialogues*', *Philosophical Quarterly* (1978).
5. Ibid., p. 303.
6. *De Rerum Natura*, I, 215–20, 265–70 *et al.*
7. 'Existence, Predication and the Ontological Argument', *Mind* (1962). Reprinted in *The Many-Faced Argument*, eds J. Hick and A. McGill (London, 1968). Page references are to the book.
8. Geach and Anscombe, *Three Philosophers* (Oxford, 1961) p. 115.
9. *The Ontological Argument* (London, 1972) p. 33.
10. 'Has it been Proved that all Real Existence is Contingent?', *American Philosophical Quarterly* (1971).
11. 'The Existence of God', a debate between Russell and Copleston, broadcast 1948. Reprinted in Russell's *Why I am not a Christian* (London, 1957) and in *The Existence of God*, ed. John Hick (London and New York, 1964) p. 169. Page references are to the latter edition.
12. *The Five Ways* (London, 1969), p. 66.
13. Lucretius, I, 155.
14. Leibniz, 'On the Ultimate Origination of Things', in *Philosophical Writings*, ed. G. H. R. Parkinson (London, 1973) p. 136.
15. *Arguments for the Existence of God* (London, 1970) p. 41.
16. Charles Hartshorne, *The Logic of Perfection* (Lasalle, 1962) p. 53.

CHAPTER 5: MEANING, SCHOOL METAPHYSICS AND DIVINITY

1. Antony Flew, *Hume's Philosophy of Belief* (London, 1961) p. 26.
2. E. J. Furlong, *Imagination* (London and New York, 1961). More alarmingly see also Flew, op. cit., p. 22f.
3. There is a spirited and well argued endorsement of my contention that for Hume ideas are *not* mental images in D. W. Livingston's 'Hume's Historical Theory of Meaning' in *Hume a Re-evaluation* (New York 1976) eds D. W. Livingston and J. T. King. Although Published before the first edition of my own book in early 1978, my typescript had gone to press before I learnt of Livingston's work. His views augment rather than repeat my arguments. More recently see also ch. 4 of his *Hume's Philosophy of Common Life* (Chicago and London, 1984).
4. Jonathan Bennett, *Locke, Berkeley, Hume: Central Themes* (Oxford, 1971) p. 229.
5. D. W. Livingston, op. cit., p. 215.
6. For a discussion of what Aquinas has to say on matters relating to 'analogical' language, if it is to avoid Hume's strictures, see Nelson Pike's edition of Hume's *Dialogues* (New York, 1970) pp. 142–6.
7. e.g. Luke XII, 5–10; Matthew XXIII, 33.

CHAPTER 6: SCEPTICISM AND NATURAL BELIEF

1. The similarity of thought to an item in Diogenes Laertius' Life of Pyrrho might be noted in view of Hume's addiction to the phrase 'Pyrrhonian doubt': 'With regard to the things about which our opponents argue so positively, claiming to have definitely apprehended them, we suspend our judgement because they are not certain, and confine our knowledge to our experience' (*Lives*, IX, 103). This is of course a very modified statement of the sort of extreme scepticism normally associated with Pyrrho and rejected by Hume. An excellent account of the place of Pyrrhonian scepticism in modern fideism can be found in Terence Penelhum's *God and Skepticism* (Reidel, 1983).
2. I say 'final' theory because it is evident from *Treatise*, 96, and other early passages that Hume hesitates at first between belief being 'A lively idea related to or associated with a present impression' and belief being 'a particular manner of forming an idea'.
3. It is interesting to note that in some chapters devoted to attacking Hume's account of belief, Thomas Reid comes to an almost identical conclusion concerning its indefinability: 'In like manner, every man that has any belief – and he must be a curiosity that has none – knows perfectly what belief is, but can never define or explain it' (*Inquiry into the Human Mind*, ch. II, sect. V).
4. Hendel has 'demanded'. Hume's final corrected edition of 1777 has 'commanded' which seems to make better sense.
5. Flew, *Hume's Philosophy of Belief*, p. 98.
6. Since Hume muffs his account of personal identity and then continues as if nothing had gone wrong (e.g. *Treatise*, 329) it could be argued that

belief in my own identity as a person going beyond the limitations of my
memory should be added as a fourth. But I am not convinced this belief
could be conclusively evidenced from within Hume's own writings.
The other three can.

7. R. J. Butler, 'Natural Belief and the Enigma of Hume', *Archiv für
Geschichte der Philosophie* (1960) pp. 73–100. This article contains much
with which I am in agreement, the argument which I refer to as 'Butler's
thesis' being only a part of it. I shall refer to it subsequently as 'Butler'
followed by the page.

8. David Fate Norton, *David Hume, Common-Sense Moralist, Sceptical
Metaphysician* (Princeton, 1982) p. 218.

9. The example is given in Hume's essay 'The Sceptic', in the paragraph
beginning 'In the operation . . .'.

10. *An Abstract of a Treatise of Human Nature* (1740), eds J. M. Keynes and
P. Straffa (Cambridge, 1938) p. 24.

11. In the argument which has led to these conclusions I have attempted to
establish a positive account which fits at least a significant part of
Hume's thought. There are other accounts of how we should use the
term 'natural belief' in relation to Hume. See, for example, chapter 1 of
Stanley Tweyman's *Scepticism and Belief in Hume's Dialogues concerning
Natural Religion* (Nijhoff, 1986). I regret that the scale and objectives of
the present undertaking do not permit me to follow the details of these
alternatives. But to do so would, in the end, not significantly alter my
own account.

CHAPTER 7: GOD AND NATURAL ORDER

1. See note 7 to Chapter 6.

2. Examples can be found in *Treatise*, 633; the essay 'The Platonist' (1742);
Enquiry, 135: 145; *N.H.R.*, 22; *Dialogues*, 214. See below, pp. 219f.

3. Terence Penelhum, *God and Scepticism* (Reidel, 1983) p. 127. The book is
of the first importance to the whole range of subjects I discuss in this and
the preceding chapter.

4. Who speaks for Hume in the *Dialogues* is a vexed question which has
always drawn the attention of critics and scholars. An impressive list of
authorities may be assembled to support Philo and an almost equally
impressive list for Cleanthes. Demea and Pamphilus have been
suggested and one commentator has even found Hume's sole personal
contribution in a passage which Kemp Smith places as a footnote on
p. 219. So far in this book I have taken the philosophical arguments in
the *Dialogues* on their own merits and given as little attention as possible
to the speakers. In Chapter 12, I shall have more to say about Hume's
own beliefs and the interpretation of the *Dialogues* but at this stage I
accept what I shall later have little occasion to amend, namely, Kemp
Smith's widely accepted thesis that, although something of Hume's own
beliefs is put into the mouths of all three characters, nevertheless, Philo
represents Hume in all he says and Cleanthes can be regarded as Hume's
mouthpiece only in those passages in which he is either agreeing with

Philo or refuting Demea. This is much the same as the opinion of the first reviewer of the *Dialogues* when he wrote: 'Philo is the hero of the piece; and it must be acknowledged that he urges his objections with no inconsiderable degree of acuteness and subtlety' (*Monthly Review*, July to December 1779, vol. LXI, p. 343).

5. Even Demea's profession 'that each man feels, in a manner, the truth of religion within his own breast' (*Dialogues*, 193) does not claim for belief in god the *universality* and *unavoidability* which would be required to make it a natural belief.

6. In *Alciphron* IV, 16–17, the sceptic Lysicles argues 'you must know then that at bottom the being of God is a point in itself of small consequence, and a man may make this concession without yielding much. The great point is what sense the word *God* is to be taken in'. He concludes 'Since, therefore, nothing can be inferred from such an account of God, about conscience, or worship, or religion, you may even make the best of it. And, not to be singular, we will use the name too, and so at once there is an end of atheism.'

7. For his earlier contribution see in particular *Hume* (London, 1975) ch. 8, and 'Hume's Skepticism and the *Dialogues*' in *McGill Hume Studies* (San Diego, 1979) eds D. F. Norton, N. Capaldi, W. L. Robison. The two more recent publications with which I am concerned are (1) 'Natural Belief and Religious Belief in Hume's Philosophy' in *The Philosophical Quarterly* (1983) and (2) ch. 6 of *God and Skepticism* (see note 3 above). In the text I shall refer to the former as Penelhum (1), followed by the page.

CHAPTER 8: MIRACLES AND REVELATION

1. Origen, *Contra Celsum*, I, 2. Translated by H. Chadwick (Cambridge, 1980).
2. R. M. Burns, *The Great Debate on Miracles* (London & Toronto, 1981) p. 242. This work is the most thorough account of the eighteenth-century controversy and of Hume's place in it.
3. George Campbell, *A Dissertation on Miracles* (Edinburgh, 1762) p. 172.
4. Note, for example, Eusebius' *Treatise*, ch. 31, where, in writing against Philostratus' *Life of Apollonius of Tyana*, having questioned the correctness of Philostratus' report, he remarks 'even if we admit the author to tell the truth in his stories of miracles, he yet clearly shows that they were severally performed by Apollonius with the co-operation of a demon'.
5. Philostratus, *Life of Apollonius of Tyana*, IV, 44.
6. A more detailed version of this section can be found in an article of mine in *Hume Studies* (1985). I am obliged to the editor of that journal for permission to re-use some of the material here.
7. *Discourse concerning Natural Religion and Revelation*, 9th edn (London, 1738) p. 388.
8. Ibid., p. 372.
9. 'Now what convictions there can be to any sober mind concerning

Divine authority in any person without such a *power of miracles* going along with him, when he is to deliver some *new doctrine* to the world to be believed, I confess I cannot understand'. Stillingfleet, *Origines Sacrae* (London, 1663) p. 143.

10. Locke, *Works*, 10 vols (London, 1812) vol. ix, pp. 256–65.
11. Toland, for example, alludes to it: a miracle in the New Testament is 'what serv'd to confirm the Authority of those that wrought it, to procure Attention to the Doctrines of the Gospel . . .' *Christianity not Mysterious* (London, 1696). Leslie, one of his orthodox critics, agrees that 'his [Jesus'] miracles do vouch the truth of what he delivered' *Short Method* (London, 1697) p. 6.
12. *Discourse of the Grounds and Reasons of the Christian Religion* (London, 1724).
13. Sir Leslie Stephen's *History of English Thought in the Eighteenth Century*, ch. IV. sect. iv, is still an invaluable guide to the whole controversy.
14. This declaration of his purpose appears near the beginning of each of the first four *Discourses*.
15. The controversy eventually lost touch with the original issues. The following remarkable heading to a pamphlet illustrates the decline. *The enthusiastic infidel detected being the trial of a Moral Philosopher before the grand senate of bedlam, on a stature of lunacy for publishing a RHAPSODY entitled the Resurrection of Jesus considered in answer to the Tryal of the Witnesses*, by a Brother Lunatic.
16. *The Miracles of Jesus Vindicated* (London, 1729) Part I, p. 25.
17. Sherlock, *The Tryal of the Witnesses of the Resurrection of Jesus*, 'London Printed, and Dublin re-printed' (1729). All page references will be to this edition.
18. Annet, *The Resurrection of Jesus considered in Answer to the Tryal of the Witnesses* (London, 1744) 3rd edn, p. 3.
19. *Hume's Philosophy of Belief* (London, 1961) ch. VIII.
20. The account which Sherlock gives (*Tryal*, pp. 62–3) of what would happen 'If one or two were to come into England, and report that a Man was raised from the Dead', makes a striking and very specific contrast to Hume's account of the way reports of Queen Elizabeth's resurrection would be received.
21. I am indebted to R. M. Burns for pointing out in a long note (op. cit., pp. 283f) that the points Sherlock makes are unoriginal, and that Hume's replies could be directed at him or at any of several other conspicuous writers. Of course I accept this; but I still think that the clarity and wide success of Sherlock's work, coupled with the particular evidence I produce, makes it probable that Hume is particularly concerned to get at the arguments as expressed by Sherlock.
22. 'Vindication of the Free Inquiry', in *Miscellaneous Works* (London, 1752) vol. 1, p. 351.
23. The points are not easily distinguishable from one another in the way in which Sherlock presents them. They are gathered from the speech of the Counsel for Woolston and from paraphrases offered by the Counsel for the Apostles and Judge.
24. Hume attributes the argument to Tillotson. It is to be found in *Rule of*

Faith (London, 1676) 2nd edn, p. 275 and in a more developed form in the *Discourse against Transubstantiation* (1684). But this attribution seems little more than a device which enables Hume to develop his sceptical arguments from the writings of a celebrated churchman.

25. The footnote was added at the end of the 2nd edn (1751), 'The Distance of the Author from the Press is the Cause, why the following Passage arrived not in time to be inserted in its proper Place.' Versions of the Indian Prince Argument occur in Locke's *Essay*, Butler's *Analogy*, and in several minor authors. Locke's treatment (*Essay*, IV, xv, 5) is concerned with the value of evidence and could have given Hume several useful hints. But Locke does not use the story to substantiate reports of miracles. Butler mentions the argument in the 'Introduction' during the course of some very general remarks concerning probability. Flew (op. cit., p. 176) says that it is Butler's version which Hume follows. I do not think this can be substantiated. It is Sherlock's *use* of the argument, not Butler's reference to it, which provides the butt for Hume's remarks. (The Indian Prince appeared again in 1825 as the Saracen in Scott's *The Talisman*, ch. 2.)

26. A critic has pointed out that few of us have much and many of us have no experience of anyone dying. I take the point, but rely upon the common sense of my readers to augment the example with such qualifications as philosophers might require.

27. See pp. 188f for Hume's use of the word 'superstition'.

28. Newman, *Two Essays on Scripture Miracles*; see also *A Grammar of Assent*, ch. VIII.

29. *Philosophers and Religious Truth* (London, 1964) p. 35.

30. 'Hume's Theory of the Credibility of Miracles', *P.A.S.*, 1916–17.

31. C. S. Pierce, *Values in a Universe of Chance*, ed. P. P. Wiener, (New York, 1958) p. 292f. Quoted in Flew, *Hume's Philosophy of Belief* (London, 1961), p. 179.

32. For Hume's use of the term 'popular religion' see below pp. 188f.

33. 'Hume, Flew, and the Miraculous', *Philosophical Quarterly* (1970) p. 235.

34. Few pieces of philosophical jargon sound more ghastly than 'nomological' used as a plural noun. In most relevant contexts it means a universal statement of some natural regularity to which we attribute a law-like character ('law of nature' is *almost* a synonym).

CHAPTER 9: THE REVELATION OF IMMORTALITY

1. See J. Noxon, *Hume's Philosophical Development* (Oxford, 1973) p. 170.

2. 1 *Cor.*, XV, 44.

3. 1 *Cor.* XV, 53.

4. *City of God*, XIII, 23.

5. The idea is powerfully conveyed by Marcus Aurelius (X, 38): 'Bear in mind that what pulls the strings is that Hidden Thing within us; *that* makes our speech, *that* makes our life, *that* one may say, makes the man'.

6. The doctrines of resurrected body and (immaterial) soul combine if it is held that the person survives and has experiences between death and the reconstitution of the body at the general resurrection of the dead in the last day. For the soul as the vehicle of identity of the person in the resurrected body, see Locke, *Essay*, II, xxvii, 15.
7. *Philosophical Commentaries*, ed. A. A. Luce (London, 1944) p. 301.
8. *Essay*, II, xxvii, 17.
9. I express myself guardedly because of Jonathan Bennett's argument in ch. 3 of *Locke, Berkely, Hume: Central Themes* (Oxford, 1971), that what we have is Berkeley's exegetical mistake not Locke's theory of substance. Bennett may well be right, but Berkeley's account of Locke's theory of substance has a life of its own which Hume took over and which I cannot ignore in this chapter.
10. I am obliged to Professor Flew for drawing my attention to this point.
11. See *Why I am not a Christian*, (London, 1957) p. 72.
12. 'Personal Identity and Individuation', *P.A.S.* (1957) p. 244.
13. See Luce and Jessop's edition of *The Works of George Berkeley*, vol. VII, p. 108. 'Nay, I defy any man to produce any parallel to this in any part of the creation, or to assign one single instance wherein God hath given appetite without a possibility of satisfying it' (Sermon VIII). In the *Guardian*, essay no. 27, op. cit., p. 181, Berkeley repeats the identical argument.
14. *Death and Immortality* (London, 1970) p. 27.
15. *God and the Soul* (London, 1969) pp. 117–29.
16. See, for example, Samuel Clarke's *Answer to Henry Dodwell* and more particularly Anthony Collins' reply in *Letter to Henry Dodwell* (London, 1709) pp. 6f. Hume seems to find common ground with Collins in much of what he has to say.

CHAPTER 10: THE CAUSES AND CORRUPTIONS OF RELIGION

1. This may seem a gratuitous undertaking. Surely his account of the causes of religious belief is well enough known already? I would have thought so myself but for an astounding comment in a relatively recent book on Hume:

> Judging by the methods employed in the *Treatise*, we should have expected him first to have considered the meaning of the word 'God'. . . . Then we should have expected Hume to give some account of the origin of our belief in the existence of God, independently of the truth of that belief. In short, we should have expected his treatment of God to follow the lines laid down in his treatment of causation, the material world, and the self. But he does not attempt this. All he does is to consider some ancient arguments for the existence of God, and expose their weakness, and conclude that belief in God is not rationally founded. (A. H. Basson, *David Hume*, London, 1958, pp. 107–8)

It may of course be that Hume's contribution to the philosophy of religion should be brushed off as 'disappointing' (loc. cit.). But disappointment need not be compounded by gross disregard of what Hume actually wrote on the subject.

2. *Prospect for Metaphysics,* ed. Ian Ramsey (London, 1961) p. 84.
3. Charles Blount, *Oracles of Reason* (London, 1696) p. 195.
4. *De Veritate,* trans. M. H. Carre (Bristol, 1937) Chapter IX.
5. E. C. Mossner, *The Life of David Hume* (Edinburgh, 1954; Oxford, 1970) p. 333. Hereafter referred to in the text as *Life,* followed by the page.
6. The three items referred to are, in order, *An Analysis of the Moral and Religious Sentiments of David Hume* (Edinburgh, 1755); *Remarks on Mr D. Hume's Essay on the Natural History of Religion* (London, 1757) p. 15; *A Letter to Adam Smith on the Life, Death and Philosophy of his friend David Hume, by one of the people called Christians* (Oxford, 1777) p. 13.

CHAPTER 11: THE CORRUPTIONS CAUSED BY RELIGION

1. Cf. J. Kahl, *The Misery of Christianity* (London, 1971) ch. 1.
2. For further developments of these ideas, and their relation to religious morality, see my 'Hume, Atheism, and the "Interested Allegation" of Morality' in *McGill Hume Studies* (San Diego, 1979) eds D. F. Norton, N. Capaldi, W. L. Robison; also 'The Obligation of Secular Morality' (*Hermathena*, 1978). I have attempted a mapping of all the main issues in *The Quest for Eternity* (Penguin Books, Harmondsworth, 1984) ch. 7.
3. The word 'frivolous' is used by Hume with reference to religious observances, and/or virtues in the *Dialogues,* the *N.H.R.* and the *Moral Enquiry.*
4. Note the similarity here (as so often in the *Dialogues*) to Cicero's *De Natura Deorum,* in the present instance to II, xxviii.
5. In a discussion of this subject it might seem desirable to distinguish between what Hume has to say about religious observances and ceremonies on the one hand and frivolous species of merit or 'monkish virtues' on the other. But the subjects are not consistently separated by Hume and any attempted distinction by another on his behalf would be tenuous and of questionable value.
6. 2nd edn (London, 1786) p. 36.
7. *Monthly Review* (July–Dec. 1779) vol. LXI, p. 347.
8. One of the reasons why he rejects the possibility is a moral reason: everlasting reward and punishment suppose two sorts of men, the good and the bad, and men do not fit into these exclusive categories. See Chapter 9 above.
9. See my 'Hume's Suppressed Dissertations: an Authentic Text' (*Hermathena*, 1968). The essay 'Of Suicide' has been much reprinted. As far as I know none of the reprints yet follow the text Hume wished to be considered as a manuscript. For a full account of the vicissitudes suffered by the dissertations see the article by E. C. Mossner in *Modern Philology* (1950).

10. If 'Of Suicide' is important in the context of *Hume's Philosophy of Religion*, the reader familiar with the 1978 edition may wonder why I there omitted all reference to it. The short answer is that the section was suppressed: not, as in Hume's case, for the exciting reason that the publisher might have been prosecuted, but, more tediously, because the MS was too long.

11. Note that in this instance the 'false religion' is going to be one of the most deeply established taboos of Christianity; 'false' only in the important sense that Hume draws attention to in the final footnote, namely that there is no biblical condemnation of suicide, but *orthodox in every other respect*.

12. *City of God*, Book I, composed in the period 412 to 427.

13. The commandment in Exodus 20, 13 is usually translated 'Thou shalt not kill'. But this is not what is meant by the original as is shown by the number of unreprimanded killings (*including* suicide) which are recorded in the O.T. The commandment is actually 'Thou shalt not commit *wrongful* killing', i.e. murder.

14. The doctrine of Natural Law is almost impossible to express in a sentence. For a short exposition see F. C. Copleston, *Aquinas* (Harmondsworth, 1955) pp. 211–28.

15. In 'An Analysis of Hume's Essay "On [sic] Suicide"', *Review of Metaphysics* (1976), T. L. Beauchamp, apart from attempting an analysis of Hume's arguments which is much more extensive than anything I can include here, offers an historical and an interpretive suggestion concerning 'Of Suicide'. The historical suggestion is that the dissertation was suppressed by Hume because he became aware of a defect in its argument, or because of its unoriginality, rather than because of his prudential concern about the adverse results of publication (as Mossner argues – see note 9 above). Beauchamp may well be right to doubt whether 'Hume's real reasons are historically recoverable' (p. 94) but I would have thought that prudence rather than loss of academic nerve is on the face of things the much more probable explanation. John Donne apart, such antecedents to Hume's arguments as can be traced *in English* are fragmentary or obscure, and it seems inconceivable that Hume could have removed the sophisticated argument of 'Of Suicide' because of a *defect of argument* while leaving in place the vapid rhetoric of 'Of the Passions'. Moreover Beauchamp makes far too little of the risk Hume was taking in publishing a direct refutation of a fundamental piece of Christian orthodoxy which had acquired the status of a taboo. Beauchamp's interpretive suggestion is that 'Of Suicide' is a 'point by point reply to Thomas Aquinas' three arguments against the morality of suicide'. Without following the matter in detail, I have to say this seems to me quite outstandingly improbable. Hume never quotes or refers to Aquinas in any published or private source, and it would be hard to think of any other outstanding philosopher *less* likely to be in the thoughts of eminent men during the enlightenment. As Hume says, he is concerned with 'the *common* arguments against suicide' (my italics). This being so, and given that Aquinas states briefly a version of what was to become one of

the common arguments, it is scarcely surprising that some of what Hume writes can be seen, as Beauchamp himself says, as 'a general and remote paraphrase' of something in Aquinas works. The point is that Hume is dealing with an accumulation of Christian arguments which set out to show that suicide is sinful or immoral, and Aquinas is part of that accumulation.

16. See Cicero, *De Re Publica VI*, xv (Somnium Scipionis) and more particularly *De Senectute, XX*, where the attribution is to Pythagoras; see also Plato, *Phaedo*, 62b.

17. One of the few recent discussions of suicide which are both scholarly and philosophically sophisticated is M. P. Battin, *Ethical Issues in Suicide* (New Jersey, 1982). See pp. 49–57 for her discussion of the issues raised by Hume.

CHAPTER 12: THE DISPASSIONATE SCEPTIC

1. His opinion is the more interesting because he gives a hint that he knew Hume personally – 'Hume was a very benevolent and amiable man . . . we *know* he was' (italics in original).

2. Kemp Smith lists earlier protagonists in the interpretation dispute in full detail, pp. 58f. His argument that Hume is Philo etc. is on pp. 58–75 and 97–123.

3. Florence, 1972.

4. James Noxon 'Hume's Agnosticism', *The Philosophical Review* (1964) reprinted in *Hume, a Collection of Critical Essays*, ed. V. C. Chappell (New York, 1966) pp. 361–83. I shall refer to this article as 'Noxon' with, where necessary, the page of the Chappell reprint.

5. Nicholas Capaldi, 'Hume's Philosophy of Religion', *International Journal for Philosophy of Religion* (1970) p. 238n.

6. *Mind* (1936).

7. *Journal of the History of Ideas* (1964). For more on the relation between Cicero and Hume see P. Jones, *Hume's Sentiments: Their Ciceronian and French Context* (Edinburgh, 1982) pp. 29–43.

8. What follows is substantially the same as part of an article of mine in *Journal of the History of Philosophy*, July 1976. I am indebted to the directors of the Journal for permision to reproduce the material here. I reproduce it, not in order to underline my disagreement with Professor Noxon whose good-tempered and generous reply appears in the *Journal* for Oct. 1976, but because his thesis is the most important statement of a position with which the whole tenor of my argument is at variance. What is more, Professor Noxon's thesis has acquired something of the character of an orthodoxy. See Nicholas Capaldi's judgement in his *David Hume* (Boston, 1975) p. 194n.

9. A somewhat similar objection to Noxon's point is made by Forrest Wood, 'Hume's Philosophy of Religion as Reflected in the Dialogues', *Southwestern Journal of Philosophy* (1971). I also agree with much of what Wood says on other matters. In particular he offers a shorter version

(with transatlantic reference) of my argument that belief in god is not a natural belief (see Chapter 7).

10. It seems appropriate to recall Hume's own reply to a critic of the dialogue which concludes the *Moral Enquiry*: 'But you impute to me both the sentiments of the Sceptic and the sentiments of his antagonist, which I can never admit of. In every Dialogue, no more than one person can be supposed to represent the author' (*Letters*, 1, 173).

11. Edited by C. McC. Weis, *Boswell in Extremes* (London, 1971) p. 14.

12. See, for example, Apuleius, *Metamorphoses* IX, 14 and Marcus Aurelius, *Meditations* III, 16.

13. An entry in vol. II of the 1737 edn of Bailey's *Dictionary* defines *deism* thus: '(deists) believe there is one God, a providence, . . . but reject revelation, and believe no more than what natural light discovers to them'. Johnson in 1755 differs somewhat. Deism is 'the opinion of those that only acknowledge one God, without the reception of any revealed religion'. When one turns to the particular writings of those whom most would agree to call deists – originally Herbert of Cherbury and later Charles Blount, John Toland, Matthew Tindal and many others – the combination of affirmation and denial recorded by the lexicographers is apparent. There is typically an *affirmation* of a rather elusive, primary, non-priestly, natural religion of mankind and of belief in a single creator god discovered through some version of the design and / or first cause arguments. There is a thinly veiled *denial* of revelation together with its supposed external authentications, namely its fulfilment of prophecies and its accompaniment by miracles. But within the full limits of what could be called deism the affirmation may be affirmed, and the denial indicated, with almost every shade of emphasis from the near orthodoxy of Samuel Clarke (marred only by an undue insistence upon rational demonstration and an Arian view of the Trinity) to the near-complete avoidance of any affirmation at all by those like Collins. (These extremes of the deist spectrum were of course identified by Leslie Stephen as 'constructive' and 'critical' deism: my additional point is that constructive deism could merge into orthodoxy, while critical deism almost certainly merged into complete atheism.) In Hume's case the denial of the credentials of revelation is complete and the affirmation very thin.

14. His letters, with one possible exception (see my article cited at the end of this note) give ample evidence both of his dislike of the title 'deist' and of the unwelcome reputation for deism which he acquired with others. Thus: In 1744, concerning his candidature for the Chair at Edinburgh: 'The accusation of Heresy, Deism, Scepticism, Atheism &c &c &c. was started against me; but never took, being bore down by the contrary Authority of all the good Company in Town' (*Letters*, I, 57). In 1752, concerning his application for Keeper of the Advocates Library: 'The violent cry of Deism, atheism, and scepticism, was raised against me; . . .' (*Letters*, I, 165). In 1757: 'My compliments to Dr Leland, & tell him, that he has certainly mistaken my Character' (as a deist – see John Leland, *A View of the Principal Deistical Writers*, vol. II, London 1755, pp. 1–135); *New Letters*, 43). In 1765, referring to his appointment as

Secretary to the British Embassy in Paris: 'So that in spite of Atheism & Deism, of Whiggism & Toryism, of Scoticism & Philosophy, I am now possess'd of an Office of Credit, and of 1200 Pounds a Year' (*Letters*, I, 510); also in 1765, referring to his *non*-acceptance of the post of Secretary to the Lord Lieutenant of Ireland, 'Perhaps, the zeal against Deists enter'd for a Share' (*New Letters*, 130). It is evident that Hume does not like his reputation as a deist (any reputation as an atheist was as bad or worse). He blames these reputations for his failures, and looks on his successes as things achieved despite them. But there is something more to all this than the grumbling irritation of a man dogged by a reputation he did not think he deserved. On at least one occasion he was provoked into a denial of deism. The story is Lord Charlemont's. He writes that Mrs Mallet: 'who was not acquainted with Hume, meeting him one night at an Assembly, boldly accosted him in these words "Mr Hume, Give me leave to introduce myself to you. We deists ought to know each other". "Madam" replied He, "I am no Deist. I do na style myself so, neither do I desire to be known by the Appellation." (Royal Irish Academy, MS 12/R/7 f 523). For more of these and other matters concerning Hume's relation to contemporary use of the terms 'atheist' and 'deist' see my 'Hume's Attenuated Deism', *Archiv für Geschichte der Philosophie* (1983). The reasons, I suggest, for Hume's dislike of being called a deist, were the degree of opprobrium attaching to the title and the undue extent to which deism relied upon arguments of natural religion which Hume rejected: notably argument to a first cause.

15. Note, for example, the tone of a letter written in 1750 at a time of alarm about an earthquake in London: 'I see only a Pastoral Letter of the Bishop of London, where, indeed, he recommends certain pills, such as fasting, prayer, repentance, mortification and other drugs, which are entirely to come from his own shop' (*Letters*, I, 141).
16. From *Private Papers of James Boswell*, eds. Scott and Pottle, vol XII. Quoted in full in *Dialogues*, 76.
17. Some years earlier Boswell had greatly upset Johnson by insisting that Hume was not afraid of death: 'I told him David Hume said he was no more uneasy to think he should *not be* after this life than that he *had not been* before he began to exist . . .' *Boswell in Search of a Wife*, eds Brady and Pottle (London, 1957; limited edn) p. 353.
18. 'Hume's Early *Memoranda* 1729–40: The Complete Text' by E. C. Mossner, *Journal of the History of Ideas* (1948). Entry 27: 'It seems to be a kind of Objection against the Immortality of the Soul to consider the trifling Accidents of Marriage. Copulation etc. that bring Men into Life.' Even this earliest extant note on the subject seems to display the scepticism which was to be confirmed by all Hume's later remarks.
19. J. Hill Burton, *Life and Correspondence of David Hume* (Edinburgh, 1846) vol. 11, p. 516.
20. *The Journal*, ed. W. E. K. Anderson (Oxford, 1972) p. 326.
21. Hill Burton, *Life*, vol. 11, p. 512n.
22. In a somewhat diffuse article in *Religious Studies* (1976), P. G. Kuntz offers the astounding summary 'Thus he was led to theistic conclusions' (p. 428). This judgement is on the face of things, and using

'theistic' in any accepted sense, simply false; nor do Kuntz's arguments justify it.

23. *Aristotelian Society*, Supp. Vol. XVIII (1939), p. 179.
24. The judgement is my own. Others may demur. But when 'philosophy of religion' is understood in its usual modern sense – as analysis of the truth and meaning of religious beliefs – it is difficult to think of anyone other than David Hume as its founder. I notice that in his book *The Emergence of Philosophy of Religion* (New Haven, 1967) J. Collins begins his account with Hume, and T. Penelhum remarks, rightly I believe, that the *Dialogues* 'is beyond any question the greatest work on philosophy of religion in the English language' (*Hume*, London, 1975, p. 171). Hume is of course not the first exponent of 'philosophies' of religion: those characteristically nineteenth-century views which treat the *phenomenon* of religion without much reference to its claims to substantial truth. The first philosophy of religion in *that* sense may well have been provided by Hegel. (Cf. B. M. G. Reardon, *Hegel's Philosophy of Religion*, London, 1977, p. 77f.).

Index

Notes are indexed only with respect to subjects and comments.

Adams, R., 82f
Addison, J., 15, 178
agent
  god as, 37
  source of order, 32f
analogy
  argument by, 28f
  in design argument, 29f
Annet, P., 145
Anselm, 74
anthropomorphism, 38f, 102f
Apollonius of Tyana, 141f
Aquinas, 11, 87f, 242n15
Asclepius, 137, 139f
atheism
  Hume's denial of, 219–22
  relative, 222
Augustine of Hippo, 167, 205

Barnes, J., 81
Basson, A. H., 240n1
Bayle, P., 1
Beauchamp. T. L., 245n15
belief
  Hume's account of, 113–15, 235n2
  in god, reasonable or natural, 121–31
  natural, 109, 112, 115–21
Bennett, J., 99, 240n9
Berkeley, Bp., 11, 21, 126, 177, 240n13
Boswell, J., 228
Broad, C. D., 140, 157
Burns, R. M., xi, 140, 238n21
Butler, Bp., 12, 167
Butler, R. J., 116, 120f, 236n7

Campbell, G., 140f
Capaldi, N., 233n27
Carabelli, G., 210, 232n9
cause
  causal explanations, 41f
  causa sui, 86f
  'external' or metaphysical, 76, 85f
  Hume's account of, 25
  infinite regress of, 88f
Celsus, 139
chance, 48f

chaos, 46, 49, 233n25
Cicero, 1, 11, 13, 212, 241n4
Clarke, Dr S., 74–6, 78, 81, 83f, 86, 88, 90, 92, 143
Collins, A., 144, 240n16
cosmological argument, see god, a priori proofs of
creation, ex nihilo, 87

Darwin, C., 45
deism
  meanings of, 244n13
  Hume's attenuated, 7, 129, 219–22
  Hume's dislike of, 244n14
Descartes, 74, 86, 91
design argument
  analogy in, 27–31, 37–41
  criticisms of, 17–47
  feeling for, 109, 126–30
  forms of, 12–17
  importance of, 7, 11
  inference to moral designer, 19–21, 53–8
  'irregular' argument, 50f, 127f
  other names for god in, 12
  outcome of critique of, 6f, 48, 221
  probable conclusion, 12, 127
  regularity (nomological) argument, 13f
  teleological argument, 14
Diderot, 220

Einstein, 11
Elliot of Minto, 1
evil
  free will defence, 69–73
  god author of, 71f
  Hume's conclusions about, 73
  inference problem of, 53–8, 68f
  natural or physical, 53f
  necessary, 62–4
  problem of, 54, 58, 69
  solutions to, 59–68
evolution of organisms, 44
existence
  necessary, 78–81

existence – *continued*
  not an idea, 90–2
experience
  limits our understanding, 104–7
  no guide to origin of worlds, 25, 47
explanation
  agent, 42f, 233n24
  causal, 41f
  internal/external, 26, 85f

Flew, A., x, 25, 52, 69f, 72, 77, 95, 146,
    153, 161f
Furlong, E. J., 97

Geach, P., 181
Gibbon, 194
god
  an agent, 37
  anthropomorphic, 37–41, 102f
  a priori proofs of, 74–92
  being of, 218, 221, 237n6
  belief in: causes of, 184–6; Hume's,
    219–23; not natural, 121–5, 130;
    not universal, 122f; rational,
    125f, 221
  general consent, 183, 207
  god and God, x
  idea of, 99
  incomprehensible, 40, 103, 225
  moral attributes of, 19–21, 67f, 101f,
    195, 221
  necessary existence of, 78–81
  see also design argument

Hall, R., xi
Hartshorne, C., 90
Hendel, C. W., 210
Herbert of Cherbury, 185
Hick, J., 61, 65–8, 88
Hume, David
  and Philo, 210–18, 236n4
  attenuated deism of, 7, 129, 219–23,
    229f, 244n14
  his beliefs concerning: immortality,
    166, 228f, 245n17; miracles, 161;
    prayer, 223f; revelation, 227;
    sincerity of clergy, 226
  works, comments on: *Dialogues*, 5,
    211–18; *Enquiry*, 2f; *History*, 3;
    Letter, 2; *Moral Enquiry*, 3, 195–7
    200–2, *N.H.R.*, 3, 184–7; 'Of
    Immortality', 4, 170–80; 'Of
    Suicide', 4, 203–7, 242n10;
    Treatise, 182

Hume's Fork, 77–84, 106
Hurlbutt, R. H., 6

ideas/impressions, 91, 95–8, 105f
immortality
  accounts of, 167–9, 240n6
  arguments against, 170–80
  Hume's disbelief in, 166, 181, 228f
  Hume's position summarized, 181
  immorality of, 179f
  soul as immaterial, 170–4
impossibility, physical, 163f
impressions, *see* ideas/impressions
Indian Prince Argument, 151f, 239n25
Irenaeus, 149

Jeffner, A., 6
Johnson, Dr, 228
Jones, P., 243n7

Kemp Smith, N., xi, 124, 127, 210–12,
    215, 217, 236n4
Kenny, A., 87
King, Dr, 54
Kuntz, P. G., 245n22

Laird, J., 210
laws of nature, 22, 160f, 239n34
  see also miracles; order (in nature)
Leibniz, 54, 62, 71, 87
Leroy, A., 210, 232n9
Livingston, D. W., 235n3
Locke, John, 104f, 143, 170
Lucretius, 79

Mackie, J., 69
Maclaurin, C., 15
Marcus Aurelius, 239n5
matters of fact/relations of ideas, *see*
    Humes's Fork
McPherson, T., 25, 35
meanings(s)
  meaning empiricism, 98–101
  Newspeak words, 101–4
Middleton, C., 149
Mill, J. S., 20, 30f, 175, 183
Miller, A., 4
miracles
  aim of Hume's chapter, 146, 158
  and laws of nature, 159–65
  a posteriori arguments against, 156–8
  a priori argument against, 151–6
  Christian use of, 138f, 141, 143,
    237n4 and 9, 238n11

Contrary Miracles Argument, 136–43
  controversy concerning, 144–6
  definitions of, 141, 153, 159
  Hume's disbelief in, 161
  Indian Prince Argument, 151f
Monod, J., 33
Mossner, E. C., 187, 212

Nathan, G. J., 45
natural belief
  characteristics of, 109, 117f, 236n11
  examples of, 116, 235n6
  in god, 121–6, 237n5
  not 'innate concept', 109
  nor irrational, 118f
  versus Pyrrhonian scepticism, 112
natural religion, 7, *passim*
  defined, 185
natural selection, 232n6
  of organisms, 44
  of processes, 45f
necessary existence, 78–80, 88
Newman, J., 154
Newton, 11, 14f
Newton's Rule, 21
Norton, D. F., ix, 118
Noxon, J., 211, 213–18, 228, 243n8

Occam's Razor, *see* Newton's Rule
Olding, A., 21
ontological argument, *see* god, *a priori*
    proofs of
Optimum World Argument, 62–4
order (in nature)
  agent given *v.* natural, 31–6
  as laws of nature, 160–4
  evolution of, 44–6
  in processes, 36, 46
  in structures, 36, 46
  mechanistic *v.* statistical, 46, 49
  principle of, 48–50
  sources of, 35f
  see also design argument
Origen, 139
Ossian's Poems, 157

paganism, *see* polytheism
Paley, W., 14, 200
Pearce, Bp., 144
Pearl, L., 35f, 44
Peirce, C. S., 158
Penelhum, T., ix, xi, 123, 126–30,
    236n3, 237n7
Phillips, D. Z., 180

Pike, N., ix, xi, 50, 63, 72
Plantinga, A., 52
Plato, 11, 168
polytheism
  attitude to miracles, 138f
  original religion, 184–6
  v. monotheism, 22, 137
  prayer, 223f, 245n15
Price, J. V., 212, 215
Pyrrhonian scepticism, 111f, 235nl

regularities
  of succession (processes), 13, 36
  of copresence (structures), 13
Reid, T., 235n3
relations of ideas/matters of fact, *see*
    Hume's Fork
religion
  and morality, 194–203, 241n2
  causes of, 184–7, 240nl
  corruptions of, 188f
  Hume, earliest comments on, 1,
    245n18
  first philosopher of, 230, 246n24
  misery caused by, 193f
  natural, defined, 185
  observances of, 224f, 241n3, and 5
  true, 187f
Resurrection, the, 147, 150f, 156f,
    238n20
revelation, 135, 143, 165, 181, 226f
Rowe, W. L., 76
Russell, B., 84f, 88, 176

scepticism
  antecedent, 110,
  checked by natural belief, 112f
  excessive or Pyrrhonian, 111f, 235nl
  mitigated, 110f, 216
Scott, Sir W., 156, 228
Shaffer, J., 80, 90f
Shakespeare Plays Argument, 34
Sherlock, Bp., 144f, 157
  Tryal of the Witnesses, 146–51
Smart, N., 154, 184
Spinoza, 173
Stephen, Sir L., 210, 238n13
Stewart, M. A., xi, 75f, 232n3
Stillingfleet, Bp., 143
Stove, D. C., 76f
Strahan, W., 228
substance, 99f, 170f
suicide, 203–8, 225, 243n12 and 15,
    243n17

superstition, 188–90
Suppressed Dissertations, *see* Hume,
    D., 'Of Immortality', 'Of Suicide'
Swinburne, R. G., 13f, 18, 21, 25,
    27–9, 35, 37, 42, 233n16

Taylor, A. E., 210, 230
thoughts
    locationless, 171f
    material causes of, 172f
    related to ideas, 96f
Tillotson, Bp., 238n24
Tweyman, S., ix, 6, 236n11

understanding, limited by experience,
    104–7

universe
    external *v.* internal causes of, 26, 85
    uniqueness of, 25

Vespasian, 139f

Wadia, P. S., ix–xi, 51
Wallace, R. C., 162
Warnock, G., 6
Whiston, W., 144
Williams, B., 177
Woolston, T., 144
world
    meanings of, 23
    best possible, 23f, 62–4
    origin unknown, 25

Xenophon, 1, 11, 13